T0265528

GROWING WINGS

GROWING WINGS

THE INSIDE STORY OF
RED BULL
RACING

BEN HUNT

HARPER

An Imprint of HarperCollins*Publishers*

HarperCollins books may be purchased for educational, business, or sales promotional use. For information, please email the Special Markets Department at SPsales@harpercollins.com.

Originally published in the United Kingdom in 2024 by Ebury Spotlight.

FIRST U.S. EDITION

Library of Congress Cataloging-in-Publication Data has been applied for.

ISBN 978-0-06-341191-3

24 25 26 27 28 LBC 5 4 3 2 1

To my children, Teddy and Rose.

CONTENTS

FOREWORD BY CHRISTIAN HORNER *1*

1 'NO RISK, NO FUN': 2004 *5*

2 THE BULL GETS ITS HORN: 2005 *19*

3 OFF TO A FLYING START: 2005 *32*

4 THE FIRST PODIUM: 2006 *47*

5 WEBBER'S ARRIVAL: 2007 *60*

6 ALL CHANGE: 2008 *77*

7 A NEW ERA: 2009 *87*

8 VETTEL GETS HIS CROWN: 2010 *100*

9 THE FULL WORKS: 2011 *115*

10 TRIPLE CHAMPIONS: 2012 *129*

11 TO INFINITI AND BEYOND: 2013 *144*

12 RED BULL RING'S RETURN: 2014 *159*

13 LIFE AFTER SEB: 2015 *176*

14 MAX MAKES HIS MARK: 2016 *189*

15 THE CHANGING FACE OF F1: 2017 *204*

16 TURBULENT TIMES: 2018 *216*

17 THE HONDA GAMBLE: 2019 *229*

18 PUT ON HOLD: 2020 *242*

19 MAX IS WORLD CHAMPION: 2021 *254*

20 BACK-TO-BACK SUCCESS: 2022 *272*

21 TOTAL DOMINATION: 2023 *288*

AFTERWORD *301*

ACKNOWLEDGEMENTS *305*

IMAGE CREDITS *307*

INDEX *309*

GROWING WINGS

FOREWORD
BY CHRISTIAN HORNER

It is incredible to think that 20 years have passed since I was in discussion with Dietrich Mateschitz around the genesis of this team. And somewhat fitting that the team's 20th anniversary comes off the back of the most phenomenal season in 2023, which saw us reach our 100th win and eclipse records the likes of which we never thought could have been broken.

Records like McLaren's spectacular season from 1988 with their fantastic drivers, Ayrton Senna and Alain Prost, winning 15 out of 16 races. To better that by winning a total of 21 out of 22 races is just unbelievable, a performance beyond any expectation. Blazing the way was Max Verstappen who won 19 of those races, which fittingly crowned him world champion for 2023; while Sergio Pérez finishing second in the drivers' championship meant it was the first time Red Bull Racing clinched a one-two in a championship.

When I reflect on my time at Red Bull Racing, I am struck by what a remarkable journey we have been on in a relatively short space of time. In many ways it seems like only yesterday that I first walked through the doors of the team's factory in Milton Keynes, which looked substantially different to how it does today. But during those 20 years, the team has risen from the ashes of what was Jaguar Racing to what Red Bull Racing is today. We came into the sport and were perceived as the party team, that we perhaps were not taking the task at hand as seriously as some of our counterparts. But we built the team up, and by 2009 we started winning. Then, in 2010, we started winning championships.

This is indicative of the team spirit that Red Bull Racing was built on and what we value so highly to this day. All the records, all the wins and all the accolades are testament to the hard-working individuals at the track and behind the scenes, in the factory. Every team member can feel incredibly proud of the role they have played in contributing to this incredible run of success. The commitment to that cause has been unwavering but we have had to keep our eye on the target, to continue to believe and to never give up. And that attitude permeates from the top down.

If people see self-doubt creep in or uncertainty from those at the top, that is quickly infectious throughout any team or business. Leading from the front, keeping the sense of team, never being afraid to take on a challenge or hire a maverick who is not afraid to challenge the establishment – all are core values within our team installed by our founder Dietrich Mateschitz. None of this would be possible without Dietrich. It was his vision that gave rise to the team and it was his belief that carried us through. It is with tremendous respect and gratitude that we carry that torch.

Dietrich took great enjoyment and pride from what we did. The subsidiary of a fizzy drinks manufacturer, as we were once labelled by an opponent, we took on the rival teams. We have demonstrated what is possible when you have the right people, the right spirit, the right culture and the right attitude. Dietrich gave this team so much and his spirit is woven in the fabric of who we are. From 2026, we will carry his initials on the engines of our cars. The first one will be the DM01, the next DM02 and so on, meaning Dietrich will always be at the heart of our cars.

In our somewhat short history, we have had a series of incredible highs coupled with some points where we were not so successful. But we never lost our ambition. We always rebuilt and, from that point onwards to where we are today, never lost sight of our goal: to get back on top.

That has come in various iterations throughout our history. In 2021 on the final lap, at the final race of the season in Abu Dhabi, seeing Max win his first world title completely against the odds, was a huge moment. It came after the most intense battle in F1 history. Another, which incidentally also came in Abu Dhabi, was when Sebastian won the title in 2010. That was the team's first drivers' championship title and, again, it was won with such drama, against all the odds in the final race of the campaign. Another moment I will never forget.

I have been there for all of the races – all of the wins and all the losses – and I enjoy each race now just as much as I did from day one. Formula One was always my goal and ambition; I was always determined to make a success of it. With the benefit of experience, you learn how to deal with some of the emotions, you mature, but the excitement of going racing, the passion and competitive spirit, it never gets old – it is just the same for me now as it was 20 years ago.

I am absolutely sure that later in life, when we look back at what we achieved in our years, we will all say, 'That was a heck of a lot in a pretty short time frame,' especially if you were to look at statistically where we sit among some of the great names and teams in this sport. That is something that everyone can be very proud of.

However, what really is exciting is what lies ahead of us. We have a colossal task with new engine regulations in 2026 and that has seen the team focused on many aspects behind the scenes with Red Bull Powertrains and our partnership with Ford.

Red Bull Racing continues to grow its wings and I trust that Dietrich is looking down from wherever he is now and smiling at what we have achieved together. Thank you, Didi.

CHAPTER 1

'NO RISK,
NO FUN'

– 2004 –

Christian Horner, the Red Bull Racing team principal, is sitting at a table on the top floor of the team's 'Holzhaus' – the largest of the motorhomes in the Formula One paddock. He is surrounded by journalists, their Dictaphones splayed out across the table, looking to capture his words. His driver Max Verstappen has just won the 2023 Austrian Grand Prix.

Outside on a grass verge, a twin-engined helicopter has landed and is being loaded with VIP guests looking to make a speedy exit from the Red Bull Ring. The sound of the engines increases as the pilot deploys the throttle for their departure, making it near impossible to hear Horner's answers. Once it has departed and it is quiet again, there is one clearly audible comment that perfectly encapsulates the spirit behind Red Bull Racing.

'No risk, no fun,' he says when asked why the team gambled on pitting Verstappen from a comfortable lead on the penultimate lap. Verstappen had been ahead of Charles Leclerc by almost 25 seconds and the time lost in making the pit stop was around 20 seconds, even disregarding the potential for a mistake from one of the pit crew. However, the fresh tyres would allow Verstappen to set the quickest lap of the race, earning him a bonus point. And ultimately he still finished just over five seconds clear of Leclerc.

'A stunning weekend from Max,' said Horner, 'and the first time we've been back here [to the Red Bull Ring in Austria] since Dietrich's [Mateschitz] passing. It felt very poignant that it was a great team performance. We decided to go for the fastest lap on the last lap, despite the risk involved in fluffing a pit stop. And it was at the back of my mind that Dietrich's mantra was "no risk, no fun".'

If one comment captures the spirit behind everything the Red Bull Racing team stands for, it is this.

. . .

Formula One teams are rarely started from scratch; they simply evolve. The staff, factories, equipment and cars all remain in place. It is the ownership that changes hands. But there was something different about the deal that saw Red Bull founder Dietrich Mateschitz purchase the failing Jaguar team on 15 November 2004. The Austrian billionaire's energy drinks company promised to bring a fresh presence to a sport that had been dominated by automotive, oil and cigarette companies.

Red Bull was an exciting brand that was at odds with the traditional ownership model for F1: teams would usually be financed by a manufacturer or backed up by a substantial advertising rate-card for sponsors. Red Bull did not have either.

Dietrich Mateschitz was born on 20 May 1944, in Sankt Marein im Mürztal, a municipality in Styria, Austria. His mother was from the region, while his father's family was from Maribor, now in Slovenia. Both his parents were teachers and he attended the Vienna University of Economics and Business, where he graduated with a marketing degree in 1972. He landed his first job with Unilever, marketing detergents. He then moved to German cosmetics company Blendax, which is now owned by Procter & Gamble, the American multinational consumer goods corporation.

One of the products Mateschitz worked on was toothpaste, and it was this which led him to Asia where he came across a drink called Krating Daeng, which locals said had an invigorating effect. According to journalist David Tremayne writing for F1.com, 'He discovered the concoction because it was marketed by a company that also happened to market that same brand of toothpaste. After sampling Krating Daeng himself, Mateschitz realised it helped with his jet lag, and became intrigued.'

Popular among Thailand's blue-collar workers, Krating Daeng was created in the seventies by Chaleo Yoovidhya, owner of T.C. Pharmaceutical. Yoovidhya was born to a poor Thai Chinese family and rose to success after setting up his own pharmaceutical company. Spotting the product's potential for success in the Western market, Mateschitz agreed a deal with Yoovidhya that saw each of them investing $500,000 in return for a 49 per cent share of the business. The remaining 2 per cent went to Yoovidhya's son, so the family retained the control, while Mateschitz ran the company.

The new company was formed in 1984 with 'Krating Daeng' translated into English as 'Red Bull'. Mateschitz spent three years developing the drink for European tastes before it was launched in Austria in 1987. He aligned the image of Red Bull with extreme sports and focused on the physical and mental benefits of the drink, later adopting the slogan 'Red Bull Gives You Wings'. The product was primarily placed in Austrian ski resorts and marketed as a premium brand, unlike the original Krating Daeng, which remained low-cost and produced in Bangkok. It was later rolled out across Europe, where it gained popularity in nightclubs as a mixer for alcoholic drinks.

Many think that Red Bull's association with motorsport came when Mateschitz entered his team in the 2005 season, but it actually started back in 1989. With the Red Bull brand still in its infancy, Mateschitz agreed a sponsorship deal with fellow Austrian Gerhard Berger, the F1 driver who was then driving for Ferrari.

Berger was a natural fit for Red Bull. Ultra-competitive but with an easy-going attitude and bags of charisma, Berger was a throwback to the old days of Grand Prix racing, someone who did not take the fast-paced world of F1 too seriously and, very importantly, liked a practical joke. He once filled a bedroom that was being used by his teammate, Ayrton Senna, with live frogs. He also once threw the Brazilian's briefcase out of a helicopter – mid-flight. The deal proved to be a landmark moment as Berger became the first Red Bull-sponsored racing driver on their total athlete programme, which now extends to an impressive roster of around 850 competitors across multiple sports and disciplines.

Berger's deal was brokered by another Austrian, with whom Mateschitz formed a crucial partnership that would span the rest of his involvement with motorsport: Helmut Marko. Marko would become Mateschitz's right-hand man for his motorsport business, acting as advisor to the Red Bull GmbH Formula One teams, and head of Red Bull's driver development programme.

Marko was born in Graz and was part of the tight-knit Austrian racing scene of the early seventies. (He was a friend of Jochen Rindt, who was killed during practice for the Italian Grand Prix in 1970, becoming the only driver to win the Formula One World Drivers' Championship posthumously.) Marko, too, was a racer, who took part in ten Grands Prix in 1971 and 1972, although he did not score a point. He had more success in endurance racing and won the 24 Hours of Le Mans in 1971, driving a Martini Porsche 917K. However, his racing career ended prematurely in 1972 at the French Grand Prix at Clermont-Ferrand, when a stone flicked up from Ronnie Peterson's March and pierced Marko's visor, permanently blinding his left eye. With his driving career over, Marko initially turned to driver management, before setting up his own race team – RSM Marko – in 1989, competing in the FIA Formula 3000 (now Formula Two) championship, the feeder series for F1.

Marko was Gerhard Berger's manager, and handled the Red Bull sponsorship deal with Mateschitz. A decade later in 1999, Mateschitz also agreed to sponsor RSM Marko, which would in turn be renamed the Red Bull Junior Team. In an interview with the *Observer*'s Richard Williams in November 2010, Marko emphasised the importance of the Austrian connection in his relationship with Mateschitz: 'I'm from Graz in Styria and he's from Mürztal, 60 or 70km away. He was always racing-minded. When we first met, he didn't have a budget to go into anything, but Red Bull became bigger and bigger and it seemed natural to come together.'

Between these two deals involving Marko, Mateschitz had also had another – somewhat less successful – foray into F1 in 1995, when he struck a partnership between Red Bull and Sauber, purchasing a stake in Sauber's F1 team. In return, Red Bull branding would be prominent on the overalls of the drivers.

Sauber is a motorsport engineering company from nearby Switzerland who ran numerous racing teams across different disciplines. Perhaps the most significant moment of Red Bull's partnership with Sauber was the arrival in F1 of Kimi Räikkönen in 2001. The Finn was not part of Red Bull's Junior Team, so Red Bull had hoped that Sauber would select their sponsored protégé, the Brazilian Enrique Bernoldi. However, Sauber opted for Räikkönen and Bernoldi would wind up at minnows Arrows, a British team that entered 394 races between 1978 and 2002 without a single victory. The Finn, who would later win the 2007 F1 title with Ferrari, helped Sauber finish fourth in the 2001 constructors' championship – the league table that measures the overall performance of the ten F1 teams. Sauber's decision to select him over Bernoldi was vindicated, but for Red Bull it proved to be the start of the decline in their relationship and resulted in them selling their share in the team to Credit Suisse in 2002.

Now, in 2004, a new chapter was starting for Mateschitz, in a move that would change the shape of the sport forever.

Mateschitz's opportunity to re-enter F1 had come about by virtue of Jaguar's parent company, Ford, who had struggled to make the team successful. Against a backdrop of some bad trading results that had limited Ford's spending on the project, and coupled with the slow realisation that it would require years of investment before the team were regular winners, the car giant was no longer able to justify the luxury of its F1 commitment. Put simply, it was concerned about the major liability a defunct F1 team would levy on the Ford Motor Company's books. The team was put up for sale publicly in September 2004.

'Ford has decided it can no longer make a compelling business case for any of its brands to compete in F1,' said Jaguar chairman Joe Greenwell at the time. 'Having reached this decision our focus has turned to securing the best future for our F1 businesses and our employees in these businesses going forward. Jaguar's presence in F1 has been a valuable marketing and brand awareness platform, particularly outside our main markets of the US and the UK. However, it was our collective view that it is time for Jaguar Cars to focus 100 per cent on our core business.'

The deadline of 15 November marked the final day by which the sale could be completed, beyond which a new buyer would not be allowed to compete in the 2005 Formula One championship. The strict timeframe was such that if no new buyer could be found, some of the existing teams would be required to enter a third car to fill the grid, at an extra cost.

Jaguar had first entered F1 for the 2000 season, the year after parent company Ford bought the Stewart team founded by the three-times world champion, Sir Jackie Stewart, renaming the team after its luxury car brand. But despite substantial investment, Jaguar had not won a single race and had ended the 2004 season in seventh place in the constructors' championship with just ten points. In their total of 85 races, Jaguar had won just 49 points, with two third places in Monaco (2001) and Italy (2002) their best-ever finishes.

'It wasn't really a shock to me,' F1 supremo Bernie Ecclestone was quoted as saying in a BBC News article published on the day of Ford's sale. 'They couldn't afford to be running around at the back of the grid with the likes of Jordan.'

Ecclestone's comments were confirmed by Ford's vice-president Richard Parry-Jones, who accused the sport of failing to distribute prize money evenly among all teams. 'The current structure of F1 does not encourage smaller participants to make an investment,' said Parry-Jones. 'I think Jaguar's withdrawal will highlight the awareness of the need for change.'

Now, just hours before F1's closure deadline, Red Bull's purchase of Jaguar Racing was officially announced. The press releases surrounding the 11th-hour offload were notably lacking in financial details, however. The BBC reported that it believed Ford had asked for 'a symbolic $1 if the new owners guaranteed to invest $400 million into the team over the next three Grand Prix seasons'; the primary focus for Ford was to pass the team onto good owners for the benefit of their workforce. Crucially, it had also safeguarded the 340 jobs at the team's HQ in Milton Keynes in the UK, plus the wind tunnel and test facilities it had recently acquired and renovated in Bicester and Bedford.

On the same day, Ford also announced the sale of Cosworth, the company who made the engines for the Jaguar Racing team, to the owners of the US-based Champ Car series, Kevin Kalkhoven and Gerald Forsythe, who would continue to supply the team with engines for the 2005 season. In the same BBC article, Kalkhoven said: 'We are strongly committed to continuing the great F1 tradition at Cosworth and take that very successful heritage into the future.'

The Red Bull deal was widely welcomed in the motorsport world. However, the sale of the Jaguar team was by no means straightforward, especially for the man charged with achieving it: Tony Purnell, team principal for Jaguar Racing.

Purnell had been the next in line to manage Jaguar after the team failed to live up to its early promise under the direction of Wolfgang Reitzle, Neil Ressler, Bobby Rahal and then Niki Lauda. The Austrian three-times world champion, with his notorious attention to detail, was dumped by Ford in 2002 and Purnell was given the reins. The Englishman had previously had an academic career in England and the United States before his early in-car telemetry company was acquired by Ford in 1999. His involvement with the F1 team meant that he was a natural successor to Lauda. However, the position became something of a poisoned chalice after he was charged with sourcing a new owner when Ford decided to sell up.

'I remember it very well indeed,' says Purnell, now a visiting professor at Cambridge University, as we discuss the origins of Red Bull over a Zoom call. 'It was probably the most traumatic year of my life. We had the R5, which was a half-decent race car, and we had made a lot of progress, particularly in the aerodynamics. We had bought the Bedford wind tunnel, which was a major step for the team, and we are all up and running. Parry-Jones seemed really happy, but then at the beginning of 2004 I was taken aside and told that it was very unlikely that Ford would continue with a Formula

One project. I was sworn to secrecy, but told to look for a buyer or partner for the team. For about six months, I had to quietly see if I could find a buyer. And I looked around and thought the most likely people were Red Bull, because they had been co-owners of Sauber and had some idea of what F1 involved.

'I started negotiating with them and began to get somewhere. Midway through the year, we got to the stage of agreeing a "heads of terms"-type partnership between Red Bull and Ford. Both would be 50 per cent stakeholders on the understanding that Red Bull would look after the car and Ford would look after the engine. I got really excited about this and I remember saying to the press that the prospects for the team were really, really good. We got to the stage where we had one of the wind-tunnel models painted up in Red Bull and Ford colours. I've still got this model; it's in the engineering department at Cambridge. We met somewhere near Coventry and they pulled a little slip of cloth off the model and the deal was done.'

Any triumph at the closure of this deal was short-lived, however.

'About two weeks later, I got summoned to Detroit and had to go up to the fifth floor to meet the Ford board. The moment I walked in the room I could smell something was wrong. They basically said, "Look, we've considered things, and we don't want to go ahead."'

It seemed Ford wanted to be out completely; they didn't want to keep the 50 per cent stake. Purnell continues: 'I had the job of phoning up Red Bull and telling them. My contact was Dany Bahar, who was Mateschitz's right-hand man, and he was not at all happy because both he and I had spent hours and hours and hours getting this deal together. Dany told Dietrich, who was actually very

14

magnanimous about it and said, "Well, you know, if it wasn't meant to happen, it wasn't meant to happen." I was really, really down.'

Despite his disappointment, Purnell was still required to find a buyer for Jaguar Racing, as the future of the team's staff all depended on it. He says Ford turned down potential bids from concerns based in China and Russia. All the while he was still hoping to entice Red Bull back to the table – this time with the aim of them being a full buyer rather than as 50:50 partners. 'I went back to Red Bull,' he says, 'but the whole relationship was busted between me and Dany and Dietrich. I kept on putting out an olive branch to them and coming up with various ideas. Oddly, one of these ideas was for them to buy two teams – Jordan and Jaguar – because it looked like it might make sense economically. I ended up taking loads of trips to Salzburg.' Red Bull's HQ is in Fuschl am See, situated in the foothills of the Alps, a 30-minute drive from the Baroque architecture and chocolate-box charms of Salzburg.

'I remember once driving all the way there and parking up outside and demanding to see them,' Purnell continues. 'I can't tell you how hard I tried. There was one meeting where Dietrich kept on banging a table, saying, "Tony, Tony, Tony, you have to understand. We will never, ever, ever, spend more than 60 million euros on the Formula One adventure per year."'

Purnell's persistence was rewarded, but only after Marko had had his say on the purchase of the Jaguar team. 'Helmut would normally keep his cards close to his chest, as he is a canny operator,' says Purnell. 'But this time Helmut said to Dietrich, "This is a good team. It's got all the assets you need to do a proper job in Formula One. The deal that Ford is proposing is good." It wasn't the giveaway as advertised, but it was still a fire sale. Helmut explained to Dietrich that he'd wanted a Formula One team all his life and that there was never going to be a better opportunity than this. Either he moved now or he forgot it. I knew then by Dietrich's reaction it was a done deal. It was all a bit last-minute but we got it across the line. In fact, we signed at the Red Bull's lawyers' place in the early hours. Oddly, even during this, one of the companies Ford had turned down was sending me texts saying they would better any offer, but Ford wanted the Red Bull deal as they were a blue-chip concern.'

Once the sale was agreed, it was inevitable that speculation would immediately switch to who would drive for the team. Somewhat ironically, given the huge part he would later play in Red Bull Racing's history, Mark Webber was quitting Jaguar to join Williams. The Australian had spent three seasons in F1 and been touted as a future star but his results had been punctured by reliability problems at both Jaguar and his previous team, Minardi. He had continued to lead the Jaguar's technical improvements and frequently outperformed his teammate, former Red Bull Junior Christian Klien, but finished the 2004 season with eight retirements in 18 races and in 13th place in the drivers' championship.

Webber's departure had been agreed long before Red Bull completed their takeover. McLaren's Ron Dennis had previously checked on his availability only for him to agree an extension with Jaguar, which wisely contained a number of performance clauses that permitted him an early exit should a better offer come along. Such clauses are commonplace in F1 contracts and allow for wriggle room on both sides of the agreement. For instance, teams can cancel contracts for underperforming drivers.

Understandably, Webber had been flattered by Williams' interest in him. In an *Autosport* article by Adam Cooper in July 2004, Webber made it clear that Sir Frank Williams had been approaching him since 2003, when he discovered his driver Juan Pablo Montoya, who had been signed to his team since 1997, was angling for a McLaren drive. Webber recalls how he first received a call from Williams after the 2003 British Grand Prix, after which the conversations 'intensified'. Williams were an established team and had produced GP-winning cars, something Webber had never got close to before. Webber said: 'Frank was keen, and so was I. When you've got someone like Frank ringing you quite a lot, it's pretty flattering.' This was the chance for Webber to progress his racing career to the next level, by challenging for victories.

Webber ended the season with Jaguar before being released from his contract to test with Williams and do fitness training with cyclist Lance Armstrong in Texas. His departure left a hole in the driver line-up for Red Bull Racing. With Klien likely to keep his seat by virtue of his junior sponsorship links to Red Bull, attention turned to Italian youngster Vitantonio Liuzzi, whom Red Bull backed to the Formula 3000 title in 2004, while German Nick Heidfeld and Britain's Anthony Davidson were also in the running. It was a decision that would be deferred for the time being.

One position that was not being debated was that of team principal, with Mateschitz asking Purnell to remain in charge of the new team for the initial period, although there was no official comment from the Austrian or from Ford.

For Mateschitz, the timing of the purchase was perfect. In 2004, he ranked 406th in *Forbes'* list of the world's richest people and was estimated to be worth around $1.4 billion. The previous year he had hit the headlines for buying the Fijian resort of Laucala. In general, Mateschitz kept a reclusive profile. However, his business was now at a crossroads.

Red Bull was faced with the prospect of defending its 70 per cent worldwide market share of the energy drinks market, thought to then be worth around £2.5 billion. Despite its limited product line, Red Bull had captured the imagination through ambitious marketing, decentralised distribution and sponsorship of extreme sports and pop culture. Its obvious success had drawn the interest of beverage industry giants including Coca-Cola and Pepsi, who looked to bring their own energy drinks to the market. Red Bull needed to do something different to keep ahead of the game and it tapped into Mateschitz's passion for motorsport.

For Mateschitz, moving into the top tier of motorsport made total sense from a branding perspective; it offered the potential for global growth, while maintaining the product's anti-establishment attitude. He had also come to rather enjoy it. After initially being cautious he soon felt at ease, telling *Autosport* on the day of the purchase: 'Our move to fully owning a Formula One race team makes good business sense for Red Bull. Add to this the opportunity of being directly involved in a sport from which I derive great personal pleasure, then it is easy to understand how delighted I am to have made this purchase. It is the logical and final step in the process we started with the Red Bull Junior programme, where we identify, advise and promote young talent through the different formula from karting to the very pinnacle – Formula One.'

CHAPTER 2

THE BULL GETS ITS HORN
– 2005 –

In the months that immediately followed Red Bull's takeover of Jaguar Racing, the initial relief that Purnell experienced at having saved his colleagues' jobs soon turned to uncertainty. He had been working closely with his managing director, Dave Pitchforth, to produce the 2005 challenger, the car that would eventually be christened RB1, Red Bull Racing's first race car. However, while Purnell oversaw operations at the factory over the winter, both he and Pitchforth quickly realised they were at odds with some of Marko's ideas. Tensions were growing between Milton Keynes and Salzburg.

During those months at the end of 2004, Purnell says he sensed that the relationship between himself and Pitchforth and that of Red Bull was not working. 'The relationship never recovered from the collapse of the 50:50 deal,' he tells me. 'When they first took over, we were delighted. It secured the future of the team, which had been weighing heavily on me, and they invited me to continue as team principal. But Red Bull were a marketing company, and a really good marketing company at that – they knew nothing about engineering or building a race car at that stage, and they did not understand how to run an F1 race team.

'We got into some real stress points. One was on the drivers that they wanted to put in. There were some names suggested that we didn't think were up to it. However, that was a minor point. The big thing was they had these crazy ideas about how to build a race car. They wanted us not to use emails, only mobile phones. There was no process. Whereas we believed that Formula One teams were a big, big thing and needed a lot of discipline and formal procedures. And, particularly, you needed a clear budget to work to. Red Bull did some things which myself and Dave were completely unaware of until the bills arrived. They spent enormous sums on things like the motorhome [the three-storey glass and steel paddock building used to host guests and provide an area for staff to have their meals in while at the track] and that led to huge tensions.'

In addition, they wanted personnel changes that Purnell found unacceptable. 'Dave was the best technical manager I had ever come across. He was an absolute megastar who would go on to become the president of Boeing Defence. Marko didn't like him, because he always pushed back when he thought an action was wrong or badly handled. Red Bull asked me to fire him, which I said was completely out of the question. I was pretty angry about it because I thought we had built something that was going places. That car in their first season was totally built using Jaguar's plans, and it came out of the box pretty nicely, running in the top six for the first handful of races, a big jump forward on the R5, the previous model. But they didn't believe in us. The relationship wasn't working.'

Despite the warning signs, the end, when it came, was still unexpected. 'They hadn't dropped any hints that they were going to fire us, so it was a shock to turn up at work and find Marko and some lawyers at the desk.'

Purnell's exit had been brutal and swift. A few years later, he was in France to attend a ceremony at which former FIA president Max Mosley was awarded the Légion d'Honneur. Purnell recalls meeting Mateschitz, whom he says was 'very sheepish' about his short tenure at Red Bull, but kind and happy to chat. 'I've never really felt any great resentment against Dietrich,' Purnell says. 'He was a fantastic businessman and quite rational. He'd always prided himself on the return on investment he got from backing skateboarders, but I think he suffered from the problem people do when they smell petrol; they go all irrational as businessmen. I don't think getting into Formula One squared with him from that point of view. So it felt like an irrational, emotionally led, non-business decision, albeit the realisation of a childhood dream. The irony of that is that it turned out to be a pretty good decision commercially. Hats off to them. They've done a spectacular job.'

Christian Horner was appointed and confirmed as Red Bull Racing's new team principal on 7 January 2005. At 31 years old, he became the youngest-ever manager of an F1 team. With two months until the opening race of the season in Australia, Horner had stepped up from running a Formula 3000 team – the series now called Formula Two – to becoming an F1 principal, going head to head with the likes of big beasts Ron Dennis at McLaren, Jean Todt at Ferrari and Renault's Flavio Briatore. And he was given an immediate example of the ruthlessness of F1, as he explains when we chat in his office in Red Bull Racing in Milton Keynes.

'It was agreed that I'd wait in the car park while [Red Bull executive] Dany Bahar went into the office to see Purnell and Pitchforth and basically fire them,' says Horner about his first day in charge, 'and they were told to leave the building immediately. I was sitting in the car park and saw them come out with a cardboard box with their stuff in. I thought to myself, "F1 is pretty brutal." And then I was brought in and all the staff were assembled. And Dany said, "Oh, we're having a change of management and here's your new team boss!" The only person I knew walking through the group was Ole Schack, who is now the front-end mechanic on Max's car, because he'd raced in Formula 3000. I think he was the only person who was pleased to see me!

'The workforce was stunned. They had gone through a lot of change. I explained that I was here to listen and learn for the first few weeks but I made it clear that the aspiration of the team is to win. It was quite simple. So the people from Red Bull went back to the airport and I went upstairs to the office, where it is now, and there's a secretary in tears because she's just lost her old boss. And I sat down at a desk and there were half-opened Christmas cards and a half-drunk cup of coffee. I thought to myself, "Where do we start?" So I asked to see all the senior people one by one and there was a guy, Graham Saunders, who was head of manufacturing. And I said, "Will you take me around the factory?" I'd only been there once before. So he took me on a walk around the factory so I could see what was going on.'

On that first walk around the factory, it quickly became apparent to Horner that there was talent within the team, but it lacked structure and technical discipline and there was no real sense of what Red Bull wanted to achieve. He had his work cut out and the clock was ticking down, with only two months to go until the opening race of the 2005 season. Horner would have to work quickly to get to know his new colleagues, and in turn they would need to familiarise themselves with the man who was about to become the public face of their team.

Now famous for his role at Red Bull Racing, and his appearances on Netflix's show *Drive to Survive*, Horner had a modest upbringing. He was born in Leamington Spa in 1973 to a family who were in the automotive trade. His grandfather worked at the Standard Motor Company in Coventry as a purchasing manager before setting up his own business. Horner told *Motorsport* magazine in January 2012:

'As a kid I pestered my parents for a kart, just to drive around the garden, and my mother found one in the local paper for £25. In time I managed to get something better, and ended up racing in a category called Junior Booster. In 1991, Renault offered scholarships to help kids move up from karts to Formula Renault, and I won one. I won a championship round and got some poles, and F3 teams started calling. So for 1993 I did F3 Class B with Roly Vincini's P1 Engineering. I had five wins, and finished second in the series.'

He persuaded his parents to agree to him taking a year off after his A-levels, in the hope of pursuing a career in racing. The deal was that he would apply for a place at university the following year if it did not work out on track. By his own admission he was never interested in his university place and claims not to even remember where he had applied to go. But the odds of making it to the top tiers of the racing world were against him, not least financially. It is now estimated that it costs around £8 million to work through the lower formulas to reach Formula One. That funding normally either comes from family, a group of investors, who would be paid back when their driver landed a lucrative F1 contract, or the financial backing of a sponsor, such as a car manufacturer or other automotive brand. Horner was required to source the investment to allow him to buy the parts – fuel, tyres, car – that would allow him to race. He moved into F3 with Fortec in 1994 but this step up, which had got him to within just two tiers of F1, had exhausted his budget.

The following year, he was determined to progress his racing career with the sole goal of reaching F1, but he was unable to fund a drive with a leading Formula 3000 team, which would have moved him closer to competing in the same events that made up the bill of an F1 weekend. It was this financial hurdle which, unbeknown at the time, would set out his career path and lead to a chance meeting with a certain Dr Marko, the title Helmut Marko still uses from the doctorate of law he achieved in 1967. 'I decided that if I could buy and run an F3000 car myself, at least at the end of the season I might still have the car left and something to show for it,' recalls Horner in the same interview with *Motorsport* magazine. 'It was a bit brave, but I thought I'd give it a go. I sold everything I had, borrowed as much as I could from the bank, from my father – who helped me on condition that I paid him back at some point . . .

'I was team manager, money hunter, secretary, cook and bottle-washer, did all the paperwork and the hassle. As mechanic we had a part-time lad who worked at the local Threshers off-licence . . . We needed a trailer and the best deal was one I found for sale in Austria. I took a cheap flight to Graz to look at it. The owner, a guy I'd never heard of called Dr Marko, drove a hard bargain, but I said I'd buy it if he delivered it to Calais for me to pick up. When I told my father I'd given the cash to a complete stranger in Austria on a handshake, and I hadn't even got the trailer yet, he thought I was mad. But Dr Marko's handshake was good, and the trailer duly turned up at Calais. By now I'd found out he was the ex-F1 driver Helmut Marko, and he was running two F3000 cars for Juan Pablo Montoya and Craig Lowndes, so I soon got to know him better.'

Horner's team, Arden – named after the area of Warwickshire where he was born – was formed in 1997 with his father, Garry, and operated on a slender budget with no room for error. Horner could barely afford the parts in the first place so spares were out of the question. If he were to have a crash, it would be a toss-up as to whether he would be able to pay his bills or spend the money on rebuilding the car. The other difficulty was that he was acting as both team principal and driver. He could not afford to be out of action for any length of time. And perhaps overriding all of that, eventually there was the painful realisation that his talent did not match up to that of other drivers on the grid, names like Montoya and Le Mans legend Tom Kristensen. The disappointing awareness that he did not possess the same level of ability left him crushed. He retired from driving in 1998, relinquishing his dream to race in F1. But, on the flipside, his team was gaining plenty of recognition.

Arden had caught the eye of Dave Richards, the senior business-man who founded Prodrive, the British motorsport and advanced engineering group now based in Banbury, Oxfordshire. Richards was vastly experienced in motorsport and had also run the successful BAR F1 team and the Subaru World Rally Team. Horner agreed to a 50:50 split of the team with Richards in exchange for some much-needed funds, which eased the pressure on the fledgling team boss.

However, after an unspectacular first season together, Horner agreed to repurchase the full ownership of the team in time for the 2002 campaign. He picked Czech racer Tomáš Enge and Björn Wirdheim from Sweden as his driver pairing. The repurchase paid off: Arden were not only competitive, they were crowned team champions. Enge won three times but was disqualified from the round in Hungary, which he had also won, after failing a drugs test. The disqualification cost him the title but Enge protested his innocence. The team believed the positive test was caused by some medication he had been taking to treat back spasms. Arden retained the F3000 title the following season, with Wirdheim this time clinching the drivers' title and US racer Townsend Bell as the team's second driver.

The success had piqued the interest of Marko, who approached Horner about running the Italian driver Vitantonio Liuzzi for the 2004 season. Liuzzi was managed by Marko, who had high expectations for him, despite his rather average performances in Formula 3000 driving for Red Bull's junior team. It was another gamble for Horner; however, after switching teams, Liuzzi did not disappoint, winning seven of ten rounds to take the F3000 title. Arden were again crowned winners of the team competition.

Three successful championship titles as a team principal had convinced Horner he was ready to make the leap into F1. If he could not make it as a driver, he'd make it as team boss. He recalls his early discussions with F1 chief executive Bernie Ecclestone, who was look-ing to help him progress into the top tier of motorsport. Ecclestone was trying to encourage Horner to buy the Jordan F1 team, but the purchase became overly difficult. 'I was looking to take that Arden team into F1 and Bernie was pushing me, saying, "We need new young blood in Formula One. I want to get rid of this guy Eddie Jordan, he's driving me mad – why don't you buy his team? I'll help you,"' Horner told the *High Performance Podcast*:

'So I looked at trying to put a deal together to buy what was then the Jordan team. But the deal just got more and more complicated, and at the same time Red Bull was look-ing to buy what was the Jaguar F1 team. They acquired it in November 2004 and later that month Helmut rang me up and said, "Dietrich would like to see you." I went to Salzburg, it was early December, and Dietrich said, "Look, I want to change the management; I've got big ambitions with this team." It was so compelling. He said, "I want it to be differ-ent, I want it to have a different energy, we're not going to be corporate, we're going to do things the Red Bull way. And I'm willing to take a chance on you."

'At 31 years of age I didn't have to think too long about it. Dietrich said, "Look, because I'm giving you the chance when you're young, I'm gonna pay you this much, but for every point you score I'll pay a healthy points bonus. Jaguar scored nine points last year [in fact, the team scored ten points], so if you score ten or eleven points that would be a success in the first year." In the first race we scored nine points. We went on to score 34 points that year and thank God we did, otherwise I wouldn't have been able to pay my mortgage!'

Reporting Horner's appointment at Red Bull Racing, Reuters journalist Alan Baldwin noted that 'Horner will jointly manage Red Bull Racing together with a new technical director, whose appointment will be announced within the next week'. Reports circulated that the German-speaking Italian Guenther Steiner, Jaguar Racing's managing director when Austrian Niki Lauda was in charge of that team, could be in line for a return to Formula One. Steiner of course would later become team principal for the Haas F1 team (until he departed in January 2024) and rise to stardom courtesy of his straight-talking and colourful language in the fly-on-the-wall series, *Drive to Survive*.

Steiner's appointment as technical operations director was confirmed on 13 January 2005. He proved to be a steady hand given the internal upheaval caused by Purnell and Pitchforth's departure. Steiner's background was in motorsport engineering. He had worked in the World Rally Championship alongside greats such as Colin McRae and Carlos Sainz. He later switched to F1 in 2001 when he was appointed by Ford to act as Jaguar Racing's managing director, having been headhunted by Lauda. Steiner quickly reorganised the team and reduced costs but the team still lacked performance and ultimately both Lauda and Steiner were axed by the US car giant in 2003.

After a spell working with Opel in the Deutsche Tourenwagen Masters, Steiner was persuaded to return to the Milton Keynes factory that was once the home of Jaguar, now taken over by the Red Bull team. However, he was struck by the enormity of the situation he faced upon his return to the factory after two years away. Very little had changed. There were still lashings of Jaguar-green paint everywhere and, predating even Jaguar's involvement, Sir Jackie Stewart's sponsorship with the luxury watch brand Rolex meant there had been large reproductions of their famous timepieces hung on the walls, which were being removed when he arrived.

Steiner would provide a crucial link between the factory in Milton Keynes and Red Bull's base in Austria. On a superficial level it was useful that he could speak both German and English, but more importantly he also benefited from his previous association with Red Bull, which stretched back to when he worked in rallying. At a meeting in the team's hospitality building at the Circuit de Spa-Francorchamps on a dreary day in July 2023, he tells me it was a logical decision for him to rejoin his former teammates and work with Mateschitz and Marko on their ambitious new F1 project. 'I had known Dietrich and Dr Marko for a long time,' he says. 'I first met Dietrich when we were doing a rally programme in Austria with Raimund Baumschlager, the 14-time Austrian Rally Champion. He was already wealthy – not like how he became, but still rich – and he was looking to buy into F1. So when they asked me it was quite straightforward. I lived there in the UK and was working in Germany, so they did not need to sell it to me.

'When I went back, it was just weird. Nothing had changed; the people were the same, the facility was the same. Nothing had changed in the two years. There were still just two buildings. I did not think too much about it, but it was nice to be back. I'd had a lot of contact with the staff in between the years I was not there. Christian had started a week earlier. He was a lot younger and less mature but I had no problem working with him. He was not difficult to work with.'

Steiner was not the only addition to Red Bull Racing's expanding team. A few weeks before Horner and Steiner were appointed, they had secured the services of experienced racing driver David Coulthard. The Scottish racer had been released by McLaren in favour of Colombian Juan Pablo Montoya. Coulthard started karting at 11 and progressed his career through British Formula Ford and Formula 3000, where he had mixed in the same circles as Horner. He was offered his F1 breakthrough with Williams in 1994 as a replacement for the late Ayrton Senna. Coulthard secured his first F1 win in 1995 at the Portugal Grand Prix before then joining McLaren. He was second in the drivers' championship to Michael Schumacher in 2001 but was unable to repeat the same level of success in 2002 and 2003, prompting McLaren to change their line-up. The offer from Red Bull suited both parties. For Coulthard it gave him an F1 lifeline with little pressure, while Red Bull Racing were getting a vastly experienced driver who had knowledge of how the larger, successful teams operated.

Coulthard signed a one-year deal with Red Bull Racing that was confirmed on 17 December 2004. He was 33 and had won a total of 13 F1 races in his 11 years in the sport. 'After speaking to team owner Dietrich Mateschitz I was impressed by Red Bull Racing's plans for the future. This is definitely an exciting new team,' Coulthard told Austrian news agency APA at the time.

Horner, who had not been privy to the discussions with Coulthard, was delighted to have such an experienced driver on board. 'I'd known David from his karting days,' he tells me. 'We had some of the same sponsors when he was in Formula 3000, in Formula Three and even in his early years with Williams. So I'd followed his career closely and I knew what he was capable of. Had he not come to us, it could have been the end of his F1 career. But we gave him the responsibility of being a clear team leader. He raised the bar and lifted everyone up. He was the guy who had come from a world championship-winning team, so he was the guy I was going to be drawing on the most and saying, "OK, how does this compare to McLaren? How did they do it?" I could draw so much out of him.'

Steiner agreed with Horner's assessment, adding: 'We had David coming into the team and he knew what to do and what direction to go in. He brought stability. He was a good racer and well respected, despite not being a world champion. He had experience and that helped the team a lot.' It was the perfect challenge for Coulthard. He was wounded and hurt that he'd been written off by McClaren, and this would be a new start. Horner's goal was simple: to rejuvenate the racer and regenerate his self-belief in the hope he would be able to carry the team forward. The team was now all in place and they were ready to make an impact.

CHAPTER 3

OFF TO A FLYING START

– 2005 –

Horner, Steiner and Coulthard were not the only new additions to Red Bull Racing in 2005. As the team hurriedly prepared for the first race of the season at Albert Park in Melbourne on 6 March, other key personnel were being brought on board. Understandably, given Jaguar's failure to produce a reliable car capable of fighting for pole positions and victories, Horner's first job was to scrutinise the team's infrastructure. Very quickly he spotted where the weaknesses were and subsequently went on a recruitment drive to fill the gaps. He also noticed morale was low and understood he needed to set about changing the culture within the team. He wanted them to feel like winners, so he scoured rival teams in the paddock looking for talent who could drive the team forward and bring the positive energy that was required. In essence, he was willing to offer them a promotion in exchange for them having enough faith in the project to jump ship.

Of course, it was a gamble. Memories of Jaguar's demise still lingered and there was no indication that Red Bull would not grow tired of F1 if they were not regular winners, and then decide to pull the plug in the same way Ford had done with Jaguar Racing. However, Horner's ability to sell the team was a considerable factor in his favour. And many of those who did decide to join Red Bull Racing at this time would remain with the team for years.

'Mark Smith was one of the first to join,' says Horner. He had come from Renault and had also worked briefly at Jordan, and he was appointed technical director working alongside Steiner. 'Then there was Rob Marshall, who joined us as chief designer; he also came from Renault. They were the two guys I went after initially, and then I felt we needed to change the team manager. I was giving people the opportunity to step up, so Rob had gone from head of mechanical design to chief designer; Jonathan Wheatley was a chief mechanic at Renault and I gave him the chance to join us later as team manager.' Other names that would follow included Peter Prodromou, who was appointed as head of aerodynamics. He had worked under Adrian Newey at McLaren. Paul Monaghan also joined after stints at Renault and Jordan. Then there was race engineer Guillaume Rocquelin, known as 'Rocky'. And of course, later, Newey himself.

One other hire was Kenny Handkammer, who also arrived from Renault (formerly Benetton). Handkammer spent 25 years in F1 and now works in the US as the Global Director of Service and Technical Operations for Lucid Motors, after a brief stint at Tesla. Handkammer was front jackman when Max's father Jos Verstappen's

Benetton was famously engulfed in a fireball in the 1994 German Grand Prix at Hockenheim, and he ended his F1 career with Red Bull Racing as chief mechanic. 'Kenny was a bundle of energy,' says Horner, 'an absolute force of nature and exactly what we needed in those early days because he was a winner.'

'Mark Smith had joined Red Bull Racing and I had spoken to him about it. He wanted to see if I was interested in joining too,' says Handkammer as we chat on the phone after negotiating the time differences between the US and the UK. 'It was funny because I was at Renault and they wanted me to be their chief mechanic as well. They were a successful team and had just won the constructors' championship. I met Mark in a pub called the Green Man near the team's factory in Milton Keynes and we discussed the situation at Red Bull Racing and I decided to give it a go. It was simply because I had been in F1 for 18 years already and I'd reached a point where I needed a change of scenery – or to get out of the sport altogether. I decided that I wanted to try something else, to see if I could have a small impact in helping another team be successful. That's what drove me forward. I could be part of building a team. It was like the early days at Benetton, and it offered me a restart. I went and handed in my notice at Renault and it did not go down very well. They were telling me I was crazy; the team had never finished any higher than seventh [on three occasions between 2002 and 2004] and effectively were a bunch of losers. And then Flavio [Briatore] tried to convince me to stay, which was quite nice, because he doesn't do that very often with many people – but I still left.'

Handkammer's account of life at the team in those early days chimes with Horner's reflections. It quickly became evident to him that a change in attitude and culture was required. 'There were a lot of things that had to change,' says Handkammer, 'because the mentality was pretty poor. Some of the staff seemed happy to settle for finishing seventh; do their job, go home, take the cash. They didn't have any kind of belief or optimism . . . We replaced those guys.'

Handkammer looks back at his decision to join Red Bull Racing as 'probably one of the best things' he had ever done. But how do you go about changing a culture within an underperforming team? 'It was about installing a winning mentality,' he says. 'You have to convince the people that you are working with that you are not the devil who is coming to disrupt the team. There were some people who wanted to stay in the team and those who didn't almost all went by themselves.

'We introduced more procedures, different procedures and better procedures. It was about getting people working better together operationally and having a structure in place. But don't forget, I had worked in F1 when mechanics would work a minimum of 20 hours on a Friday – every Friday. We'd probably have gone on longer but the curfew stopped us from doing that because we had to be in a hotel for a few hours or something. It was all about the challenge. I wanted to be that creative person who was 3D-printing things overnight and coming in and putting them on the car. We'd miss breakfast to fit them on the car to get some performance and everybody would have a big smile on their face.'

The combination of the new arrivals, renewed ambition and substantial investment being made by Mateschitz meant Red Bull Racing became an obvious target for the media, some of whom had labelled the team as a potential surprise package for the season. It was a tag that Horner was keen to play down when he spoke at the team's car launch in Jerez in southern Spain in early February.

The car launch is a key part of the winter schedule and represents an important deadline for the factory, while the marketing and communication departments focus on this date to build a constructive campaign and decide how best to use the launch images to gain maximum exposure. However, given the limited timeframe and the influx of new staff, Red Bull Racing's 2005 car launch was a rather low-key event. Constructed by designers Mark Smith, Rob Taylor and Ben Agathangelou, who had the job of bringing Pitchforth and Purnell's vision together, the RB1 was very much a Jaguar-designed F1 car, powered by a 3-litre V10 Cosworth TJ2005 engine. It featured a dark-blue livery with key Red Bull branding across the front and rear wings and the sidepods. It also carried the 'Sun and Bulls' logo that is now synonymous with the team's cars on the engine cover, behind the air intake.

The unveiling of the RB1 at the venue used for pre-season testing was underwhelming compared to some of the more audacious launches we have seen throughout the history of the sport. But the understated approach was fitting, given Horner's messaging that the team were very much in their infancy.

'We want to punch above our weight and grab any opportunities as they present themselves,' he said in a BBC News article on 7 February, the day of the launch. 'I've inherited a car and engine from a previous management and this year will be putting in the foundations and a structure for the future. We were mainly running for some film we were shooting, but both chassis one and chassis two completed a few laps in wet and mixed conditions and both did exactly what we expected. I haven't had an input into this car but it looks like they have done a pretty good job with it. I am very impressed with what I have seen so far. The team is very motivated and there is a great deal of drive there which I can identify with. Certainly the power of the engine looks respectable. Obviously, reliability is going to be key this year. We will have a step forward on the engine halfway through the year but they are competing against some very big opponents and it's enormously difficult.'

The driver line-up was yet to be completed as Red Bull Racing weighed up which of the two Red Bull-sponsored drivers – Christian Klien or Tonio Liuzzi – would partner Coulthard. All three drivers were present at the launch. Coulthard's decision to grow some stubble drew some light-hearted reaction among commentators when the images were released to the press. Perhaps he was trying an alternative look to keep in with Red Bull's anti-establishment attitude? Horner says the look received the full support of Mateschitz, who told Coulthard to keep it. Photos of Klien and Liuzzi dressed in the team's race suits were also distributed, though they both looked a little awkward in them as neither actually knew which one would be selected to drive for the team. After the initial shakedown, where a car is put through its paces to see that all the systems work correctly, Horner would have to make the decision who would be offered the opportunity to drive the second car. He was more familiar with Liuzzi, having run him in Formula 3000, but the Austrian Klien was the popular choice for Red Bull.

'In David we have a fantastically experienced driver who has won 13 Grands Prix and been on the podium 50 times,' Horner explained in the same BBC article. 'He brings a wealth of experience to the team. He is 33 but he has plenty more to give and at the moment he is our biggest asset. We have a test in Barcelona next week and we will decide after that. Christian and Tonio are two young chargers. Christian will benefit from a second year of racing and Tonio was outstanding in Formula 3000. He is undoubtedly a star of the future. We are very happy with what we've got.'

Pre-season testing is a curious time for F1 teams. It provides a first opportunity to see a glimpse of your opposition but the reality is you never really know what you are up against until the very first qualifying session of the season when the cars and drivers are running at full tilt. While in recent years F1's increased popularity has seen the pre-season laps televised, in 2005 the running was only witnessed by journalists at the track.

The Circuito de Jerez was a popular choice for F1 testing. The circuit had suitable facilities as it has previously held the Spanish and European Grands Prix. It is located 90km south of Seville so escapes the harshest weather of winter, and it's in Europe, where all the F1 teams are based, making it an obvious choice logistically. The lap times are largely unhelpful as a public indication of performance, given that the speed of the cars depends on their weight, which in turn depends on their fuel loads – a figure that remains unknown outside their own garages. However, one clear marker is the number of laps a team is able to complete as the new cars are tested for any signs of mechanical failures.

Encouragingly, on their opening day Coulthard managed 38 laps while Klien racked up 49. Interestingly, their lap times were very similar, with Coulthard just 0.1 seconds quicker than the Austrian. On the second day it was Klien who was 0.4 seconds quicker than his teammate. However, it was the third and fourth days of testing in Jerez that pricked the curiosity of those at the circuit, as Coulthard posted times that were quick enough for sixth and fourth place respectively on the timesheets. The fact that Klien had been selected for the first test over Liuzzi placed him in pole position to drive alongside Coulthard. Liuzzi's first test run would not come until 28 April, also in Jerez, where interestingly he posted a quicker lap time than Coulthard.

The good progress continued too at the second test at Barcelona later in February. This time the Circuit de Catalunya, home of the Spanish GP, provided the venue for three untroubled days of testing where the team simulated a Grand Prix distance and handed a shakedown to their back-up car. In the quote for the press release that accompanied the positive end to testing, Horner is clearly upbeat, although there is an undeniable sense of him trying to keep expectations low-key: 'Barcelona was another positive test for both the team and the new RB1. During the three days of testing we have completed a considerable amount of mileage and have gained a good initial understanding of the new car. The car has proved to be reasonably reliable and following a final test at Silverstone next Monday, we are looking forward to Red Bull Racing's debut race in Melbourne.' Steiner added that 'the RB1 proved to be reliable and technically mature' and that 'all in all, we can go to Australia full of confidence'. The team were all set to head down under, with Klien having been selected over Liuzzi to take the position of Coulthard's teammate.

There is something special about the first race of an F1 season being held in Australia. It is probably partly due to the fact that, from a European perspective, it conveys the nature that it is a global championship. There is simply no easy way to make the journey to Melbourne. Wherever you change planes in the airline hubs of the Middle East or Asia, you are still looking at over 26 hours of travel before you even factor in the time to and from the airports.

Albert Park is set just outside of Melbourne, towards the bustling beach resort of St Kilda, and it is a popular destination for those who work in F1. There is something satisfying about arriving at Tullamarine Airport and feeling the warmth on your face after a winter in the UK. Largely speaking, the food is good and the coffee even better. Given Red Bull's marketing history and the ambitions of Mateschitz, it was inevitable that they would not let the occasion of the team's first race in F1 go uncelebrated. So it was fitting that Pink would perform at Red Bull's season-opening party. It was the hottest ticket in town, with the singer flanked by Coulthard and performing to a backdrop of a digital screen playing a video of a car driving around a racetrack. The concert was held in the Docklands area where 1,300 guests and VIPs were treated to a champagne reception and 50 kilometres of electrical cables powered a spectacular light show to thrust Red Bull Racing into the spotlight.

The party also served to provide a reality check for Horner, who recalls heading into the first race with some trepidation. 'I'd never gone as far as Australia,' he says. 'I soon realised that it's a bloody long way! I remember being in that paddock for the first time and there was the realisation of what we were going into. There was this big party for the Australian market that had been organised and

Pink played and the drivers got up on stage and suddenly you start to realise that this is very real and that it was quite a big step from where I came from. But it was still a car with four wheels in a series.'

The team had the youngest driver in the field in Klien, who was 22, as well as the youngest team boss in Horner at 31. In the team's press release ahead of the race, Coulthard, who had won in Australia twice before in 1997 and 2003, said: 'This is the start of an exciting adventure for Red Bull Racing, and following a promising winter-testing programme, I am looking forward to making my debut and I am optimistic for the season ahead.' Horner's quotes from the same release were equally mundane, although he alluded to the fresh presence that Red Bull Racing looked to bring to the sport. He said: 'This is obviously a significant event for Red Bull Racing who will enter F1 this Sunday. We have prepared within the time available to us as fully as possible and I am delighted with the effort and commitment made by the team. Hopefully people will identify Red Bull Racing as a team bringing new ideas as well as new spirit to F1.' Certainly, their decision to throw open their doors and welcome in the media went against the grain of some of the larger teams, who generally wanted to keep them out.

Somewhat unusually compared to modern F1 weekends, opening practice was then a chance for teams to not only test their cars, but also their rookie drivers. So Red Bull Racing now handed Liuzzi his chance behind the wheel, after losing out on the second seat to Klien. He seized his first opportunity in F1 and got off to a flying start, topping the first practice session of the year. Running against other reserve drivers including Pedro de la Rosa for McLaren, Ricardo Zonta for Toyota and Robert Doornbos for Jordan, Liuzzi proved he deserved his shot. Well, initially he did: in the second session, he spun at turn three, which left him beached in the gravel. Embarrassingly, he had to climb out from his stranded car and trudge back to the team's garage on foot to await the car's transportation back on a low loader.

Attention switched to qualifying, which initially saw the introduction of a new qualifying format. It was the third time in five years that the FIA – Formula One's governing body – had tinkered with the rules with regard to forming the grid for Sundays' races. Position was determined by the aggregate time of two single-lap flying runs, one being set on Saturday afternoon and one on Sunday morning. The new system meant that for the opening race, the order was run in reverse from the final race in 2004, the Brazilian GP, and proved bewilderingly complicated for fans to understand, as the two lap times set on different days were totalled up to determine the grid. Thankfully, the concept was dropped after only six races for a more simplified one-session qualifying format.

A heavy shower arrived when Sauber's Felipe Massa started his flying lap on a set of slick tyres – tyres that are completely smooth and have no tread, so they have a larger contact with the surface and more grip. This enables drivers to take corners at quicker speeds in dry conditions, but they are disastrous in the wet. While Ferrari's Michael Schumacher had time to select the wet Bridgestone tyres, he was only able to set a time that was good enough for 18th. Red Bull Racing's duo lucked into the healthy combination of a dry run and a scrubbed-up track that provided some grip, thanks to others putting down a layer of rubber. Coulthard duly qualified in fifth and Klien in sixth. McLaren's Montoya (ninth) and Räikkönen (tenth),

Ferrari's Rubens Barrichello (11th), Renault's Fernando Alonso (13th) and Ferrari's Schumacher (18th) were all out of position, as all had expected to be higher up the grid and battling for pole.

At the start, Mark Webber, who had qualified in third for Williams, was quickly passed by Coulthard, who had leapfrogged the Aussie by turn one. At the front was Giancarlo Fisichella, who had qualified on pole for Renault and was able to hold off Jarno Trulli's Toyota while Coulthard was caught in the battle for third place with Webber. The two came close to making contact on lap 15, causing Webber to run onto the grass while Alonso and Barrichello battled back into the top three behind Fisichella, who won. Somehow, Coulthard came home in fourth place ahead of Webber's Williams, while Klien, to his credit, was seventh. For the briefest of moments it had looked as though Coulthard was on for a podium himself. 'A podium finish was achievable today,' he said after the race. 'That would have been a dream start for Red Bull and at one stage I was beginning to dream a little, but I can't complain about fourth place. It is much more than we expected. With Christian scoring points as well, it is a fantastic start for Red Bull Racing.'

Horner admits his flight home was 'more enjoyable' than the slog to Melbourne, as the team left Australia placed in third in the constructors' championship. 'We were a little fortuitous,' he says as he sits in his office in Milton Keynes, 'because we had to go out in order for qualifying, and we had benefited from the conditions. In the race, DC [Coulthard] was running in third place for a long percentage of it and in the end, we just did not have enough pace. But we had a double-point score in our first ever Grand Prix. It was such a result for a team that had turned up and which nobody was taking very seriously. They thought we were just a party team and yet there we were, just one place from a podium. It felt like a win. I remember DC coming back to the garage after the race and just giving him a big old hug. I don't think he'd ever seen a team so excited to finish fourth! He joined from McLaren where winning was the expectation, but that result was a clear statement of intent that got us off the mark.'

Steiner recalls his conversation with Mateschitz soon after the chequered flag. 'I remember speaking to Mr Mateschitz after the race and saying that we got lucky there and he said, "I agree with you on that one!" We had no expectations, we were just trying to get our feet off the ground and we were fortunate. The car was decent and we made points, there were a few incidents that helped us, but it absolutely was a good start to the season.'

Finishing in the points, however, was no fluke, as Coulthard managed top-ten finishes in three of his next four races, although Klien did not enjoy the same good results. After stalling on the grid in Bahrain, the third race of the year, he was swapped with Liuzzi – a move that in hindsight Horner admits was not beneficial to either driver. Liuzzi did not fare much better than his opposite number and the swap left both drivers unhappy.

By the time the season had moved around to the Monaco GP, however, nobody was focused on the team's drivers. It was all about their mechanics – and the motorhome. Red Bull Racing had agreed a promotional partnership with Hollywood director George Lucas to run a special promotion for the *Star Wars* film, *Revenge of the Sith*. Monaco is just down the coast from the famous Cannes Film Festival and this offered Lucas an ideal opportunity to promote his latest blockbuster. The partnership would see the team's mechanics wear iconic white Stormtrooper outfits, while logos were also placed on the race cars. Characters from the film would attend the Energy Station, the three-tiered hospitality building, which was being used for the first time, and which had drawn so much criticism from Purnell. It took 25 people to build it and 11 trucks to transport it and the music thumped from it all weekend, unlike their rivals' equivalents.

The whole mentality behind the Energy Station was one of confident self-promotion and to create a fun vibe in keeping with the drink's non-conformist reputation. 'We all know what Red Bull are capable of doing,' says Steiner as we sit in his tiny office in the Haas F1 team motorhome when we speak ahead of the 2023 Belgian Grand Prix. He is fidgeting about and at one point a member of staff interrupts to ask him the whereabouts of one VIP guest, but his mind is back in 2005 and those early days of Red Bull Racing. 'The marketing ideas of Mr Mateschitz and the money he put into it was amazing, so it made a big impact,' he continues. 'On a personal level I was not surprised by the motorhome because he had the creativity, he had the means to do it and he wanted to do it because there was a good reason – to get attention. We are talking about it now. He took F1 into a new era of marketing and opened it all up. Formula One was lucky to get Red Bull into the sport because they have done so much for it. It is like what Ron Dennis did at McLaren. Ron had taken a racing team into a corporate set-up and then Dietrich came and moved it up to the next step, by using the motorhome as a proper B2C [business to consumer] marketing tool. It was not just a shiny crystal palace, it was something more – and it moved F1 and raised it a level.'

At the following race, the European Grand Prix at the Nürburgring, Coulthard came agonisingly close to earning the team their first podium. At one point in the race he was running in first place, but a mistake in the pit lane when he was caught speeding triggered a penalty that cost him his spot in the top three. In his haste to get ahead of a Minardi, Coulthard had released the speed limiter button a fraction too early. 'It was an incredible race,' says Horner. 'I just think the Minardi distracted him and he came off the speed limiter just a moment too early. Without that penalty, it would have been a podium for him.' His fourth-place spot marked the team's last real chance for a podium that season.

Despite this minor setback, Coulthard continued to pick up points, along with the returning Klien, who had moved back in favour, partly due to Liuzzi's double retirement in Spain and Monaco. The target Horner had been set by Mateschitz was to beat Jaguar Racing's previous year's total of ten points. In the event, Red Bull Racing finished their debut season with 34 points, just four points behind BAR Honda, and ended up in seventh place in the constructors' championship. However, despite still searching for their first win, undoubtedly their biggest victory came at the end of the year – with the unexpected capture of the F1 design supremo Adrian Newey from McLaren.

CHAPTER 4

THE FIRST PODIUM

– 2006 –

Newey's appointment was confirmed on 8 November 2005 and in the accompanying press release Horner is quoted as saying, 'It sends out exactly the right message that we are totally serious about what we want to achieve. Adrian was keen to take on a new challenge and I'm delighted that we managed to get him to join us.'

Newey is considered the best Formula One designer of all time. Using 2B pencils, he has designed several world championship-winning cars for different teams. He arrived at Red Bull Racing from McLaren, where he had only recently been offered a new contract, with the Woking team believing that he was committed to them for the long term. In their PR riposte after his departure was announced, McLaren's wording was interesting, with the press release saying: 'The pressures of working for a front-running Formula One team are intense and we have been aware for quite some time that Adrian was looking for a new challenge with a smaller team. The decision to leave McLaren was both amicable and mutual and we wish him all the best in the future.'

Newey's capture was a landmark moment for Red Bull Racing, but the origins behind his move are quite revealing. Horner recalls how their first discussion came about because of Newey's curiosity about their motorhome at the 2005 Monaco GP. The designer had been lured by the razzmatazz surrounding the *Star Wars* partnership and his inquisitiveness had tempted him inside the Energy Station. Mateschitz's attention-grabbing brainchild – and the 'enormous sum' it had cost, in Purnell's words – had paid off in the most unexpected way.

'My first interaction with Adrian was when I saw him outside the Energy Station in Monaco,' says Horner. 'He was standing there and looking up at this new hospitality unit and I invited him in for a drink. The *Star Wars* movie was of course coming out and they wanted to do a big number in Monaco where they were holding a screening. I asked Adrian if he wanted to come to the premiere with his wife, who must have been totally pissed off with me for making her sit through a three-hour *Star Wars* movie! That's how it started. He was just interested in what we were doing. McLaren was very different – you needed 15 different passes to get in. The Energy Station had neon lights and music pumping out. We didn't have any sponsors, so everyone was invited in. Adrian finished his drink and went back to the morgue-like facility at McLaren next door.'

Horner turned to Coulthard, who knew Newey from his time at McLaren, for some more insight into how he worked. Coulthard had a good relationship with him and knew the best way to reach him.

'I met Adrian again in Montreal for the Canadian GP,' recalls Horner. 'I said to DC, "Look, I really think we have got a chance of getting Adrian. He's interested in this project." DC quickly said, "Well, his wife makes all the major decisions. You know, let's get dinner together."'

Horner arranged a dinner at Bluebird in London. He continues: 'The more Adrian and I talked, the more we realised what we had in common: where he grew up, where he went to college, which was just up the road from where I grew up. We just hit it off – not talking about racing cars but our different career paths. I just had a huge respect for him and the cars that he designed – he'd designed a car for Nigel Mansell, who was my hero! We had a really pleasant dinner. We were getting warmer and warmer. I spoke to Dietrich about it afterwards and he said, "We'll bring him to Austria and show him the world of Red Bull."' Now with the full support of Mateschitz, Horner was able to pull out all the stops in an attempt to convince Newey to jump ship. Results had been going well on track, but adding a designer of Newey's ability to the team would clearly be a huge coup and Horner knew he was close to getting his man.

'Dietrich sent his plane over and we flew from Luton to Salzburg. And because he was under contract to McLaren, his wife at the time, Marigold, was paranoid about him being seen speaking to Red Bull. So, she put a cap on him and gave him some dark glasses; he almost went with a false moustache!' recalls Horner, laughing. 'Then as soon as we got off the plane, there's a group of Japanese F1 fans who see DC and they all want to take his picture. Only Adrian has forgotten his cap, and Marigold's going mad, worrying if Ron Dennis would see the photos . . .'

Horner remembers how things got even more surreal once they were in Salzburg, when Mateschitz met up with them at one of his hotels. 'He turned up on a Harley-Davidson and then disappeared inside for a bit,' says Horner. 'He just came out, had a bit of apple strudel with everybody and laid out his vision for the future. He said that he wanted to have two teams in F1. Then he said, "See you later," got back on his bike like *Easy Rider* and rode off. That was it.

'We put Adrian up in a hotel and later we went off in a sea plane and landed on a lake. He got the full experience. There were all these people in rowing boats and we had to get them all out of the way so we could land this plane on the lake. We had something to eat there, and then took off again.

'That was going to be the point I came out and asked him to join us. We all went out, and I had a [salary] number in my head that was so bloody far below what turned out to be the reality. So I asked him, "What would the number be to get you to Red Bull Racing?" and Marigold said to me, "Well, this is what Adrian's on at McLaren," and she told me the figure. I asked if we were to offer something similar, would he be prepared to come, and he said, "I think I'd be up for the challenge."

'So I went out of the restaurant to phone Dietrich and I said, "Dietrich, I've got some great news: Adrian has agreed to join us." And he said, "That's fantastic. It's the best thing for our team. This is game-changing for us, it's a statement of intent." And then I said, "The bad news is it's this many million a year . . ." He said, "That's obscene, send him back on the plane, it's ridiculous!"

'Two minutes later I was working my way back to Adrian and thinking that maybe I could split the sum between bonuses because

I could not let this opportunity go, and Dietrich rang me back and said, "No, this is a game-changer for our team. Go for it."

'Wow! And that was it. So we celebrated with a few drinks and went to some dodgy Salzburg nightclub. And then at ten o'clock the next morning, Adrian was sent up in an Alpha Jet. He's in an ex-military plane and the pilot, Ziggy, was about 87. I think at one point Adrian was inverted over Innsbruck at the speed of sound. He was probably trying to work out where the flaps were. He got out looking so green. But that was his introduction to the world of Red Bull.'

Newey's acquisition was recognised along the paddock: Red Bull Racing had secured the most coveted designer in the sport. Indeed, Newey would go on to shape the future success of the team.

Purnell hailed the signing as 'a masterstroke', although he makes the point that Newey had been used to substantial budgets at McLaren: 'Adrian, more than anything, unlocks budgets. His attitude to money is beyond cavalier. He'd just look people in the eyes and say, "I thought you wanted to win. You know, if you don't want to win, I shouldn't be here, so spend the extra million." It sounds like I'm condemning this; I'm not, I'm admiring it. Adrian was a big step towards really getting Red Bull to spend.

'He believes in poaching the best people and having the money to react to anything. And that works; it's the traditional way of running a Formula One team. Adrian also had the best wind tunnel in F1 to work with. It's not hyped up like the others,' says Purnell. This is a reference to the team's now-former wind tunnel, which was based at the old Bedford research site of the Royal Aircraft Establishment and fitted out with a variety of testing equipment. It had undergone significant refurbishment at the start of the 21st century, surpassing the equipment used by other teams. 'It was originally built in the Cold War,' adds Purnell. 'It's like a cathedral. It was and is quite different from anybody else's. And really the fuel Newey needed wasn't petrol, it was money to spend. When you have those two [the technical genius of Newey matched with the resources], it is one almighty combination.'

Despite the excitement generated by Newey's arrival, he was unable to influence the RB2 for 2006, which had already been designed under Steiner's watch. In fact, he did not spend too much time with the design team during that first season. He oversaw the first few races in 2006 and was then redeployed on a new project for Red Bull, who were simultaneously exploring a project racing in the US NASCAR series.

Sadly, the RB2 proved anything but a monster on track. The winter testing had confirmed the team's fears that it was not only slower than expected, but it was also unreliable. Horner wryly observes that it must be the only F1 car that could overheat at a cold Silverstone Circuit. According to Horner, when Newey saw it, he declared that he would focus on the following year's car instead.

Newey quickly drew a line in the sand, stopping all the development on the RB2 and announcing he wanted all the wind-tunnel time for the RB3. That prompted a few awkward discussions between Horner and the design team who had been putting the RB2 together. He had to tell the team that all the development was dead.

At the season-opener in Bahrain, there was another Red Bull launch party at the Ritz Carlton Hotel, a beautiful venue within the capital of Manama, where Newey arrived wearing 'the most lairy

T-shirt', as Horner describes it. Clearly Newey was 'fully embracing the rock and roll theme of Red Bull'. Perhaps it should not have been such a shock, for despite his calm demeanour, it is worth remembering that the great designer was expelled from school at 16 – or 'asked not to return' as he puts it – for tinkering with cars and getting drunk at a sixth-form concert where he jumped on the mixing desk, pushed the sliders up to the maximum and turned the music up so loud that it rattled the windows out of their lead fixings. Maybe this was just another case of him deciding to cut loose ahead of what was going to be a difficult year scrapping for points.

The start to the 2006 season also featured another sizable breakthrough in the realisation of Mateschitz's dream: the establishment of a second team called Toro Rosso – Red Bull in Italian. The name was picked for a reason. In the same way that Mateschitz purchased Red Bull Racing from struggling Jaguar, this time he bought the struggling Italian team Minardi from its owner, Paul Stoddart.

Stoddart was an Australian businessman who had had previous dealings with F1 teams Tyrrell, Arrows and Jordan before he bought Minardi in 2001. As Mateschitz had outlined to Newey in Salzburg before riding off on his Harley, he wanted to have two teams in F1. Minardi were based in Faenza in northern Italy and the plan was for Red Bull to keep the team located at the factory there, with Italian still used as the principal language.

The idea was that by having a second team, they would create an extra level for the Red Bull Junior programme, this time in F1 itself, acting as a feeder team for Red Bull Racing. The only slight difference from the Red Bull Racing deal was that this time, Mateschitz approached his friend Berger to agree to a 50:50 joint ownership deal, tying the former F1 driver to the team, a position he held until Red Bull regained total control in November 2008.

The deal was an audacious one and took the competition by surprise. Minardi had been in F1 since 1985 but in that time had failed to reach the podium. As a result, they were looked down on by their larger rivals on the grid, despite attracting a considerable fanbase. It was another perfect opportunity for Mateschitz to defy expectations and preconceptions. When asked about his decision at the time, Mateschitz told Horner, 'It's the exuberance of the challenge.'

Toro Rosso was kept apart from Red Bull Racing; it would assume its own identity and have its own separate HQ. But there was one notable overlap: the Italian team had a chassis that was a modified version of the 2005 Red Bull Racing RB1, which was of course a design from Jaguar. They also used Minardi's contracted supply of engines, which followed the previous year's specifications. This consisted of a 3-litre V10 engine that had its performance slightly limited, after smaller teams were given special permission to use them because the new V8 engines were too expensive to buy. Horner's team, however, were running the all-new 2.4-litre V8 Ferrari power unit.

Horner recalls how the initial plans would have seen 'one design house and one production company based in Milton Keynes that would design a car for both teams. One, Toro Rosso, that would turn out to have a Renault engine installation and one, Red Bull Racing, that had a Ferrari installation.' Red Bull Applied Technologies would supply two teams.

However, this plan caused huge uproar and a flurry of challenges to the Concorde Agreement, the legal contract that ties the FIA, the teams and the owners together. Rival teams were upset that Toro Rosso were not producing their own car, as one of the key F1 rules is to require a team to act as a manufacturer. The smaller teams felt that Toro Rosso were effectively being handed a free chassis, meaning they could not remain competitive. Consequently, in 2009, it was decreed that any technological ties between the two teams should be cut and that Toro Rosso and Red Bull Racing would become separate entities. The 2010 Toro Rosso car, therefore, was the first to be designed and built in their own factory in Faenza, Italy.

The opening rounds of the 2006 season saw Alonso and Schumacher trade places for victories and Renault trade positions with Ferrari. For Red Bull Racing, however, their only top-ten finishes occurred when Coulthard finished eighth in Australia and Klien was also placed eighth in the opening race in Bahrain. It was shaping up to be a miserable season and a slip back to the Jaguar days of battling to remain off the foot of the constructors' championship table. So it was a huge surprise for everyone when Red Bull Racing achieved their first podium finish – at the 2006 Monaco GP of all places.

Red Bull went into the race with low expectations, having broken down or overheated in the first six meets of the season. The famous street circuit is notoriously difficult to make up grid positions, so qualifying is vital and the team were hamstrung by their car's performance. But that had not dissuaded former F1 driver-turned-commentator Martin Brundle from making a bold prediction over dinner with Horner on the Wednesday before the race. Horner remembers that Brundle said Coulthard always went well around Monaco – the city in which the Scottish racer had made his home – and predicted him to finish on the podium. Horner replied, 'Martin, we will not be anywhere near the top ten, let alone the podium!' He subsequently proposed a bet that if indeed Coulthard did somehow defy the odds to make the podium, then he'd strip naked and jump into the new swimming pool that had been added to the gigantic Energy Station – or 'floater home' as it was dubbed, because it floated in the Monaco harbour of Port Hercules. The extravagant swimming pool was an additional hospitality area that had been constructed 40 miles away in Italy and floated on a six-hour journey down the coast to Monaco where it was attached to the Energy Station building.

Qualifying for the race was a cut-throat affair, as Schumacher and Alonso battled for the all-important pole position. In the final moments, just as Alonso was on a flying lap and setting quicker sector times than Schumacher, the German inexplicably slid his Ferrari into the barriers at the final turn, the Rascasse corner. The error caused minimal damage to his car, but it was enough to force the other cars on track to slow down, with Alonso having to abort his attempt.

In the post-qualifying interview, Schumacher said he 'locked up the front and went wide' before adding, 'I wasn't sure what was going on after this because of the positioning of the cars and so on; I was not aware. In the end, I checked with the guys what the situation was, where did we end up . . . and they said P1, so I was glad, considering what had happened. I tried to engage reverse but it didn't engage, and I didn't really want to back up just by myself without knowing what was coming around the corner – and then, finally, it stalled.'

Alonso was clearly none too impressed. When asked by Byron Young from the *Mirror* if he thought any less of Schumacher after this incident, the Spaniard said: 'I have my opinion and I won't tell it here.'

Having worked with Young for a number of years and become good friends with him, I know him to be a tenacious journalist, and he was clearly not going to let this questionable incident go unchallenged. He turned to Schumacher to ask him outright: 'Michael, do you think you cheated today?'

Schumacher's response was curt: 'No. And I don't know why you ask such a bad question. I think it is pretty tough, I have to say. If you were to drive around here at Monaco, you would probably not ask this question.'

Unfortunately for Schumacher, people continued to ask questions and he was subsequently punished by the race stewards and sent to the back of the grid. Alonso was promoted to pole. Ferrari were furious, with managing director Jean Todt openly disgusted by the verdict.

However, the opinions of other racing professionals were very clear. 'It was the cheapest, dirtiest thing I have ever seen in F1. He should leave F1 and go home. There was absolutely no way it could be an error. He parked the car to stop Alonso doing his fast lap,' the 1982 world champion Keke Rosberg said on the BBC Sport website on 28 May. Jenson Button, who was driving for Honda in the race, is also quoted as saying, 'Anyone who knows anything about Formula One knows it was done on purpose. It was too obvious.' Perhaps the most incendiary quote came from former F1 world champion Jacques Villeneuve, who said: 'You cannot win seven world championships and do that. It is unacceptable. It shows that every time in the past that he has done something like that – and people have given him the benefit of the doubt – that it was obvious. I hope it was deliberate, because if that was a mistake, he should not even have an F1 super-licence. I don't know what goes through your mind when you decide to do that, when you know that the rest of the world can see. I don't understand it, it's stupid. He didn't need to do that, he's a seven times world champion, he was on pole position. Why do that? It's only going to make him look bad. This is embarrassing.'

In all the rumpus, it was missed that Renault's Giancarlo Fisichella was also penalised for blocking Coulthard and as a result he was dropped five grid places. In the aftermath, and some hours after qualifying had finished, Coulthard had made up two places and would line up in seventh place.

For the Grand Prix itself, Coulthard was having an unspectacular race until several cars in front of him started to have problems. Webber was first, retiring his Williams with an exhaust problem. Räikkönen was next when his McLaren caught fire and the Finn famously retired to his private yacht, rather than the team's garage. Sauber's Villeneuve and Rubens Barrichello at Honda both were issued with penalties that promoted Toyota's Jarno Trulli to third and Coulthard to fourth place respectively. And then mission impossible was achieved when Trulli's Toyota suffered a catastrophic hydraulic failure that shut the car down on the way up to the casino, promoting Coulthard to third.

'I thought, "He's going to blow up or something's going to happen," ' says Horner, 'but he got the job done – and we sent him up on the podium in a Superman cape! The most sacrosanct podium on the calendar and he was there dressed like Superman because, like with *Star Wars*, we had done partnership with the *Superman Returns* movie. He went up in this red cape and it flew in the face of all the traditions. No other team would do that.

'As he was up there, my phone started going bonkers. I read off a text from someone who used to work for me saying, "So looking forward to seeing you get your clothes off later!" I wondered what they were talking about. And then I found out that Martin had mentioned on ITV's coverage that "this third position is going to cost Christian Horner a naked jump into the swimming pool", as he told the world about our bet! I knew I'd have to fulfil it and was planning to do it late at night when nobody was really around, but as I walked back from the garage to the Energy Station, everybody was there waiting for this moment. DC had been winding them all up, saying, "Christian's got to jump in there." There was no way I was jumping in the water in front of that lot, so I said, "Give me your flippin' cape," and I nicked his Superman cape. That protected my modesty while I jumped in!'

As the season fizzled out, Dutchman Robert Doornbos replaced Klien for the final three races of the season, but by then Red Bull Racing had already secured a new driver for 2007 who would partner Coulthard – one of two new drivers who were welcomed into the Red Bull/Toro Rosso fold that year. One of the faces was a very familiar one for the team at Milton Keynes . . .

CHAPTER 5

WEBBER'S ARRIVAL

– 2007 –

Selecting a driver line-up is always about getting the right balance for your team at any given point – whether that means running a stellar driver alongside a consistent and low-maintenance foil who is there to capitalise whenever they can, or picking two inexperienced racers to provide some excitement and development, as was the case with Toro Rosso. It is all about managing the right level of competitiveness between the two drivers without allowing a rivalry to overstep the mark and cause a division within the team.

F1 is considered to be the ultimate team sport given there are in some cases thousands of people working towards getting their two cars around the track in the quickest time possible, so a cohesive approach is often what works best. It therefore made total sense for Red Bull Racing to sign Mark Webber as Coulthard's teammate for the 2007 season, bringing the Aussie back to Milton Keynes to rejoin the team he left when he moved to Williams.

Webber's time at Williams had been cut short after the team had decided to promote their Austrian reserve driver Alex Wurz alongside Nico Rosberg. Red Bull Racing seized the opportunity and confirmed his signing back into the fold on 7 August 2006, while also confirming that Coulthard would be retained. In the press release that accompanied the breaking news, Horner says: 'David has continued to lead the team well and demonstrate the form he showed during 2005 . . . He has shown commitment, determination and motivation to deliver at the highest level in Formula One. It was therefore an easy decision from both sides to extend the relationship for 2007. He's still one of the best drivers on the grid and we're delighted to have him in the team.' Explaining the decision to pick Webber, Horner adds: 'We chose him for a number of straightforward reasons. One, he obviously has undoubted speed and ability, and two, he appears to have the determination and motivation needed to succeed. We're entering an exciting new phase in the short history of Red Bull Racing and Mark was an obvious candidate for us . . . We believe that together he and David will form a very solid partnership, which will give us one of the strongest driver line-ups in the field.' Webber's arrival meant that Klien was released at the end of 2006. After being dropped by Red Bull, the Austrian's F1 career quickly fizzled out and he subsequently turned to racing sports cars in other categories.

Webber's decision to join Red Bull Racing was a sensible one. He had first-hand experience of the team having worked in Milton Keynes with Jaguar, only this time it was married with the ambition and financial means that Mateschitz brought to the outfit. In the same press release, Webber says it was 'fantastic to be joining Red Bull Racing', and that 'it's clear that the team is very hungry for long-term success'. He mentions his original decision to leave Jaguar before the Red Bull takeover was completed, saying: 'After I left Jaguar Racing at the end of the 2004 season and discovered that Mr Mateschitz was taking over the team, I said that I felt the team had been placed in very good hands and had an assured future. As a team, it seems to be very realistic and knows the challenge that lies ahead.' Webber was 29 and at a career crossroads. He could look at moving back into sports cars or switch back to Milton Keynes and continue his F1 career. It was a no-brainer given how hard he had worked to reach F1.

Webber is one of F1's colourful characters, who perhaps does not get the level of respect his racing career deserves. Straight-talking, no-nonsense; an interview with him is always interesting and insightful and accounts for why he now has a successful career as a TV pundit. He was born on 27 August 1976 in Queanbeyan, a small town in New South Wales near Canberra. His father Alan earned a modest living as the owner of a petrol station and a motorcycle dealership – and he was also a huge F1 fan. Battling against unfriendly time zones, he would frequently wake his son up to watch races on the other side of the world, only to fall asleep himself on the sofa.

Webber was a talented athlete and represented his high school in athletics and rugby league, and he was keen on swimming, cricket and Australian rules football. He'd also taken to riding dirt bikes on his grandfather's farm. He was, however, dissuaded from taking up racing them by his father, who had sponsored some of the other younger riders and was fearful for his son of the accidents those riders had been involved in. Instead it was deemed safer for the young Mark to race go-karts, leading to his first venture on four wheels aged around 13 – considerably older than the age at which the majority of the F1 grid got their first introduction to karting.

Mark honed his racing in karts at the Canberra Go-Kart Club and other local races. His father funded his son's career as he progressed to the junior level in 1991 when he was 14, and he won the Australian Capital Territory and New South Wales State Championships the following year. In 1993, he won more titles, including the New South Wales Junior National Heavy Championship.

The 1994 season would see Webber move into the eight-round Australian Formula Ford Championship, driving an RF93 Van Diemen F1600 car that his dad had somehow scraped together enough money to buy. However, in his debut season he finished outside the top ten in the championship. It would also be the same year he would meet his future partner and personal manager, Ann Neal. Webber's father was only able to fund his son's racing career up to a certain point, so he turned to Neal, who at the time was the media officer for the Australian Formula Ford Championship, to help find sponsorship.

Webber and Neal hatched an ambitious plan to reach F1 that first saw him relocate to Sydney before moving to the UK, where he quickly made an impact, finishing second in the 1996 British Formula Ford Championship – a competitive single-seater series which was considered to be the next step after go-karting

The following season Webber progressed another rung up the ladder into the competitive British Formula Three Championship that featured considerable talent – the previous year Montoya was driving in the series, as was Horner. Webber would drive for a team owned by fellow Aussie Alan Docking, where he came fourth overall and was voted Rookie of the Year. However, success had come at a considerable cost and the Webber coffers, both his own and his father's, had run dry. It is here where his rise to F1 takes another twist.

In the November 2010 edition of the *Red Bulletin* – the life-style magazine published by Red Bull – an article looks back on how Neal and Webber joined forces with Australian rugby legend David Campese, who had just retired from playing and was seeking out a new career in athlete management. Campese's attempts to drum up sponsorship for Webber among fellow businessmen failed, with Campese saying: 'I tried to explain to these guys how important funding was to a guy trying to make it in motorsport but there was no interest. Nothing. I remember saying to Mark afterwards, the most important thing was to just remember these guys who said no. And when you make it and they want a piece of you, tell them to get stuffed.' The *Red Bulletin* claims that Campese then put in £100,000 of his own funds to help progress Webber's career, which has since been repaid.

With funding now in place, Webber was starting to get the recognition for being a quick and tidy racing driver, while his straight-talking had impressed Norbert Haug, the former vice president of Mercedes-Benz motorsport. Haug offered Webber the chance to drive for the team in the 1998 FIA GT Championship, racing GT sports cars with roofs, as opposed to the open-cockpit single-seaters Webber had been racing. He was driving along-side Mercedes' German Touring Car legend, Bernd Schneider, who acted as a mentor to him, and the two won five races and took eight podiums to finish runners-up to Mercedes' second team.

Webber's decision to race in sports cars would not detract from his goal to race in F1. His side venture, however, nearly cost him his life. During the warm-up for the 1999 24 Hours of Le Mans race, his Mercedes had a major aerodynamic fault where the design caused air to build up underneath his car, creating more lift than downforce. The result was catastrophic. As he sped between the Mulsanne and Indianapolis corners, his Mercedes launched into the air and spun into a terrifying flip before it came crashing down outside the barriers and catch-fencing (the wire mesh fence that allows spectators to see through but is critical for catching debris). It was a narrow escape. In December 2015, Webber was interviewed about the accident by BT Sport's Clare Balding. Reflecting on the crash, he said: 'I was thinking it was all over. If I go in the trees, I had no control over it. The windscreen in those cars is super-thin if branches or trees come in. It was in slow motion. You think about family, you think it is not good.'

Miraculously, Webber escaped unhurt, but the accident ultimately prompted him to turn his focus back to European single-seater racing, with Neal encouraging him to join the International Formula 3000 series. Webber secured his place in the series driving for the Arrows F3000 team. He finished the 2000 season in third place and won at Silverstone with podiums in Imola and Hockenheim.

The following year Webber, who was now 24, moved to Super Nova Racing, an F3000 team who were affiliated to the Benetton F1 team, and who he and Neal believed would offer him the best shot of progressing to F1. He achieved three wins and finished the season in second place. Benetton boss Flavio Briatore was suitably impressed by Webber's ability to offer him terms to become Benetton's reserve and test driver for the 2001 season. He would be responsible for developing the car for the team's first-choice driver pairing of Button and Fisichella, driving it between races and trying new parts, such as front and rear wings, after they had been tested in the wind tunnel. He would also deputise for either should they be unable to race.

Flavio Briatore was a shrewd operator with a background in business rather than motorsport. He had a chequered past in his native Italy where he had faced multiple charges of fraud, though he was ultimately acquitted. He had found his way into F1 via Luciano Benetton, who had founded the fashion company of the same name and later made Briatore commercial director of his Formula One team, Benetton Formula Ltd, after buying the Toleman team in 1985. Briatore was later promoted to managing director before eventually becoming team principal.

Webber would also join the Italian's management company, and Briatore brokered his move to small Italian team Minardi in 2002, the team which had struggled for points and would later be bought by Mateschitz, and of course become Toro Rosso. He replaced Fernando Alonso and made his F1 debut in Melbourne in the Australian GP where he defied the odds to drag his under-powered Minardi PS02-Asiatech to fifth place. But he was unable to better the result and, aside from an eighth-place finish at the French Grand Prix, he was hamstrung by the poor reliability which had been a constant theme for the team.

He subsequently moved to Jaguar Racing, spending two seasons with the team before his move to Williams. The dream move to the legendary Oxfordshire-based motorsport giants saw him land his first podium, coming third at Monaco in 2005, but the switch did not live up to his expectations and the allure of driving for such a historic name fizzled out. The relationship with the team broke down as Williams struggled for sponsorship and the promise of racing a competitive car quickly dried up. Nonetheless, he had proved his ability behind the wheel and showed that he deserved his place in F1.

Webber says a meeting with Mateschitz in Jerez, plus the lure of working with Newey, were considerable factors in the decision to join Red Bull Racing. 'Obviously Adrian was a big attraction,' he says when we discuss his route to F1 in the McLaren motorhome, where he is working in his current capacity as the manager for Oscar Piastri. 'But I think that as I spent more and more time with Dietrich, I understood that the chances of this going in the right direction were getting higher and higher. It was great to meet him. I'm a sports fan myself, so irrespective of what he was doing with me, and with our team and Formula One, what he did with other sports was also something mighty.'

Webber was also processing the unravelling at Williams, which had forced his hand. 'They were tough years at Williams. There was great ambition to what we were hoping to achieve there. But then there was a big realisation that we were in a tough spot. BMW had quickly left and taken their technical support, and some of the sponsors had also left too, resulting in a lack of investment. It was a pretty tough 24 months. In my mind, when Red Bull asked, I thought, "I don't like chopping and changing teams." But when I got back to Milton Keynes, there were a huge number of people that were still there from Jaguar, so that was a positive thing for me. And when I looked at the journey they were going on, it was not hard for me to get my head round it.'

Horner recalls how the decision to sign Webber was a by-product of his discussions with Briatore about Renault supplying Red Bull Racing engines – a partnership that would prove instrumental in the team's future success. Briatore, who had run the Benetton F1 team, was now not only both Webber's manager and the team principal of the Renault team (after the French car giant bought the Benetton team in 2000), but also, on top of that, part-owner of a London football club, Queens Park Rangers.

'In 2006, things were not going that well for Williams,' says Horner. 'I had been speaking to Flavio about getting a Renault engine – I'd even been going to QPR matches to convince him to give us a Renault engine – and that's when we started talking about Mark. Nobody else was that keen on him; the others wanted Montoya, who was racing at McLaren but was unhappy and seeking a change. But I rated Mark from my F3000 days and we made a deal for Williams to release him early from his contract so we could sign him. It was nice and straightforward. It was a case of "that's the fee, let's get on with it".'

Horner was not the only person glad to see Webber join Red Bull Racing. Handkammer recalls how his arrival gave the team a boost. 'I've known Mark since he was 21 years old,' he says. 'When both he and DC joined the team, they knew things needed to change and they were looking forward to it. It was a tough experience in the first few years, but it was a *good* experience. Once they were in the team along with Adrian, from that point onwards, that's when the belief started happening. On track it wasn't the greatest time, but things soon improved dramatically to the point we had almost won the championship in 2009. It was all about getting the right people together, having that belief and just trying to help the team. We didn't have answers at the beginning; it was a case of figuring everything out as you went along.'

The 2007 season would mark a significant moment for Red Bull Racing as the team were granted an Austrian racing licence. Previously, had the team won a race in their first two seasons, then the Union flag would have been flown on the podium while the British national anthem would have played. That was changed to reflect the Austrian ownership. However, it would be some while before 'Land der Berge, Land am Strome' would be played at a Grand Prix in victory.

Meanwhile, there was scant chance of achieving a win in 2007, for while the RB3 proved to be quick over a lap, it was painfully unreliable. Newey's design was brought to life at the season-opener in Melbourne, with Webber impressing and qualifying in seventh place. However, he dropped back in the race and ended in 13th, while Coulthard was sent out of the race after a collision with Wurz. It would prove to be the first of seven retirements for the Scottish driver during the 17-race season. Interestingly, Webber would also retire from seven Grands Prix.

'The problem was that Adrian had designed something that the team were not yet able to deliver or produce for him. Reliability was just horrible, but you could see the basis of the car was there,' says Horner.

A rare highlight was the 2007 European Grand Prix, which was held at Nürburgring in July, so-called because the Hockenheimring held naming rights for the 'German Grand Prix', and an agreement to share them could not be reached. Webber had qualified in sixth while Coulthard would start the race down in 20th place after the team had sent him out on track too late in Q1, the first session of qualifying, which determined the grid for Sunday's race. Heavy rain on the formation lap of the race caused mayhem and quickly saw plenty of drivers pitting for tyres and subsequently changing positions in the race. However, at one point conditions had deteriorated to the extent that race director Charlie Whiting was forced to stop it. The race proved to have a high level of attrition with nine drivers failing to finish, having spun off or suffered a mechanical failure. But somehow, Webber had managed to steer clear of the carnage to come home in third place, taking the team's second-ever podium.

In the post-race press conference, Webber was understandably pleased given the huge unreliability issues that had plagued both him and Coulthard over the season. 'It's a bloody huge relief for the whole team and for myself,' he said. 'We've been ripped off quite a lot in the past but it is always down to preparation. It's not due to luck, it's not due to this and that. No one is interested in excuses; we have to get the results ourselves.' When quizzed by the US journalist Dan Knutson at *National Speed Sport News* whether he feared retirement in the final few laps due to yet another breakdown, Webber replied: '[It was] absolutely horrible, because I wasn't that confident, to be honest. If you look at our reliability record it has been quite poor.' He added: 'Once we had done our second stops, and I had a comfortable third going on the slick tyres, I thought, "Just stay together, just stay together."'

Maybe it was the increase in confidence? Perhaps it was the frustration at all the DNFs (Did Not Finish results) over the season?

Either way, Horner had noticed that a competitive rivalry was beginning to develop between his two drivers. 'The relationship was good,' says Horner. 'You could see that Mark wanted to establish himself as the lead driver and DC likewise. So there was a healthy tension between them. I think it was in Australia – certainly one of the early races in the year – that DC got somebody to knock on Mark's door in the middle of the night, just to cause a bit of mayhem.'

But while both drivers were helping the team progress, it was clear that their rivalry was also starting to cause some friction. It reached a head at the 2007 Chinese Grand Prix held in Shanghai, where Coulthard finished eighth and Webber in tenth place. 'Mark was hugely quick over a single lap,' Horner continues. 'But I remember when we got to the back end of the year, it all got a bit spicy between the two of them in China. DC decided not to listen to team instructions. It was clear that Mark was quicker and they were on different race strategies. There came a point where they would just ignore my messages over the radio and start racing each other hard. You could see it was going to end up in a mess. So, I remember after that race I gave them both an almighty bollocking. It shocked DC. I don't think he'd ever seen me get revved up before. So they had a respectful relationship, but they certainly weren't close in 2007.'

The season finished with Coulthard in tenth place in the drivers' championship while Webber was 12th, with the team placed fifth in the constructors' championship. But they were left counting the cost of a total of 14 retirements, with Red Bull Racing recording just four races where both cars finished the course.

Red Bull Racing's inconsistent performances, however, were nothing compared to the misery experienced at their sister team,

Toro Rosso. Poor reliability and driver errors had been an ever-present theme throughout the year, with American racer Scott Speed being replaced after the European Grand Prix, where he had spun off in the wet. Speed's luck – and more importantly the patience of team boss Franz Tost – had run out and he was removed from the team after three straight DNFs. His replacement, however, would have a huge hand in shaping not only Toro Rosso's but Red Bull Racing's future.

Sebastian Vettel was still just a teenager when he proved in a single race that he had the speed and the talent to make it in F1 by becoming the sport's youngest point-scorer at the time. At the 2007 United States Grand Prix, the young German had filled in for the injured Sauber driver Robert Kubica where he finished eighth to score a point. Kubica had suffered a high-speed accident in the previous race, the Canadian GP, where he made contact with another car and was subsequently launched into the air before hitting a concrete wall. The impact was measured to have a peak g-force of 75g and he was travelling at over 186mph when he first made contact with the barriers. After a brief spell in hospital in Montreal, Kubica was released and his intention was to race in Indianapolis as planned. However, when a driver has been injured, they are required to pass an FIA fitness test, which he subsequently failed. It left BMW Sauber's founder Peter Sauber and team principal Mario Theissen with a decision to make. They could either replace him with German Timo Glock, who had raced in four Grands Prix for Jordan in 2004, or hand an F1 debut to his fellow countryman Vettel, who was only 19 but who'd had a glittering career in the lower formulas. Plus, he was already up to speed with the team's procedures, having completed many test days.

Vettel had integrated himself into the team in meticulous fashion. While other drivers would look to get out of the paddock as soon as possible after a test run, Vettel would spend hours with the engineers refining the processes and studying every piece of data. It was a practice he had learned from his idol Michael Schumacher and he'd continue right up until his retirement.

BMW opted for Vettel and he soon proved his speed, finishing second in final practice behind Alonso and following that up by qualifying in seventh on the grid. In the race, Vettel made a slow start and an error at the first turn when he ran across the grass and dropped positions. But he recovered from his early setback to land the eighth-place finish and take the final point available. He was 19 years and 11 months old and set a new F1 record, but his age proved to be a limiting factor when it came to the celebrations, according to Beat Zehnder, BMW Sauber's team manager. In an interview with F1.com's Lawrence Barretto in 2022, Zehnder recalled: 'It was something worth celebrating so we took him to the Slippery Noodle, which is Indiana's oldest blues bar, they say, in the States. But he was too young to enter. They didn't let him in as when they saw his ID, he wasn't 21. He'd just scored a championship point in his first F1 race – and they said, "no way". We stayed; he had to go back to the hotel!'

Vettel's performances in the US, coupled with Speed's deteriorating relationship at Toro Rosso, had prompted Marko to speak with Theissen about signing Vettel for Toro Rosso, especially as Red Bull had an existing partnership with him as he was part of the team's young driver programme. There was another reason for Vettel to leave BMW: despite his impressive result, BMW wanted to keep

Kubica and Nick Heidfeld for the 2008 season, as the team were on an upward trajectory. It was impossible to know at the time just how good Vettel could become, and he was still seen as a risk. The simple fact was there was no space for him at BMW.

Toro Rosso, however, could offer Vettel an opportunity to drive in F1 immediately. It was a smart choice. He could progress to F1 with a smaller team where he could do his learning and make his mistakes without the scrutiny and pressure of driving for a manufacturer or leading F1 team.

Horner's early recollection of Vettel comes from when he was racing in Formula Three in 2005. After a comprehensive win in the Formula BMW ADAC championship the previous season where he had achieved 18 victories in the 20 races, Vettel was driving for ASL Mücke Motorsport in the Formula Three Euro Series. At the end of the season, he was the best-placed rookie in fifth and had been offered a test with Williams and then Sauber, who signed him up as a test driver for the following season, while he was also competing in the 2006 Formula Three Euro Series, the Formula Renault 3.5 Series and the Masters of Formula Three.

'While he was delivering in Formula Three, that was when he really came to our attention,' says Horner. 'Red Bull had this joint tug of love over him with BMW. Before then, I first met him when he came to the factory one day. He'd passed his driving test and was a Red Bull Junior driver. He'd gotten in his BMW and driven all the way from Germany to Milton Keynes to ask for a look around. I was just very impressed with this young guy who turned up uninvited and said, "Hi, I'm Sebastian Vettel. Can I have a look around?"

He'd literally just rocked up and was very polite and we showed him around and he was very grateful. After that, whenever he turned up at the factory he did so with boxes of Swiss chocolates for the secretaries and receptionists.'

Ironically, Vettel would lock horns with his future teammate in the 2007 Japanese Grand Prix when he crashed into Webber. Perhaps it provided the perfect precursor to their relationship in the team, which would become turbulent and result in some high-profile bust-ups. Somehow, Vettel had defied all expectations to be running in third place behind Lewis Hamilton and Webber, who was looking good for a career-best second place. That was until lap 46 when Vettel drove into the back of the Red Bull, sending them both out of the race.

Somewhat embarrassingly for the 20-year-old, the accident happened when they were both driving behind the safety car, deployed due to the rain. Reporting afterwards, Reuters' Alan Baldwin quoted Webber saying: 'Hitting cars behind the safety car is obviously a bit of a no-no. He [Vettel] did a good job of driving in the bad conditions and then stuffed it up in the easier situation. It was clearly a lack of experience . . . it's the old thing in this game, small mistakes sometimes look massive and that was a small mistake on his side that looked like an absolute howler.' Vettel was apologetic, saying, 'I am very sorry for Mark. I had no intention to put him out. In the end we cannot rewind the race . . . of course I am disappointed in myself. I destroyed his and my race.'

Horner recalls meeting the young racer after his collision with Webber: 'After the race, we ended up in some filthy dive in Tokyo where it serves shots. I remember Sebastian coming up and finding me and just apologising for what happened. I suppose Mark saw him as a bit of a risk as a young junior that was waiting in the wings to come through.'

A week later, however, and it was a completely different story as Vettel posted an astonishing fourth-place finish in the Chinese Grand Prix, despite starting in 17th place. Big things were starting to happen.

CHAPTER 6

ALL CHANGE
– 2008 –

Over the winter break, the positive end to the 2007 campaign had increased morale within the factory. The design of Newey's second Red Bull Racing car, the RB4, had progressed well, and there was more confidence in the reliability of the all-new Renault R27-2008 engine. The challenger was officially launched on 16 January 2008 in Jerez, with both Horner and Newey dressed in thick overcoats when the official photos were taken outside of the team's garage. In contrast to the bleakness of their dark coats and the puddles on the ground was the striking livery popping in the gloom. The pinstripes that had featured on the RB3 were extended along the dark blue bodywork while the now-iconic bright yellow was retained for the nose cone and the airbox.

There is a widely held belief, among journalists at least, that if a car looks quick when it is still, then it usually performs well on track too – the sleek-looking FW14 Williams from 1992 and the McLaren MP4-20 from 2005 both being good examples. The livery also helped the car stand out from the rest of the grid, while the addition of the radical new fin-shaped engine cover, which would become widely known as the 'shark fin' – designed to improve rear-end stability – made it unique upon its launch, though it soon became a staple feature on many other cars.

The car itself was an evolution of the previous year, with the team hoping their painful issues with the reliability of the RB3 had been put firmly behind them. The crucial failings of that car had come as a result of a disjointed technical process, a notable hangover from the transition from Jaguar Racing. The team needed to analyse why parts were failing and ensure that matters were rectified in time for the 2008 season, which, crucially, would be the first opportunity for Red Bull Racing to carry Newey's design ethos all the way through production. It meant the transition from one model to another was smoother than in the team's previous years, where they had inherited a design from the previous team or been placed under extra pressure due to a late engine change.

The 2008 season marked a fresh start and the feel-good factor was evident from the first shakedown, a trouble-free run in southern Spain that took place immediately after the gloomy-looking photo shoot. There was a positive mood at the winter test too; reliability looked markedly improved and the team were able to build on the pace their drivers had shown at various times in 2007. The solid performances in the winter test had not gone unnoticed by the media, who had Red Bull Racing earmarked for a spot in the 'best of the rest' category behind Ferrari and McLaren.

Amid the busy pre-season testing sessions there was also a run out for Vettel in the RB4, when he deputised for the injured

Coulthard in Barcelona after the Scot had trapped a nerve in his neck and shoulder and needed time to recover. Vettel was the logical choice given he was a Red Bull driver with Toro Rosso, and he welcomed his run on 19 February, racking up 109 laps with a best lap time that was good enough for seventh on the timesheets. Meanwhile, Webber's quickest time during his 58 laps saw him placed in 17th.

The decision to have Vettel deputise for the injured Coulthard was sensible for Red Bull Racing but also for Mateschitz. The previous season Vettel had excelled at times and made mistakes at others but one of the pillars Mateschitz had installed early on in the team's history was his desire to have a production line of talent. It was wise to have a ready-made replacement for whenever Coulthard did decide to quit – and Vettel knew it.

Despite the pre-season optimism, the 2008 season got off to the worst possible start for Red Bull Racing with a double DNF in the Australian GP. Things had started brightly enough with Webber looking quick in practice, but then it started to unravel in qualifying with the Aussie suffering a brake failure and spinning off, meaning he qualified in 15th. Coulthard qualified in eighth on the grid.

But during the race, any hopes for a turnaround were dashed when, on the opening lap at turn three, Webber, Anthony Davidson, Jenson Button and Vettel all made contact and all four were forced to retire. Then Coulthard saw his race ended after only 25 laps following a collision with Massa, with the Brazilian retiring from the race himself just three laps later with an engine failure.

At the following race in Malaysia, Red Bull Racing were summoned to the stewards after Coulthard's car suffered a suspension failure during practice. The FIA were concerned about the safety of the RB4 but after a thorough investigation the team were granted permission to compete. The decision was welcome, but the delay had denied them running in second practice, robbing them of crucial track time used for refining the car's performance. In the race, Coulthard finished out of the points in ninth and Webber was seventh, taking two points. It began a steady run of finishes in the points for the Australian who was seventh in Bahrain, fifth in Spain, seventh in Turkey, and then fourth in Monaco.

Coulthard, on the other hand, was yet to get off the mark and crashed out in Monte Carlo, where Vettel had finished fifth in the Toro Rosso, despite starting down in 19th place. Horner had seen enough to know that he needed to rethink his driver line-up and decided to speak to Coulthard about calling time on his career.

'DC had reached a level of performance where he did a lot of crashing,' says Horner. 'I spoke to him at the Canadian GP and said to him, "Let's announce it at the British Grand Prix that you're going to stop and that you can become an ambassador for the team" – which he still is. We discussed it through and DC liked the idea that it would be announced on his terms. Anyway, he goes to the toilet just before the first session and he bumps into Helmut [Marko], whom I had informed about what was going to happen and explained the plan. And he goes straight up to DC and says, "So, you're stopping in Silverstone and Vettel will replace you." DC came out of the toilet and back to the garage and said to me, "I think I've just been fired!" I explained to him he wasn't and that he'd go on until the rest of the season.'

Somewhat ironically and most definitely fittingly, Coulthard went on to finish third in the Canadian GP for his first podium since the 2006 Monaco Grand Prix. In the post-race press release he said he was 'delighted to get a podium for the team' and that 'the strategy worked well and all the credit to the engineers, mechanics and everyone back at Red Bull for all their hard work'. Horner, meanwhile, paid tribute to Coulthard's result 'after such a tough start to the year'.

Coulthard's imminent retirement soon became the sport's worst-kept secret. In an interview with *Autosport* a week prior to the British Grand Prix at Silverstone, he told Simon Strang that 'in theory it should be', when asked if the 2008 race would be his last home GP. Coulthard added, 'I'm quite a realist. When something has happened, or a decision has been taken or whatever it happens to be, it's not something I dwell on, I just get on with the next thing.' He then said: 'There will be a point, naturally, where that's not going to continue.'

Given all the speculation, when Coulthard called a press conference for 3pm on Thursday 3 July, ahead of the race, everyone present realised it was likely to be his moment to break the news officially. Coulthard's statement said: 'I would like to announce today my decision to retire from racing in F1 at the end of this season. I will remain actively involved in the sport as a consultant to Red Bull Racing, focusing on testing and development of the cars. I have an open mind as to whether or not I will compete again in the future, in some other form of motorsport, so I am definitely not hanging up my helmet!' His plans would include working as part of the BBC's Formula One coverage and three years driving in the German Touring Car series.

Coulthard had called time on a stellar 15-year F1 career that had given him 13 wins and 62 podiums. He went on to thank his parents for their support, along with a host of others, including Mateschitz and Horner, 'for his open and professional management style in association with Helmut Marko'. Horner had formed a close friendship with his driver, which is unusual in the sport but perhaps understandable given their proximity in age. In a statement released by Horner, he described Coulthard as 'a consummate professional', adding: 'He has demonstrated that he is a real team player, a fact reinforced by the statistic that he has only driven for two other F1 teams in his career. He scored our first point, our first podium and was the first of our drivers to lead a Grand Prix. Above all, he is a gentleman and I regard him as a good friend. His retirement brings to a close not just his career as a Grand Prix racing driver but also a chapter in the history of Formula One, if one considers the changes the sport has been through while he has been involved with it.'

Sadly, Coulthard's final British Grand Prix appearance lasted less than a lap after a collision – with Vettel, none other.

Just two weeks later, on 17 July 2008, Red Bull Racing confirmed Vettel's promotion from Toro Rosso for the 2009 season. The news broke on the eve of the German Grand Prix at Hockenheim, where it was also confirmed that Webber would be remaining in the team. The smart money had been on Vettel to replace Coulthard but there were rumours within the media that they would agree a one-year deal with Alonso, ahead of his move to Ferrari in 2010. Those rumours proved unfounded.

'We are delighted that Sebastian will be joining us next year,' said Horner in the press release accompanying the official announcement. 'With David Coulthard announcing his retirement as a Formula One driver a fortnight ago at the British Grand Prix, after careful consideration, it seemed natural to announce his replacement here at Sebastian's home race in Hockenheim. As he was already part of the Red Bull family, choosing Sebastian as Mark Webber's team-mate was not a difficult decision. However, we have always stated that our aim is to have the strongest available driver line-up and Vettel's selection also matches these criteria. Having only turned 21 at the last race and with only 17 Grand Prix starts to his name, he is still on a learning curve, but it is clear that he has plenty of ability and speed. We are confident that Red Bull Racing will make the most of these attributes and believe that, in Mark and Sebastian, we have a very competitive driver line-up for 2009.'

Vettel had been promoted after his excellent season with Toro Rosso but when I asked him about how he came to join Red Bull in the first place, he provides a wonderful anecdote about his first few encounters with Mateschitz, revealing how the tycoon had been single-handedly responsible for getting him into F1. 'My very first meeting with Dietrich would have been at the Red Bull Ring in 2001 when the Red Bull Junior Team was launched,' he says when we discuss the early years. 'It was funny because Helmut [Marko] said to me, "OK, so you're karting and you can start international go-karting," and I said to him, "Yeah, well, I just came back from the European Championship that I won!" He didn't know it at the time. But for Dietrich, it must have been a quick hello. Let's say the first proper meeting was in 2007. I was with BMW and they didn't really commit to F1 and then this seat was opening at Toro Rosso. We were in negotiations with Helmut, Franz [Tost] and Gerhard [Berger], and they were like, "Shall we give him a chance? I don't know. It's a risk . . ." Nobody really had the balls to make a decision and then

Dietrich put his fist down on the table and said: "Give this boy a chance. If he's good, he's good. If not, then we'll take somebody else. Give him a shot." So obviously nobody disagreed. And that was that. He made it happen and the rest is, you know . . .'

In the same press release that accompanied the announcement, Vettel was clearly delighted that Mateschitz had given him the opportunity: 'I am very proud to be joining Red Bull Racing and it's always good to have an early decision on what you are doing next year. As a driver your target is always to be with the most competitive team possible and, over the past couple of years, Red Bull Racing has proved it has great potential, so this is a good move for me. I have been part of the Red Bull family for a long time and with its Junior Team since 2000. Throughout my career, they have offered me great support and now, to drive for their senior F1 team is a dream come true and I am looking forward to having a great season next year, even if I still have a lot to learn about F1.'

Despite being part of the Red Bull young driver programme, Vettel's switch to the senior team was not met without resistance from some within the organisation – namely Toro Rosso, who wanted to retain the German, having seen the progress he had made during his short time with the team. Many within the sister team felt that he would do better to spend another season there, but Red Bull had already seen enough to be convinced he was ready for the next step in his career.

'He was just a kid,' says Horner, 'a really nice guy. Very fresh, very eager but also demanding. He knew what he wanted in terms of support and was really into the details. He was shrewd. He knew the people in the team who could help him and he would really put in the effort with them. Mark was already popular within the team. But Sebastian started spending time with the designers, started going up to people and really listening to them. He'd also visit the factory because he wanted to know what was going on. It was all about the detail, detail, detail.'

If anyone needed any final convincing about Vettel's potential in F1, then they were left without any doubt when he won the 2008 Italian Grand Prix at Monza while still driving for Toro Rosso. It was a seminal moment for Vettel, as he achieved the first of his 53 wins in F1, but it would also be the first victory for Toro Rosso. Vettel had qualified on pole in wet conditions and in the race he was leading while Webber looked good for third place until he spun, spoiling what would have been a sensational result for Red Bull as he finished in eighth place.

Vettel's victory meant he became the youngest driver ever to win an F1 race – he was just 21 years and 73 days old. It was a mightily impressive result, especially considering the Toro Rosso was powered by a 2007-spec Ferrari engine. Vettel would use the result in Italy as a springboard for the rest of the campaign, scoring solid points in Singapore, Japan and Brazil. 'We had signed him quickly,' says Horner, 'and then he won the race in Monza. The chassis on the Toro Rosso started to come alive and the Ferrari engine was pretty potent and Sebastian was starting to get more out of the car.'

While Vettel impressed in his last season with Toro Rosso, there were contrasting fortunes at Red Bull Racing, as Webber managed just three points in the whole of the second half of the season. Coulthard, meanwhile, mustered only two points, which came courtesy of a seventh-place finish in Singapore. At the season-ending

Brazilian Grand Prix, Coulthard's F1 career came to a disappointing end with a DNF. His RB4 was decorated with a special one-off livery in the colours of the Wings for Life charity to raise awareness of spinal-cord injuries. However, his race was over on the opening lap when he was hit from behind by Nico Rosberg, sending him into a spin. He then made contact with Rosberg's teammate, Kazuki Nakajima, which broke his suspension.

'I'm pretty gutted; it's not how I wanted to end my career,' said Coulthard in the post-race press conference. 'I took a cautious approach into turn one and left plenty of space for the car on the inside, but unfortunately I think Rosberg hit me through turn two, which spun me round. I thought it would be OK, but then Nakajima ran into the front of my car and took off the front corner. I was going to do some doughnuts for the crowd, which is something you normally get fined for! But it didn't work out. I can't complain, though – I've had a good career, so thank you to everyone who has supported me. I've been overwhelmed by the level of support I've had from the paddock this weekend; it means a great deal to me that so many people have taken the time to say, "Nice career and good luck with the future." And, in the absence of a world championship, I think if I can leave with that, then that's a good ending.'

CHAPTER 7

A NEW ERA
– 2009 –

Red Bull Racing's new era with Vettel and Webber suffered an early setback before a wheel had even turned in the 2009 season. It came in the form of a freak accident for Webber during a charity bike ride in Tasmania in November, which left him with a broken leg among other injuries. Webber was struck by a car in Port Arthur where he had been taking part in the Mark Webber Pure Tasmania Challenge – a 250km endurance event consisting of mountain bike riding, kayaking and trekking on the Australian island. The 32-year-old was airlifted to hospital where he underwent surgery on his right leg.

'Mark's in good spirits,' said the event's director, Geoff Donohue, to the media. 'The broken leg is the injury, and beyond that, he's in really good shape. He has a little bit of a graze on his left forearm, but he has had full scans and everything else is clear. He'll be in hospital for at least three days, for sure under a week. I was speaking to him before the operation, and he was already thinking about his rehabilitation.'

Webber's injury significantly impacted the team's pre-season testing schedule. Horner was unaware of the severity of his accident until meeting up with his driver in person. 'When he arrived back in the UK in January we went for dinner,' he says, 'and not only did he arrive on crutches but he also had his arm in a sling. He didn't tell me that he had also broken his collarbone! It was touch and go as to whether he would be able to drive the car for the first race of the season – he was still going in ice baths and he had this great big scar on his leg. He was a bit paranoid because he thought he would be asked to jump off a box and onto his bad leg to demonstrate that he could do it.

'To be honest, by the time we got to the first race, he was still in recovery on that injury and it was still hurting him. So he came into that first season with Seb on the back foot, with an injury – and now he's got this hotshot teammate and suddenly the dynamic in the team had all changed.'

Webber's injury left him with a new sense of vulnerability. Not only did he have a new teammate to contend with, but the emergence of the Brawn GP F1 team meant a new title contender had entered the race. 'The injury definitely wasn't ideal,' he tells me. 'I missed some winter testing and I used to pride myself on being physically in very good nick. That wasn't the case then and I was certainly behind the eight ball. I hadn't been laid up in a hospital ever in my life before, so it was reasonably traumatic for me. The other thing was that Brawn had come out of the box and their car was like a missile, so we were on the back foot and we did not have an answer to them for the first part of the year.'

The formation of Brawn GP and their incredible world title success in 2009 is one of F1's great stories. Rather like Ford's exit in

2004 due to financial pressures, Honda's exit from F1 in December 2008 was a consequence of the global downturn in the automotive industry. Incredibly, an 11th-hour management buyout led by former Ferrari team principal Ross Brawn had kept the team in business and saw them retain Jenson Button and Rubens Barrichello – plus, crucially, the car, which had been developed with Honda's resources. As it would happen, it also turned out to be blisteringly quick during pre-season testing.

The regulation changes for the new season had been substantial in a bid to make the sport more entertaining, with huge aerodynamic alterations that would play straight into Newey's hands. He now had larger front wings to design, improved grip from slick tyres and the added power for some cars, not all, from the Kinetic Energy Recovery System. However, one aspect that perhaps Newey had overlooked was the 'double diffusers' that had appeared on the Brawn, Williams and Toyota cars, which created extra downforce. Despite several protests from rival teams who questioned the legality of the design within the new regulations, the FIA passed them off, giving an edge to the three teams that had them.

Despite this disadvantage, at the season-opening Australian Grand Prix, Vettel overcame a hydraulic failure in practice to qualify in third place, while Webber, still nursing his injuries, qualified in tenth but was promoted two spots after both Toyota cars were disqualified for running illegal rear wings.

The race itself proved eventful and somewhat frustrating for the Red Bull Racing duo. On the opening lap, Webber was bashed by Barrichello, who was recovering from a poor start. This sent Webber into a slide and he made contact with Nick Heidfeld and then Heikki

Kovalainen. The damage was significant to Webber's car and he was required to pit for some repairs after only one lap, before dragging his broken Red Bull to a 12th-place finish.

Vettel's race, however, was running smoothly: he was in second place behind Button and looking strong for a podium on his debut for the team. Yet three laps from the end of the race he made a mistake going into the first turn, which opened the door for Robert Kubica. The two made contact and both drivers lost their front wings. The aerodynamic drop-off impacted both: Kubica understeered into a wall and was sent out of the race, while Vettel also struck a wall, bending his front-left wheel in the wrong direction. He valiantly battled on in an attempt to score some points but his hopes of finishing the Grand Prix were finally terminated with his car coming to a halt before seeing the chequered flag.

However, his decision to plough on in his doomed attempt to finish the race, scattering debris across the track in the process, had resulted in a safety car finish. Perhaps unsurprisingly, the stewards had taken a dim view of the incident and, after a post-race investigation, Vettel was deemed to be at fault for crashing into Kubica. Red Bull Racing were also fined $50,000 for allowing him to try to finish the race with a damaged car, rather than stopping him from doing so in an order over the radio. Worse still, Vettel would be slapped with a huge ten-place grid penalty for the next race, the Malaysian Grand Prix, as the stewards made their feelings clear.

Vettel apologised in his post-race media duties for his 'stupid racing accident', adding, 'I'm sorry to the team and also to Robert as it didn't just mean the end to my race but also his.' With such a strict penalty in place, the Malaysian GP was always going to be a struggle for Vettel to score some points. He had qualified in third place but the demotion meant he started the race in 13th, while Webber in fact benefited from his teammate's penalty and was bumped forward to fifth on the grid.

To add to the drama, Sunday's race was hit by a heavy downpour, resulting in it being red-flagged and stopped on lap 31, rather than lasting the scheduled 56 laps. As the race had not reached the required distance of 42 laps to trigger full points, half points were awarded to the top eight, which included Webber, who was in sixth. However, Vettel had crashed shortly before the race was halted, having made his way into eighth place, and he was ultimately classified in 15th. The frustrating start to the campaign had yielded few points and quite a lot of time in the stewards' room, yet there were positives to be taken. Through a few tantalising glimpses, the opening two races had provided enough evidence to the team that there was performance in the car, providing they could unlock it. They just needed a clean, penalty-free and mistake-free weekend – and it came at the following race: the third GP of the season at the 2009 Chinese Grand Prix.

Red Bull Racing's first victory in Formula One was understandably a landmark moment. The Shanghai race was only the 81st Formula One Grand Prix that the team had entered – a timescale that had exceeded expectations for many, given they were going from backmarkers to the very top step of the podium. Yet within Red Bull Racing, the victory in China only served to provide an appetite for more success.

The race weekend had started on the back foot for the team, with a split driveshaft boot seal limiting both drivers' practice runs.

In an interview on Red Bull Racing's website looking back to the 2009 win, Ole Schack, who was then working as Vettel's front-end mechanic, admitted that while the reliability issue had unsettled the mechanics, Vettel had remained calm. 'Seb chatted to us in final practice and said the car was feeling really good,' said Schack, 'but that little problem crept up on us, and it looked like we might not be able to deliver on that potential. All Seb could see, when he looked in his wing mirrors, was a load of worried mechanics huddled round the back of the car – but he wasn't frustrated; he was as calm as could be.'

The mechanical issue did initially prove to be a problem for the young German, who was 13th in Q1 with Button and Barrichello again looking strong. However, the RB5 came alive in Q2, as Webber traded positions with Button for P1 before Vettel posted an even quicker time. The result had heightened anticipation within the garage that there was a real chance of taking pole position. In Q3, Webber took provisional pole before Barrichello snatched it back, but both drivers were usurped by Vettel who fired in the quickest time of the session in his one and only attempt. 'With two minutes to go he was in tenth place and hadn't done a lap,' said Schack on Red Bull's website, 'and to then go out and move from the bottom of that Q3 timesheet to the top was just incredible. The whole garage absolutely erupted. I remember I even lost the little pin in my watch that holds the strap on. I was clapping so much and so hard that it just popped out!'

Sunday's race would prove to be another nail-biter and heavy rain ensured it would be anything but straightforward. The rain scuppered the strategy calls and it became a race of reactions to unexpected scenarios. Vettel and Webber held their nerve, while the team executed their pit stops with aplomb, to achieve first- and second-place finishes.

'On Sunday morning, I remember opening the curtains in the hotel and it was absolutely teeming down with rain,' recalls Horner on the Red Bull Racing website. 'The race started under the safety car and Sébastien Buemi nearly obliterated Sebastian [Vettel], nearly took him out of the race behind the safety car, so there was a little bit of luck on our side as well that day. Sebastian rode it out and it was just an amazing feeling to see our cars bring it home first and second . . . seeing the joy and elation on everybody's faces. It was an amazing moment for the whole team not just to win the race but a one-two finish. It was a massive thing to go and pick up the constructors' trophy, even though it was broken and missing one of its handles! It was the breakthrough victory. I just remember the feeling of getting on the aeroplane, still smelling of champagne, and just thinking that this one had been so special. It felt really good going back as a Formula One winner and we'd definitely need to feel that sensation more times in our careers.'

The broken trophy was not the only quirk either, as the British anthem of 'God Save the Queen' was played to celebrate the winning constructor, rather than 'Land der Berge, Land am Strome', the Austrian national anthem as per the team's racing licence. It had also meant that Newey had become a Grand Prix winner with a fourth F1 team.

Writing in the *Independent*, journalist David Tremayne also praised the arrival of the former Williams and BAR-Honda technical director Geoff Willis, whom he hailed as 'instrumental in improving the reliability and helping Red Bull Racing to become a serious contender'. He added that the one-two finish in Shanghai 'owed as much to the engineers back at the factory in Milton Keynes as it did to the race team in China'.

Webber also gave credit to the backroom team. 'You have no idea what the guys went through last night,' Webber said. 'The cars were breaking their driveshafts after just three laps in practice. They did some work at the factory last night to understand this particular problem and they made a change that turned out to be an inspired one. It was something one of the guys in our technical department did.'

The victory had also allowed Mateschitz to celebrate his investment in F1. The marked improvements had been enjoyable, but Vettel's win for Toro Rosso had only served to increase the pressure on the A-team to deliver. With this victory, it would alleviate that stress and also silence the rumours that Mateschitz had been growing impatient at the lack of success for his investment. Ironically, too, it supported Purnell's claim to Ford that it would take five years for the team to be challenging for wins.

Results continued to be strong throughout the rest of the season. In Bahrain Vettel was second and in Spain he was fourth, while Webber was third in Barcelona. However, it was the Brawn duo who remained the quickest, as they utilised the gain provided by the diffuser design on their car. By the time the season had clicked around to Monaco, Newey had designed his own interpretation for the RB5: a two-tiered diffuser that would hopefully quash the advantage enjoyed by the Brawn drivers. Despite the fact that the tight, twisty street track through Monte Carlo would prove to be a difficult testing ground due to the limited aerodynamic opportunities, and Vettel crashed out at Sainte-Dévote after 15 laps, Webber finished a credible fifth.

The first proper test for Newey's design would come at the Turkish Grand Prix where Vettel took a scintillating pole. However, his ambitious three-stop race strategy, where he made three pit stops to have fresher tyres for the duration of the race while other teams opted for just two, dumped him behind his teammate. They finished with Webber placed second and Vettel in third, much to the German's frustration.

Nevertheless, qualifying had proved that the pace had been unlocked from the car and it led to a growing sense that another victory was looming. It would come at Silverstone, the home of the British Grand Prix, less than 30 minutes' drive from the team's factory at Milton Keynes. Vettel was again victorious as the redesigned RB5 was simply unstoppable in the cooler temperatures. He had taken pole the previous day and converted P1 on the grid to take the top step of the podium, while Button had struggled. For good measure, Vettel had also set the fastest lap of the race for a hat-trick of accolades.

Webber too had excelled, passing Barrichello after some stubborn defending by the Brazilian to take second place. Another one-two finish – and Vettel coming out on top meant his second win of the season had cut Barrichello's second-spot advantage in the drivers' championship to just two points. Webber was a further 3.5 points behind, but it had now become apparent that Red Bull Racing were closing in on Brawn for the constructors' title.

Having seen his younger teammate triumph on two occasions, Webber arrived at the German Grand Prix, the race immediately after Silverstone, determined to break his duck. He'd felt that his opportunity to win the previous race had been taken away due to an error during qualifying where he was caught behind a slow Räikkönen, who was hogging the racing line (the preferred position on the track around each corner that leads to the quickest lap time), earning a rebuke from Webber in the post-qualifying press conference. 'I would have liked a slightly cleaner run on my last lap,' he said. 'Kimi was, I don't know, drinking some vodka or dreaming or something . . . I don't know what the hell he was doing. He should have been on the right and he's on the racing line, dreaming, so that wrecked my rhythm.'

The German Grand Prix gave him a fresh chance to turn his fortunes around. He arrived in inspired form, taking his maiden pole position in qualifying. In Sunday's race he was pressed hard by Barrichello and the two banged wheels at the first corner, earning Webber a drive-through penalty. Undeterred, he battled back through the field after serving his punishment and crossed the line ahead of Vettel by over nine seconds to become the first Australian to win an F1 race in close to 30 years. Alan Jones was last to achieve it with his victory in the 1981 Caesars Palace Grand Prix.

'It's an incredible day,' said Webber after the race in an outpouring of emotion that can perhaps be partly attributed to the fact he was still contending with an injured leg. Webber continued: 'I wanted to win so badly after Silverstone, as I thought I had a good chance there, then after yesterday's pole I knew I was in a good position to try and win the race today. The only thing that I thought was going to test me was the rain, but even that held off. I lost Rubens completely at the start; I thought he was gone a little bit to the left so I went to the right and banged into him. That's not normally my style and I got a drive-through penalty for that, so had to recover. My engineer kept me calm and I pushed as hard as I could when I needed to, so it's a great day.

'It was a difficult winter. Sebastian showed in winter testing what the car could do, so that kept my motivation very high when I was hurting a lot with all the rehab. I had great people around me to recover from all the injuries I had and the team have been incredibly patient with me as well.' There was also some delicious baiting as he remembered Campese's advice to those who had turned down the chance to back him earlier in his racing career. 'I want to thank Dietrich Mateschitz, Red Bull and everyone at Red Bull Racing for what they did for me over the winter, and everyone in Australia who has supported me on the way through my career. And there are a few people that doubted me too, so hello to them as well. It's just an incredible day for all the people who have helped me get to where I am today.'

Horner added that it was 'a brilliant team performance' and paid tribute to Webber's determination, saying his driver had 'been on it all weekend and, after all the difficulties that he's been through over the winter, I'm absolutely delighted that he's managed to get his first win. He thoroughly deserves it.' For his part, Vettel complimented his teammate on his success, but it was perhaps interesting to note that this time, he felt the victory had slipped through his grasp, as the inter-team rivalry heated up. 'I'd be lying if I said I'm very pleased with second, as of course I wanted to win, but yesterday Mark did a better job and that's why he totally deserves the win – it's a good fight between us, so I'm looking forward to the next.'

Looking back on his first victory now, Webber recalls what a seismic shift it caused, not only in his career, but also how important the back-to-back wins were for Red Bull Racing's success. 'It was massive,' he says as he reflects on his first season against Vettel. 'I mean huge. I felt that Silverstone was one that got away, but I had a bit of a mishap with Kimi in qualifying. So I was put onto the second row and Seb won the British Grand Prix. I thought we had a car that could win that race, so I was pretty shattered and regretful that I didn't get the British Grand Prix victory. I went to Germany trying even harder but it just turned out that on that weekend, I made all the right decisions. I did get a drive-through penalty at the start when I shit myself and I went off-line. I was creeping across and – genuinely, on my mother's life – I'm like, "Where is Rubens?" And the next minute we touched.

'I think we both scared the shit out of each other – we both went so fast in the opposite direction as we didn't expect to see each other. I got a penalty but ultimately my drive that day was very unique to me. Everyone else had a smooth day – all the big dogs. There was no attrition, I just put them to the sword and dominated the day, which had been a long time coming. That's also when we really started to know that we had sorted out the car's floor. We could now race the Brawns.'

Ultimately, the points accumulated at the start of the season by Brawn's duo proved too big a hurdle to overcome. Despite wins for Vettel in Japan and Abu Dhabi and Webber's victory in Brazil, double successive DNFs for Red Bull Racing's drivers proved costly. Vettel didn't finish the Hungarian or European GP in Valencia, while Webber was forced out of the races in Italy and Singapore.

Button secured his one and only title 11 points ahead of Vettel, who finished the season in second place in the drivers' championship. After his victory in Turkey, the seventh race of the season and Red Bull Racing's first chance to run their diffuser, Button did not take another win that season. Meanwhile, Webber was fourth after narrowly missing out on third place to Barrichello, despite his obvious pain and discomfort caused by his pre-season accident. Nonetheless, Red Bull Racing had defied expectations to finish second in only their fifth season. The momentum was building.

CHAPTER 8

VETTEL GETS HIS CROWN

– 2010 –

The 2010 season would prove to be an unforgettable one for Red Bull Racing as the team secured their first drivers' and constructors' championship titles. It was a rollercoaster campaign that ultimately kick-started a period of domination but also ignited an inter-team rivalry between Webber and Vettel that would last for the duration of their time as teammates. The competitiveness was played out both on track and in the press, occasionally making things difficult inside the team in what proved to be a compelling season.

The new campaign was again heralded by a fresh set of regulations that had put Newey to work. A radical shake-up had seen the elimination of refuelling rigs, so mid-race top-ups were no longer acceptable. The decision had come about in order to reduce the logistical cost of transporting the extra equipment, but also with a view to making the sport more exciting and easier to understand. The result was that cars would now be heavier to accommodate the larger fuel tanks that were filled to the brim to last the full-race distance.

Put simply, designers would be tasked with repackaging their cars to accommodate the extra bulk and weight, without compromising performance.

As with every regulation change, it is all about which teams explore the grey areas of the rulebook and implement some lateral thinking to achieve the best result while conforming to the rules. If Newey had been left smarting at his failure to produce a double diffuser the previous year when Red Bull Racing ended the season as runners-up to Brawn, he would not be making the same mistake twice. Newey knew that if they had added the part to their car at the start of the campaign, then they'd have had a good chance of winning in 2009. So, his fresh sheet of paper allowed him to improve the RB5, seeking gains rather than dealing with challenges. Confidence was high in Milton Keynes that Newey's design for the RB6 would give the team an upper hand. On the operational side of things, the team also enjoyed an advantage: Red Bull Racing had maintained continuity with their key staff, whereas there had been several changes at rivals McLaren and Ferrari, notably behind the wheel.

There were certainly no poker faces at the launch in Jerez, Spain, on 10 February. 'This car is a limousine. We had only small aerodynamic changes so we didn't go crazy,' Webber told the assembled journalists, adding: 'It shows how clever Adrian is that a lot of people copied our car [last year].' The RB6 was longer than the previous year's challenger to accommodate the bigger fuel tank, but the shark-fin engine cover was retained. Webber went on: 'Continuity is a very good thing, particularly when it comes to drivers and their engineers and understanding what you need. I think the team has some very good, high expectations. We had a great season last year and we are not looking to go backwards from that position, so we have some tough goals to meet.'

In the press coverage for that early part of the season surrounding the launch, there were some notable stories that would become a familiar narrative. The first would centre on Vettel's fellow countryman Schumacher, who was rejoining F1 after coming out of retirement to drive for the new Mercedes team, which had taken over at Brawn. The seven-time Formula One world champion was Vettel's boyhood hero and the two would become close. There were similarities in their paths to F1, with both coming from modest upbringings to reach the top and family values remaining a high priority for both men. The other similarity was the meticulous level of detail both drivers would expect from their team and themselves.

In Vettel, the German media had found an heir apparent to Schumacher's reign as their country's leading F1 driver, to their collective relief. Others had not got close to matching him in terms of success or appeal, but Vettel, with his boy-from-Heppenheim charm, was someone to get behind. It was an easy story to write.

Consequently, Vettel was labelled 'Baby Schumi' in the media, and the somewhat lazy moniker was given more column inches as the press speculated on what Schumacher would do on his return with the Silver Arrows. Vettel, now 22, was naturally asked about the return of his sporting icon, but quickly turned the story round to himself, following his four victories in the previous campaign. 'I think there are going to be more rivals than just Michael,' he told reporters in Jerez. 'My goal is to be world champion.'

There was only one problem with that ambition: the driver in the other garage at Red Bull Racing had the same goal. A notable rivalry was developing, one that was quite literally spelled out in the *Guardian* on 8 March 2010 in an article bearing Webber's byline. The headline blazed: 'I'm not losing any sleep worrying about Vettel' – just so the reader was left in no doubt as to the content of the piece. The article itself is a reflection on the new regulations and the winter testing, plus a look ahead to the season-opening race in Bahrain, yet halfway through there is the line which caught the sub-editor's eye. The full quote reads: 'A lot of people see my team-mate, Sebastian Vettel, as my biggest rival this year. I have to say that there's a lot of quick drivers out there and some pretty good teams. Seb is going to be a quick driver, no question about it. But I'm not going to bed thinking about him; I'm going to bed thinking about myself and doing the best job I can, to get the best results I can, for myself.'

In the *Guardian* the following day, journalist Donald McRae led with a colourful anecdote about Vettel speaking at winter testing, where he declared there was less interest in him this season, 'because some old German guy decided to come back. He is keeping all the German writers very busy and that's good for me.' The article addresses Schumacher's return then circles back to Vettel's rivalry with Webber. 'I think the most spectacular combination is me and Mark, because everyone knows we don't have a problem,' Vettel is quoted as saying. 'Of course I want to beat him every time, and he wants to beat me, but we get along well.' The article references their prang in the 2007 Japanese GP when Vettel was driving for Toro Rosso and repeats Webber's quip in the aftermath: 'It's kids – they fuck it all up.' Vettel declared he liked the bluntness of his straight-talking teammate. 'So after that crash in Japan he was direct,' he said.

'He was angry and I was angry but, afterwards, I was sorry. We've never had a problem since.'

As the season moved closer to the opening race in Bahrain, Webber did an interview with Bob McKenzie of the *Daily Express* in which he revealed he was five kilos too heavy at Christmas and had been working hard to shed the weight. He'd nudged 80kg and it was a constant struggle to maintain his weight, especially given his height at just over six foot. That was a considerable disadvantage against his smaller, lighter teammates, such as Vettel. Nonetheless, Webber explained, 'If Sebastian is one of the favourites then I suppose I need to be one as well,' adding: 'I accept that I might be a bit of a dark horse but that is a good position for me to be in.'

The opening race of the 2010 campaign had so many storylines: Button and Hamilton now together at McLaren; Schumacher's return to F1 alongside his compatriot Rosberg at Mercedes; and the question of whether Red Bull Racing could maintain their pre-season form into the opening Grand Prix. Vettel answered that latter question emphatically in Bahrain by taking pole, with the German's scorching lap a full second quicker than Hamilton's time, who qualified in fourth. Schumacher was a further 0.5 seconds behind while Webber's best was only good enough for fifth on the grid. Come the race itself, Vettel made an excellent start and had looked comfortable out in front until he started to slow around two thirds into the race distance. The cause of the mechanical problem would not be known until a few days later when it turned out to be a faulty spark plug, but the drop in performance was significant and Vettel was passed by Alonso, Massa and Hamilton, leaving him to fend off

Rosberg to take a disappointing fourth-place finish while Webber crossed the line down in eighth.

At the following race in Australia, there was more bad luck and disappointment. After Vettel and Webber qualified in first and second place respectively, the team failed to deliver, with Vettel spinning out from the lead due to a brake failure that sent him into the gravel trap on lap 26. Webber was also guilty of a mistake that proved costly as he tangled with Hamilton. While the McLaren man – who had been told off by the local police for performing a burnout in his road car on the Friday night – battled with Alonso, Webber tried to leapfrog the Brit. However, in doing so he missed his braking point and locked up, hitting the rear tyres of Hamilton's car. Webber was required to make a pit stop for a new front wing and subsequently finished a lowly ninth.

After the double disappointment, the season hit upward momentum at the Malaysian Grand Prix. Webber took a brilliant pole position after opting for the quicker, intermediate tyre in the wet, beating Rosberg and Vettel, who qualified in P2 and P3 on the grid respectively. In Sunday's race, Vettel quickly passed Rosberg and Webber to take the lead and managed to hold on to the position. The team duly recorded their first one-two finish since the final race of the 2009 season.

In the post-race media sessions, Webber admitted an error at the start had cost him a shot at winning. 'The first part of the race is critical,' he said. 'I had a little wheel spin and gave Seb a big tow . . . The spirit and chemistry in our team is awesome and we fought well. Seb got the better of it but it could have gone either way.' Vettel too was complimentary towards his teammate, saying, 'It's good that we can fight each other but you should keep the respect and I am glad that we have done that; I am sure Mark would do the same as I did.'

Fresh from their one-two result in Malaysia, Vettel took pole in China with Webber starting second, but a messy race with tricky conditions resulted in them coming home in sixth and eighth respectively. 'It was a very chaotic race,' said Horner to the media in his post-race interview. 'Both drivers elected to stop early on when the rain came. Unfortunately, Mark hit the front jack and damaged his front wing which cost him a bit of time. Sixth and eighth isn't the result that we were looking for from first and second, but it is such a lottery in chaotic conditions.'

Things then turned around, for Webber at least, with wins in Spain and Monaco: two superb back-to-back victories. He converted from pole in Barcelona, with Handkammer going on the podium to receive the winning manufacturer's award. 'Today was a special day, no doubt about it, and I'm very happy to capitalise on the pole position,' Webber said after the race. 'It felt like the longest Grand Prix I've ever done, though. With the other victories there has been a bit more going on as I wasn't always in the lead, but today was all about watching the lap board go down and, my God, it just takes forever!' Webber's win in Monaco was equally impressive. He set a scintillating lap for pole and then, as is frequently the case at the notoriously tight track, he was able to hold on to his position for the duration of the race to win the showpiece event. In winning, Webber moved to the top of the drivers' championship standings on 78 points, the same tally as Vettel; but with two victories to his name, the Australian was placed in first position.

The cracks in the two teammates' relationship were already starting to appear, but the tempestuous Turkish Grand Prix would spark irreconcilable differences between the pair. The two clashed on lap 40 in what had been shaping up to be a thrilling end to the race. Webber – who, as previously mentioned, is heavier than Vettel – was ordered to switch to fuel-saving mode to allow him to complete the race distance, effectively turning the power of his engine down. Sensing that his position was under threat, he asked the team to instruct Vettel to do the same, given his proximity. This would mean Vettel would effectively act as a buffer to the chasing pack and the team could maintain their advantage, with Webber reaping the benefit as he was the race leader. However, his request was declined, so Vettel was able to power alongside Webber on the back straight – and as they both approached turn 12, wheel to wheel, they made contact. Vettel's wheel struck Webber's bodywork, sending them both flying.

The damage proved terminal for Vettel, who was sent into a spin and nearly hit Webber a second time. Webber suffered damage to his front wing and was required to pit, eventually coming home in third place. The flashpoint was captured on TV, with commentator Martin Brundle adamant that Vettel was to blame for the coming together, saying, 'I am giving that 100 per cent Vettel's fault.' Coulthard, on co-commentary, was initially cautious about judging his former team before weighing in: 'I think Mark was holding position. As uncomfortable as it is to call that between those two guys, I've got to say that there was no need for Seb to be pulling right there. He had the position.'

Vettel, for his part, was livid, making a gesture to suggest Webber had been crazy after climbing from his wrecked Red Bull. He shouted over the team's radio: 'What the fuck are we doing here?! It is a stupid action,' before somewhat comically adding, 'I am going home!' in the vein of a petulant adolescent. Alongside the driver reactions, it was interesting to note the not usually animated Newey sitting on the pit wall, stretching his arms out in exasperation before wrapping his head in his hands as he processed what he had just watched.

It was natural that this collision would drive a wedge between the drivers, but what followed would only serve to increase the tensions. Marko was interviewed by a TV crew about the incident and his opinion was telling. '[Vettel] was already ahead by at least two metres. There was a corner coming and he could not brake or he knew what [would] happen.' When pressed if he was implying that Webber was at fault, Marko stopped short of allocating blame and simply added: 'Unnecessary, the whole situation.'

The incident in Turkey had captured the media's attention. Coming togethers are common in F1, but are rare between two teammates, and then, usually, once the red mist has burned off, the team quickly moves on. But this time resentment appeared to be festering. Horner was caught in a tricky position. Unlike the collision in Japan when they were at separate teams, now he as team principal was caught in the middle and walking a diplomatic tightrope. 'They should have given each other more room,' he said after the race. 'Sebastian had a pace advantage on that tyre. Mark kept his line and squeezed him . . . We have given away 28 points and it should have been a one-two. This will be dealt with before we go to [the next race in] Canada.'

Both drivers, however, remained unrepentant. Webber claimed Vettel had turned in on him, whereas Vettel continued to insist his opposite number was to blame. Webber's opinion of that race has not changed in the years that have passed. When we discussed it in the McLaren motorhome in Monza, the topic was clearly still raw, with Webber admitting it was the 'start of the tension' between the two. 'I will never forget Flavio [Briatore] saying, "You can't leave Barcelona in the lead, Monaco in the lead [i.e. having won both races]; something's going to change. This won't continue," ' says Webber, when he recalls speaking to his manager about the start of the 2010 season. 'And he was spot-on. That race suddenly changed everything.'

The race may have been the catalyst, but for Webber there were already resentments that had built up before the collision. When we spoke he mentioned how he felt he was receiving the updated car parts later than his rival – that in effect Vettel would try them first before they were then fitted to Webber's car. An F1 team's factory can only produce so many parts at a time and, over the course of a season, the development race – to bring new, upgraded parts to improve a car's performance – becomes as fierce and important as the races on the track. In the past, F1 teams have rushed parts to races, in some cases hiring private jets to bring them in just in time for qualifying, because they believed the new element would make a substantial difference in lap time. So timing was everything, as Webber would have known when he noted that he 'got some of the wings late' in the build-up to the Turkish GP. It would be a hot topic that would resurface a few races later.

Meanwhile, recalling the collision, Webber still firmly believes Vettel was only able to close the gap because he himself had turned his engine down to save fuel so he could reach the end of the race. 'The fuel consumption was such that it was a bit of a stalemate until he started to win a bit of fuel back in the race by using the slipstream, so I rang up [i.e. used the team radio] to say they had to turn his engine down as well. And then he came down the inside and made a pretty strong move to the right and we made contact. That was the start of the tension, I suppose, and it was really shit for the team because [until that point] I had the race all under control.'

The tension was revisited before the Canadian Grand Prix despite Horner insisting that his drivers were given equal treatment and that there was no favouritism. The rift had captured the imagination of the media, who zeroed in on the relationship between the two, with Horner caught in the middle. In a move presumably intended to dampen the flames, Red Bull Racing confirmed Webber's seat alongside Vettel for a one-year contract the following season. Webber – then aged 33 – commented: 'I'm happy to take one year at a time at this stage of my career. It is widely known that I am not interested in hanging around in F1 just for the sake of it.' He clearly felt he still had a shot at the title and was not simply staying in the sport for the money.

At the race in Montreal, a gearbox penalty cost Webber second place on the grid as he was demoted to start seventh, at the same time promoting Vettel to second place. But neither driver was able to challenge for the victory, with Vettel coming fourth and Webber fifth. There was more drama at the European Grand Prix in Valencia where Webber had yet another lucky escape with his life. The video of his 190mph crash is still a harrowing watch, as his RB6 is propelled into the air following a collision with Heikki Kovalainen. Webber has no control of the car, which is flipped upside down before it comes crashing down on the track and is sent skidding into the tyre barriers. It was a huge smash yet miraculously he was unharmed. In fact he quickly started moving once his car had come to a stop, not only to pull himself clear of the danger but also to send a crucial message to both Ann and his parents that he was OK as they watched on TV. Vettel, meanwhile, secured the victory to move up to third in the championship behind Hamilton and Button.

The British Grand Prix came six weeks after their collision in Turkey and, if there was any doubt about the two drivers' growing discontent, then it was dispelled when the gloves came off at the post-qualifying press conference at Silverstone. Refreshingly for leading sports stars – particularly ones whose overalls are covered by sponsors paying, in some cases, millions of pounds – Red Bull Racing drivers have always been allowed to speak their minds, even when it makes things uncomfortable for the communications department. So when Vettel took pole position for the race after being the only one to receive the team's newest front wing, Webber did not hold back with his comments. 'I think the team is happy with the result today,' he snapped, before taking a swig of his glass of water and emphatically thumping it down on the desk while Vettel was starting to speak, leaving the media in no uncertain terms what he thought. Horner was left to try to justify the rationale behind the decision, explaining that Vettel was placed higher in the championship and given the new parts to boost his title chances. 'Mark knows the way we operate as a team,' he said. 'He knows there was no malice behind it, there was no manipulation.'

Webber was clearly furious but determined not to suffer at the hands of his teammate during the race itself. At the start, Vettel pushed Webber into the approach to the high-speed Copse corner, but the Australian held his position and would not be bullied. That forced Vettel into a battle with Hamilton and the two made contact, with Vettel picking up a puncture. Webber would go on to take the chequered flag and was congratulated by Horner over the team's radio as he crossed the finish line. 'Well done, Mark, you've won the British Grand Prix,' Horner said. To which his victorious driver replied: 'Not bad for a number-two driver, cheers.'

Webber was still smarting in the post-race media session and claimed he would not have signed a new deal with the team had he felt there were double standards, this time choosing to make it clear to the media that he felt parts were arriving later on his side of the garage. 'Yesterday was really a unique situation,' he said, 'and it was the first time we had one bit' – in other words, there was only one new car part available, which he implied went in Vettel's direction (normally upgraded parts, usually items such as front wings, are produced in pairs so that both drivers can benefit from the design improvements). 'I would never have signed a contract for next year if I believed that was the way going forward. I have had a few hurdles in my career, sometimes privately as well, so I think you can judge a person's character by how they come back from adversity. Some drivers have that; I've had a bit more than others.' When quizzed by the media if he felt that the win was poetic justice, he said: 'An appointment with karma? Yeah.'

As the season came down to the wire, the two traded wins before Red Bull Racing wrapped up the constructors' championship in Brazil, the penultimate race. The drivers' championship is the most coveted prize, but the constructors' title is the crucial one for the team, for the higher you finish, the more prize money the team earns. Vettel's victory and Webber's second-place finish ensured Red Bull Racing could not be caught at the season finale in Abu Dhabi. It was a landmark result after what had proven to be a difficult season for the team.

'In six years, Red Bull has come from a team that no one took seriously – that everyone thought was a party team – to the 2010 F1 constructors' champions,' said Horner. 'We have finished ahead of teams with far more experience and heritage than ourselves – we took them on and we won, thanks to the tremendous dedication of every single team member, the incredible support from Red Bull and the vision and unfaltering commitment from Mr Mateschitz.' Horner was of course right; winning an individual Grand Prix is one thing, but putting the results together to sustain enough victories to win the constructors' title against the likes of Ferrari, McLaren, Mercedes, BMW and Williams was an entirely different achievement.

The result in São Paulo meant that the drivers' championship could be won by any one of three drivers at the final race of the season in Abu Dhabi. Alonso was leading the championship on 246 points, Webber was on 238 and Vettel had 231. The build-up centred on the Red Bull Racing pair, with mounting speculation as to whether they would be allowed to race by the team – without the influence of team orders – to decide the outcome of not only the race, but the championship. In the event, both Horner and Mateschitz, who rarely commented in the press, were adamant they would not inter- fere with the outcome. In an interview in *Autosport* ahead of the race, Mateschitz said he would prefer his drivers to lose out 'under the correct circumstances'.

'To interfere with the drivers was never a possibility for us,' he said. 'A second place under correct circumstances might be better than a win on grounds of orders and confirmations.' To Mateschitz's credit, recognising his debt to Webber in the constructors' championship, he hinted that he would be prepared to help him out, if required. 'If the situation occurs on Sunday,' he said, 'then we know we are driving for the team. We have had some occasions where we got close and it didn't get too good, so the main target is not to repeat that. And the rest, we will see.'

As it turned out, Vettel did not play the supporting role, neither did he require any assistance from Webber, as he landed his first world title in a breath-taking finale. The young German qualified on pole while Webber started fifth, and Vettel would consolidate his position on the grid by going on to win the race, taking the top spot in the championship for the first time that season. He clinched the title by four points from Alonso while Webber was third, a further ten points behind. It was hard on Webber, as Vettel had mounted a late surge with three wins and a second place in his final five races. But it was indisputably a tremendous victory. In winning the title, Vettel became the youngest ever F1 world champion at just 23 years and 134 days old.

CHAPTER 9

THE FULL WORKS

– 2011 –

The aftermath of the turbulence of 2010 weighed heavily on Red Bull Racing and especially on one of its drivers. Webber had seen his younger teammate defy the odds to win the world championship that he had so badly wanted. Not only that, suspicion and distrust had invaded his mindset and he was finding it hard to move on. Webber had been so consumed by the internal politics that the straight-talking racer was now struggling to process his relationship with the team. Things had reached such a low that he was contemplating retirement from F1 due to the pressure.

When I ask him about how close he got to retiring at the end of the 2010 season, he explains how he had been left conflicted by such incredible highs and lows throughout the year. 'There was a lot going on, for sure,' he says in his typical understated manner. 'I was doing everything I could in my power to stay in the title fight, which went to the last race. The other drivers had had their moments during the season, and I had them in Valencia [the 190mph crash] and in Korea [the race-ending accident with Rosberg where Webber lost grip in the wet, spun and, after hitting the wall, rolled back on track to make contact with the German, forcing both of them out of the race after only 18 laps]. That was the first time that year I actually spun the car 360 degrees! It was intense and all about trying to maintain the momentum.'

Stopping short of laying out just how close he came to leaving the sport, he was able to provide some light on how it was his relationship with Mateschitz that had given him the strength to continue with the team. 'Ultimately, he was the boss,' says Webber. 'So I tried to keep in contact with him as much as I could and be as transparent as I could and tell him how I was feeling in the team. Sebastian and Helmut had a very, very tight relationship and I didn't have that relationship. I get on with them fine today. Obviously there were flashpoints when I was racing there, of course, and this was all very new for Christian to deal with.'

Webber's difficulties had not just lain in his relationships within the team. He revealed in his book *Up Front: A Season to Remember*, which was published in Australia in December 2010, that he had also been contending with a secret injury that he had been hiding from his colleagues. Webber had broken his shoulder in a mountain-bike accident soon after the Singapore Grand Prix in September 2010. He had been due to compete in Japan a few days later, only heavy rain saw qualifying cancelled and moved to Sunday, allowing him an extra day to recover with the help of a dose of painkillers. 'I was riding with a great friend of mine,' Webber says in the book. 'Suddenly, he crashed in front of me and I had nowhere to go but straight through the ears of the horse. I suffered what they call a skier's fracture. Suzuka is a brutal track, so it was a blessing that the Japanese weather gave me an enforced rest day on Saturday and a pre-race injection helped, too.'

The only people who knew of the injury were his trainer and F1's senior doctor, Dr Gary Hartstein, and the details were even kept secret from Horner. Webber drove with cortisone injections, which allowed him to race in the Grands Prix that followed his accident. Of course, it is impossible to predict whether the injury impacted on the results of the final four races of the season, where he missed out on some crucial points. But clearly, the accident had come very soon after his other bicycle incident in Tasmania, which was also continuing to limit his manoeuvrability. 'It was just frustrating because the original procedure, when I had the work done after the accident, wasn't overly smooth,' Webber tells me. 'We had a few issues that we would have liked to address, but I couldn't do them in seasons. So I was dealing with pain while trying to minimise how many times we had to go into the leg and do the work. It also affected my training and my ways of trying to keep my weight down while Sebastian's weight was eight kilos lighter.'

During the pre-season testing, one of the reasons Webber had decided to stay in F1 had become clear. That year's challenger, the RB7, would prove to be unstoppable and one of the most dominant F1 cars ever produced. It was also the first Red Bull Racing car to have the full support of the Renault team: it had effectively become the works team of the French car giant, meaning Red Bull Racing would now have the full technical support of Renault, who were continuing to supply them with engines. Webber knew the main benefit of being a works team is that Red Bull Racing would receive the newest and in theory best parts available, whereas some engine suppliers in the past have been accused of delivering engines to their customers that were not produced to the latest specifications, putting them at a disadvantage. It also means that Red Bull Racing's designers could work much more efficiently as they would have the benefit of knowing the weights and dimensions of the engine well in advance, so the integration of the engine to the chassis would be a much smoother process.

Things had been going rather well too on Vettel's side of the garage. Ahead of the new season, he had been offered a new contract with Red Bull Racing which would ensure he remained with the team until the end of the 2014 season. The contract was rumoured to have quadrupled his salary and was thought to be worth around $9 million a year. In announcing the deal, Red Bull Racing fended off their competitors' interest in F1's youngest world champion but also signalled a statement of intent for the team, with Horner revealing how Vettel had brokered his own terms with Mateschitz rather than having an agent or manager acting on his behalf.

'Seb had a contract for a while longer but we both felt that the future should be addressed and he reached agreement quite quickly,' said Horner after confirming the deal. 'He is comfortable with the team, having been with Red Bull in the juniors. I am sure he has had lots of approaches and inquiries and that is why we moved to stop speculation in the coming season. For sure, McLaren and Ferrari have demonstrated interest in him but they have long-term drivers at the moment. But any team with serious ambitions would want Seb. It is very unusual and refreshing in this day and age that he does his own negotiations, but he does his own thing; he is his own man.'

Vettel's services were secured along with a new deal for Newey, as Red Bull Racing tied up their assets, with Horner commenting, 'Hopefully, Red Bull will be the last team he [Newey] works for in Formula One. He is enjoying racing again and there is no sign of his passion waning.'

While all the bumper pay-days were being handed out, Webber was left waiting. In fairness, his rolling contract had been renewed some six months earlier and would take him up to when he was 35 – but clearly it also made sense for Red Bull Racing to keep their options open. Horner was very pragmatic about the fact that his two drivers were at different stages of their careers. 'At 34, Mark is not just starting out,' he said. 'He has done almost 160 Grands Prix. When the time comes with Mark, if he still has the motivation, desire and is competitive, it's logical to talk about extending his contract. But it's too early for either him or us to be having that conversation at the moment. Mark knows this year is a big year for him, that he will get equal support. He also knows he is not setting out at the beginning of his career. He is a shrewd enough guy to work that out for himself without me having to explain that to him.'

Webber's plight made him a ripe target for the media. His straight-talking had already put him in favour with the press, who would frequently turn to the senior driver for his opinions on the sport when the younger drivers were perhaps too timid to give them the answers they were seeking. Webber was not afraid to tell it as he saw it – and there were a number of talking points in the run-up to the new season, such as the politically charged concept of racing in Bahrain in 2011, given the country was caught in the Arab Spring uprising and subsequent anti-government protests. In a number of interviews, including one in *Autosport*, Webber had made it clear he did 'not feel comfortable' with the prospect of racing in the country.

Webber's opinions were also sought regarding his pre-season preparations. He did not hold back. It made sense for him to be open with the media at a time when he needed allies, so he was happy to give colourful answers. In one interview with the *Evening Standard* in London, Webber explains how he adopted the 'Ricky Hatton approach' to dieting, named after the former boxer, whose weight would increase substantially between fights. 'For five weeks I relaxed and, if I felt like eating sausages, I'd bang them on,' he said. 'It was just good to take that time off as I'd not done it for a long time. I'm not normally good at doing nothing, but it was needed after two really hard winters where I was either on crutches or having surgery. It's left me refreshed and feeling mentally ready.' And then in *The Times*, he explained how he 'liked to be the underdog, on the ropes a little bit'. Maybe it was coincidence, but the boxing analogies make it clear that he still very much had the stomach for a fight and he was sizing up for another heavyweight season.

Vettel, on the other hand, was more coy with the media. His interviews were centred on playing down expectations, but there were glimpses of a sense of humour as he made it known he was something of an Anglophile, who loved British culture, particularly its comedy and music. He often quoted lines from *Little Britain* or *Monty Python*, and he had a big interest in The Beatles. Despite this, he was generally outshone in the press by his teammate. Vettel's narrative was one of caution, consisting of blander statements such as: 'I might have the number one on my car but that is about last year and it doesn't make me any faster this year.'

Vettel got his title defence off to the perfect start with two pole positions and two victories in the opening two races in Australia and Malaysia. Meanwhile, Webber could only muster fifth in Melbourne and fourth in Sepang. By the time the third race had clicked round in China, Webber was seething after a disastrous qualifying session meant he was knocked out of Q1, the first session in Shanghai, and had qualified in 18th while Vettel was on pole again. Webber had come unstuck with an electrical problem in practice and he berated the team's decision not to send him out on track early enough to give him enough time to heat up his tyres so they achieved the necessary levels of grip. Not only had they not allowed him enough time, but the team had also gambled on using the hard tyre compounds, rather than the softs, which essentially have a shorter life span but quickly become more grippy. The durable hard tyres require a longer process to prepare for the quickest lap time.

Webber didn't hold back, saying: 'When any top team goes out in Q1, we all put the hindsight goggles on and go, "Shit, we should have done this or that." The timing was the problem, not the tyre.' In the race itself, his frustration was tempered by a brilliant and gutsy recovery that moved him from 18th to third place. Vettel came second behind Hamilton's McLaren. Afterwards, it was all too clear that Webber was pleased that his teammate had not won again. 'Congratulations to Lewis. It was good that someone finally—' he said, before stopping himself from putting his foot in it. 'Of course, Seb is in the same team, but he's been on a phenomenal run and we're all here together fighting for victories,' he continued hurriedly. 'It's a shame McLaren won in a way, but also we can't let Seb get too far away.'

With tensions in the team delicately poised, it was always going to be interesting to see the build-up to the Turkish Grand Prix. The circuit on the outskirts of Istanbul had provided the setting for the pair's explosive encounter the previous season and heading back would reopen the wound. Horner played down the significance of returning to Istanbul Park and the first European race of the season. 'Obviously last year, what happened, happened,' he said ahead of the race. 'Lessons were learned from it and we are looking forward to going back to Istanbul.' But for all the bluster about returning, the race had little in the way of controversy with Vettel and Webber qualifying P1 and P2 on the grid and converting them into the same places on the podium. Vettel had now opened up a 34-point lead over Hamilton in the drivers' championship, while Red Bull Racing were 43 points clear of McLaren in the constructors' championship.

Vettel was simply unstoppable, winning again in Spain, where he celebrated on the team's radio on his way back to the pits by singing the 'Crazy Frog' song. He followed that with victory in Monaco to make it five wins in six races, but it was far from a straightforward race. It was chaotic and captivating, with two safety car periods: one coming just ten laps from the end when Toro Rosso's Jaime Alguersuari collided with Renault's Vitaly Petrov, causing a brief stoppage in the race. The upshot was a safety car restart, with drivers pootling behind the pace car before being set free to race the final five laps. Vettel came under pressure from both Alonso's Ferrari and Button's McLaren but held his nerve to win his first Monaco Grand Prix. The race had proven to be a thriller – unusual for Monaco, as the narrow streets tend to make the event a procession rather than a race due to a lack of overtaking opportunities. But this was different to previous races; it was genuinely exciting. Indeed, the only thing that was unsurprising, given their dominance, was a Red Bull winner. Vettel was now leading the championship by 58 points over Hamilton; there was a sense that the competition was over for everyone else.

Vettel's success contrasted with Webber's inability to get off the mark in 2011. He had taken just two podiums in the opening six races in which his teammate had dominated. His contract ran until the end of the season but, given Red Bull Racing's success, it had become a valuable seat in the F1 paddock. Clearly, other drivers would be circling around to be in contention when the seat came up for grabs.

However, it was still something of a surprise when Lewis Hamilton made a very public approach to the team at the Canadian GP. The McLaren man went into the Red Bull Racing hospitality area and personally sought out a meeting with Horner – somewhat ironically given his earlier criticism of the team in Melbourne back in March, when he had dismissed them with the comment: 'Red Bull are not a manufacturer, they are a drinks company.' At this point it is worth explaining that while it is common for team principals to enter one another's motorhomes or hospitality, it is rare for a driver to do so, especially without a prearranged appointment. Hamilton had also taken the unusual step of employing artist manager Simon Fuller's XIX Entertainment company to represent him. Hamilton and Horner spoke briefly for 15 minutes but his presence in the company of McLaren's rivals would have set off alarm bells in the Woking-based team.

Hamilton was still under contract until the end of the 2012 season but his inability to add to the world title he won in 2008 was weighing heavily on him, for he felt he should have been winning more regularly. His curiosity had been piqued by Red Bull Racing and it would be interesting how this would shape his perception of both the team and of Vettel in the years to come. Hamilton owed it to himself to seek out a position at rival teams, and it would also help him drive up his value when it came to negotiating a new deal if it was suspected that another team was interested. This wasn't necessarily just about the salary. For an F1 driver, contracts are not only about the duration of the deal and the amount being paid. Often the most problematic part of the negotiations relate to the number of media and sponsor days a driver is obliged to work each year. Another considerable part is the flexibility to broker their own private endorsements. This was something that had been limited at McLaren, who had a strict policy when it came to sponsors – they had to be the right fit for the ethos of the company.

Ironically, Webber and Hamilton would make contact in the Canadian race itself – a rain-delayed four-hour epic that was won by Button after Vettel made a mistake on the final lap while leading.

The two Red Bull Racing drivers' turbulent relationship resumed at the British Grand Prix when Webber ignored team orders not to try and overtake Vettel. Webber had been told several times to hold position behind the German but he nevertheless launched an attempt to pass his teammate over the final few laps, ultimately failing to snatch second place and coming in third. His failure to respect his team's orders over the radio reignited speculation about him being dropped in favour of Hamilton for the following season.

Horner was frank about his thoughts on the behaviour of the 34-year-old. 'I am surprised Mark ignored orders,' Horner said in plain terms. 'The team is the biggest thing and no individual is bigger than it. It makes no sense to allow them to continue to fight. We risked giving away 33 points by allowing our drivers to fight it out. As we have seen previously, that can have dire consequences.' Webber also spoke plainly and faced up to his crime, saying he ignored the team on purpose as he hoped that the eventual winner, Ferrari's Alonso, would not reach the end of the race. He was furious he had received the order in the first place; his face was like thunder in the post-race press conference. Horner had said that his driver should have been 'fine' with the team's decision – but that was clearly not the case. 'I'm not fine with it, no,' Webber snapped. 'If Fernando had retired on the last lap then we would have been fighting for victory. I was fighting until the end. I ignored the team because I wanted to try and get another place. Seb was doing his best; I was doing my best. I just wanted to race to the end, but with four or five laps to go they started to chat to me about holding my position. Of course, they want the points, but I also need to try and get some points.'

Horner admitted the latest flare-up between his warring drivers would require some further in-house management, adding: 'We'd have looked pretty stupid if they'd crashed. Both drivers are now first and second in the world championship, and we're not going to do anything to jeopardise that. I can understand Mark's frustration in that, but had it been the other way round, it would have been exactly the same. I made it clear in front of the engineers the biggest thing was getting a team result in front of all of the staff who put in so much effort into both those cars.'

While Webber fumed, Vettel continued to excel and it became evident that if ever the team wanted to prioritise their pairing, he had become the de facto number-one driver. He won three races in a row in Belgium, Italy and Singapore, also taking pole position in all three. His haul of points enabled him to win the drivers' championship title in Japan; such was his dominance that he did so with four races to spare in the season. He won it in Suzuka with a third-place finish behind Button and Alonso, which gave him enough points to ensure he would not be caught. He'd taken nine wins and had finished runner-up on four occasions over the course of the season to date. The 24-year-old had become the youngest driver to win back-to-back titles, eclipsing Alonso in 2006 by nearly a year. 'We have had a fantastic year, and the good thing is it is not over yet,' he said after the race. 'We put ourselves in a very, very strong position and it is great to achieve the goal we set ourselves going into this year already.' He also had the grace to say a quick thank you to Webber.

The team wrapped up the constructors' championship at the following race in Korea. Vettel's victory and Webber's third place behind Hamilton ensured the team were 140 points clear of McLaren with three races left. 'For a drinks manufacturer to win two constructors' and two drivers' championships, it's not bad, is it?' said Horner after the race – a clear reference to Hamilton's comment earlier in the season. Hamilton, to his credit, would later admit he had got it wrong when he was dismissive of Red Bull Racing. In 2022, he said: 'I think years ago I said something about them being a drinks company and stuff like that. But they've proved me wrong, and everyone, and they've done a great job.'

Vettel won again in India but his unblemished scorecard suffered a blot at the penultimate race of the year in Abu Dhabi. He had taken pole but a puncture on the first lap forced him to retire the car and he failed to finish. The abrupt end stopped him from equalling Schumacher's record of 13 wins in one season, while Webber's fourth place meant it was the only race that season in which neither driver achieved a podium finish.

At the final race of the year, Webber was able to exhale a year's worth of frustration and anger. He'd come into the campaign promising to fight for the title but he was unable to match the results of his teammate, who had had a sensational season of complete domination. Webber had to make do with podiums, pole positions and fastest laps, but, until Brazil, a victory had eluded him. So it was somewhat fitting that he'd take the chequered flag in São Paulo on the final day of the season. For once, the reliability impacted Vettel's race as a gearbox issue slowed his progress and allowed Webber to overtake him on lap 30 for the win, while the German finished second.

Post-race, Webber was left thanking his good fortune: 'I had the rub of the green. It would have been nice to have had a race with Seb all the way through, but he had a problem. It's a win I'll take for sure because I've had bad luck, or whatever you want to call it. It's an important win for me and the team to finish on a high.' The win had cemented his third place in the drivers' championship, as he finished 12 points behind Button – although a whopping 134 points off champion Vettel. Horner conceded that the win for Webber was vindication for a tough campaign, adding: 'Mark's had a tough year, but he's kept his head down. He wanted to finish the year on a high after facing a driver in the form of his life and he's done that. I'm sure he'll come back stronger next year.'

The duo's double podium took the team's tally to 27 podiums for the season in an unprecedented display of dominance. Everything had come together perfectly. Yes, Vettel had enjoyed the lion's share of the success and Webber had been there to sweep up the points left on the table, but they had done so with reliability from Renault that had made the season seem almost effortless.

CHAPTER 10

TRIPLE CHAMPIONS

– 2012 –

If there was a sense that Vettel's success in 2011 had made the sport somewhat predictable, given his sheer dominance, then the start of the 2012 season was to prove that was anything but the case. Seven different winners in the opening seven races set the tone, and the volatility lasted until the final race of the year, ensuring that this season would remain captivating to the last. It is always a good barometer to measure a sport's popularity when you hear people speaking about it in public. I remember overhearing a conversation in the supermarket at the time, with someone asking their friend, 'Did you see last Sunday's race?' It showed that people were tuning in to see who would win, and that was certainly the situation in 2012.

F1 was in good health. There was a competitiveness across the grid that had come from some stability in the regulations. There had been no sweeping changes to the rules, which enabled those teams who had previously struggled to effectively copy Red Bull Racing's homework and produce a similar car to catch up. The convergence resulted in a feel-good factor in the paddock and a sense that a number of teams had a chance of fighting for a victory. It was an almost unique situation for F1, given how many previous seasons had been dominated by one team or another.

Horner had drawn a lot of respect for his ability to manage the relationship between Vettel and Webber. The latter would be retained for another season on a rolling contract. Vettel, however, was the star of the show and his second world title saw his global profile move up a notch. Whenever a sports star scores another goal, touchdown or wins a race, there is the notion that their life will inevitably become more public. However, that was certainly not the case with Vettel, who would defend his right to a private life during his F1 career to the extent that when his wife and children attended races, they would not come into the paddock where they would be the centre of attention and photographed. Instead, they would watch with his friends and family in the grandstands, blending in with the crowd, so that the people they were sitting next to had no idea that their neighbours were cheering on their father or husband.

I caught up with Vettel ahead of the 2012 season in Jerez where we met in the team's motorhome, a smaller version of the Energy Station, which was used for F1 testing and some MotoGP races, after persuading his long-time communications manager, Britta Roeske, to grant an interview that subsequently ran in the *Sun*. Remarkably, given his reluctance to be in the public eye, Vettel had recently done a TV advert in Germany for shampoo brand Head and Shoulders, and he joked with me about keeping his shirt on in the ad – unlike Button, who had taken his off in a similar advert in the UK. 'Of course, I've had a little bit of mickey-taking from doing the advert,' he said. 'Filming it is one thing but seeing myself on TV is always a bit weird. At least I never took my shirt off!'

Vettel explained how he would still occasionally watch his football team, Eintracht Frankfurt, from the stands rather than take a VIP box. I left the interview reminded of just how down to earth he was. He was still only 24, a double world champion who travelled the globe receiving adulation wherever he went, but his values had remained in place. 'The best thing about my friends is that they still see me as they always have done,' he said at the end of our chat. 'For them it hasn't changed a thing, despite being a double world champion in F1, or earning more money than they do. If we go out we can have a good laugh. I'm still the same guy and you need to be that way. It keeps you grounded. Life is hectic enough.' Another insight into his personality came when he revealed that he kept his world championship trophy on the kitchen table at home, right next to a packet of cornflakes.

The new season kicked off in Melbourne where Horner had backed Webber to end his wait for a victory in his home race. Horner had praised the way the 35-year-old had lost weight and trained hard over the winter now that he was free from the pain of his cycling accidents. 'I think Mark is going to be a contender this year,' Horner said in the build-up to the race. 'He has come back lighter and fitter than he's ever been. He has worked hard on his weight because he was giving away a fraction in terms of set-up of weight to Sebastian, who is a few kilos lighter than him. He was determined to narrow that band and has been very disciplined with his diet.'

Horner had also addressed the rumour that surrounded Hamilton's future, as the British driver neared the end of his

McLaren contract that would expire in December that year. 'It's difficult to envisage Lewis in our team,' he said. 'He's comfortable in the environment he is in and we're comfortable with the two drivers we have. We also made a decision to invest in youth. We have two exciting youngsters in Jean-Éric Vergne and Daniel Ricciardo – both really talented drivers who deserve that opportunity. It will be fascinating to see how they evolve over the year. So we're more likely to look inwardly than outwardly.'

The opening race was won by Button, while Vettel, who had christened his RB8 car 'Abbey' – the previous two years he'd driven 'Kinky Kylie' and 'Luscious Liz' to glory and had never given a particular reason for doing so – was second and Hamilton third ahead of Webber.

In Malaysia, Vettel was furious with HRT's Narain Karthikeyan after the backmarker got in Vettel's way while being lapped, causing the German to pick up a puncture that resulted in him finishing down in 11th place. Vettel slammed the Indian driver as an 'idiot' as it cost him a haul of points, while Webber was again fourth and just off the podium. The Mexican driver Sergio 'Checo' Pérez, who would later move to Red Bull Racing, was a surprise in second place for Sauber. There were further mixed results in China where Webber and Vettel came home fourth and fifth at the Shanghai International Circuit, as the two drivers also took the same places in the drivers' championship standings. At the next race in Bahrain – which had been overshadowed by anti-government protests, leaving some teams caught in the middle of a teargas and petrol bomb exchange between police and protestors – Vettel reflected on how they had had their wings clipped by their rivals at the start of the season, but he was now relieved to be taking his first victory of the campaign. 'This year we'd have loved to be in a better place to start,' he said after his win. 'We've only had four races and I'm not entirely happy with where we are, but I think there's great potential in the car. You have to give yourself time to try different things and see what works best for you.'

Even though Red Bull Racing were certainly not having it all their own way, their rivals were nevertheless not satisfied that the RB8 was entirely legal. It is an open secret in the paddock that each team employs a 'spy photographer', required not only to shoot pre-requested meet-and-greets or social media campaigns, but also their rivals' cars. For the majority of a race weekend, F1 cars remain in their respective garages, which are off-limits to opposing teams. Consequently, the only time they are really able to see what they are coming up against is when the cars are on track. The spy photographers are therefore on hand when the cars are out to snap the other teams, usually with a brief to get a shot of a particular part, such as a rear wing, which can then be sent immediately to the pit wall or the designers at the factory. It is a smart practice when the goal is always to be abreast – or ideally ahead – of the development curve.

However, it also means teams are open to scrutiny from rivals and the 2012 Monaco Grand Prix proved to be an example of this. It was the first instance of an ongoing theme of the season where Horner and his design team were hauled in to see the stewards, to explain their interpretations of the rulebook. For Red Bull Racing, it was the start of a growing feeling that they were being reined in, which particularly impacted Newey, who was required to show his workings. At Monte Carlo, the focus was on a new slot on the floor of their car, which had appeared at the Bahrain GP. Their rivals were suspicious and called for the FIA to investigate. At the summons, Red Bull Racing were able to successfully argue that the design had been passed by the FIA scrutineering sessions in Bahrain and that therefore it was legal. The purpose of the scrutineering is to ensure that all the cars meet the requirements, such as height and weight and structural integrity, as stipulated in the rules. In Monaco, therefore, they successfully defended the accusations, although the FIA issued a clarification ahead of the next race in Canada, making the slot illegal.

The wrangle with the stewards took the gloss off Webber's win in Monaco, a victory that moved him to joint second alongside Vettel in the drivers' standings, just three points behind championship leader, Ferrari driver Alonso. Horner hailed Webber's performance as he crossed the line in first place, saying: 'The hardest position is when you are leading a group, especially around Monaco when it gets slippery, because everyone else can judge their grip by looking at what you are doing. But Mark drove brilliantly. I think all three victories here have been sweet. You don't become triple winners in Monte Carlo by luck. Mark has become a double winner and joins an elite group.'

As news broke that Red Bull Racing would be forced to change the floor of their car in response to the FIA clarification, it created a sense that in some way, despite being cleared, they had done something wrong. Technical journalists dug away and came up with theories as to what the purpose of the slots was. Ultimately it must have proved beneficial when the car went around the corners or, presumably, it would not have been outlawed. Horner explained how the rules are 'open to interpretation and our interpretation of that particular rule was accepted', adding, 'We were always confident that our car complied fully with the regulations.'

Webber, however, felt the accusation was a slight on his victory in the blue-ribbon event. 'I am happy to be called lots of things and have criticism about my driving but I will not take talk about the car being illegal,' he said sternly. 'The car passed every single technical regulation after the race. All the teams against it did not make any protest after Monaco; the car passed the test after Bahrain and passed the test after Monaco. There has been a clarification and the rule is now different. We had a car that was legal for the start of the season, but the rule has been changed and we will race on.'

Webber's contractual situation was again resurrected in the summer as speculation started around whether he would remain at Red Bull Racing for another season. It was inevitable, given Vettel had a long-term deal, that it would be the Australian who would face the questions. However, this season the narrative would be different from previous years as there was now a strong possibility that Ferrari were interested in signing him, particularly after his victory at Silverstone in the British Grand Prix in July. Monaco and Silverstone are two of the most demanding tracks, mentally and physically, on the calendar, and now he had won at both, allaying any lingering concerns around his fitness. Webber, now 35, looked rejuvenated and was being earmarked as a potential candidate to replace Felipe Massa at Ferrari. The lure of driving for F1's most famous team was obvious. It would also take him away from the stress that he felt existed inside his current team.

Horner, however, dismissed the speculation, saying that 'very simply, we have a great relationship with Mark' and that he wanted him to remain at the team for 2013. Horner added that Webber had also 'given every indication that he is very happy'. Perhaps inevitably, given these comments, Webber would sign a new one-year extension a few days after his win at Silverstone. Webber had felt that Red Bull Racing offered him the best chance of success and he had reason to feel optimistic as he was now second in the championship behind Ferrari's Alonso – and a full 16 points ahead of Vettel, who was third. The quotes that accompanied the news perhaps over-egged the inter-team harmony: gushing comments in which he labelled the team 'a nice big family' were toe-curling given the evident frictions.

At the German GP at Hockenheim, the team would face fresh accusations that their car was illegal. However, unlike the claims at the Monaco GP, this charge was noticeably more serious, primarily because there was no physical evidence, unlike the previous case with the easily identifiable holes in the floor. The accusation related to a convoluted element of engine mapping – essentially the software that overrules the performance of an engine. Changing an engine map can deliver more revs or power than is allowed. In this scenario it was the engine map that manipulated the difference between the torque generated by the engine and the amount the throttle was open. Put simply, more air was able to run through the exhaust and over the diffuser, creating more downforce, which allowed their drivers to get more grip in the corners and take them faster.

Again, Red Bull Racing saw the stewards and again they were cleared of any wrongdoing; they had not actually broken any rules, they had simply exploited an area that had not been covered by the regulations. And once more the FIA were forced to amend the rules in time for the next race, in Hungary (resulting in an extremely complicated amendment). On both occasions, in Monaco and at Hockenheim, Red Bull Racing's advantage had been reeled in by the governing body. Their hard work to create a smart solution to gain an advantage had been taken away in the name of maintaining the competitiveness of the sport. Understandably, it left both Newey and Horner exasperated, given that the essence of F1 design is largely about lateral thinking and coming up with solutions.

Vettel, too, had been hit with a substantial 20-second time penalty for an illegal overtaking move on Button where he went off-track, which dropped him from second place to fifth in the classified results. 'Unfortunately, when you have a quick car it's inevitable that questions are asked, and F1 is a competitive business,' said Horner in his usual post-race media session. 'Initially, we were called to the stewards to have a discussion about some technicalities on the car. But the rules are pretty black and white and, having listened and looked at the data, the stewards were fully satisfied. That's the nature of F1, and you are always going to get other teams who are going to speculate. As for Sebastian, the stewards ruled he gained an unfair advantage, and the only penalty available to them is the equivalent of a drive-through penalty [where a driver is forced to take a long lap into the pit lane, costing them time], which is 20 seconds. The penalty doesn't fit the crime, even if, in our opinion, there was no crime.'

Tensions between the FIA and Red Bull Racing were running high, so a third dispute at the Hungarian Grand Prix was equally poorly received. This time it was an accusation that the team had made changes to the height of their car when it was placed in *parc fermé*. The term relates to the moment a driver is out of the car and it can no longer be worked on by the team until it has been assessed or scrutinised by the FIA for any irregularities. The charge dated back to the Canadian GP, where the team had indeed changed a part on the request of the FIA but had in no way altered the height of the car, which would have been a breach of the regulations. Nonetheless, it was the third time Red Bull Racing faced accusations and so it then became an interesting game of finding where the rumour was emanating from within the paddock. Usually, it is a rival team feeding a story to a member of the press, by way of either seeking clarification on a particular clause in the rule-book, or maybe deliberately stirring up some controversy in the hope that it will distract a team from their goal of trying to win races.

By mid-October, Horner was faced with another firefight – this time to address speculation that Vettel would be leaving the team for Ferrari. At this point of the season, Vettel had won three races in a row in Singapore, Japan, Korea, and would soon make it four with victory in India. He was looking strong for the title, but that had not stopped stories circulating about a link with Ferrari. Horner had to assess if the rumour was real or just a mischievous story planted to cause chaos within his ranks while they battled with the Italian team for the drivers' and constructors' championships. Horner said there was 'not a shadow of a doubt' that Vettel would not be driving for his team in the foreseeable future. In an interview with the BBC, he added: '[Vettel] has made it quite clear he hasn't had any dialogue and hasn't signed anything with Ferrari, but the rumour mill will always continue . . . Most of our team has [supposedly] been going to Ferrari at some point, be it Adrian, Mark, Sebastian – even myself, I'm supposed to be going there.'

It prompted a glorious reaction from the flamboyant Luca di Montezemolo, the Ferrari chairman at the time, who said he was not interested in Vettel alongside Alonso as he did not like to have 'two roosters in the same henhouse', referring to having two number-one drivers in a team. While Red Bull Racing always maintained their drivers had equal billing, Ferrari had notoriously opted for a number-one and number-two driver approach in the past. The brinkmanship between the two teams was wonderful to report on as Ferrari looked to win their first constructors' title since 2008.

Vettel was now in pole position to win a third straight title after a sensational run of results. But if he was expecting some help from his teammate, the one who had so enthusiastically celebrated his re-signing to the 'big family', he was not going to get it. In the media, Red Bull Racing had diligently said they would not use team orders to help Vettel's race, yet behind the scenes it is common practice for teams to back their driver who is leading the championship and in this case that was clearly Vettel. However, Webber stubbornly maintained he would not be helping him out while he could still win the title himself. 'It's going to take a lot of smelly races for Seb and Fernando,' he said ahead of the Indian Grand Prix. 'Mathematically, I have a chance [of winning the title], so if I'm in the lead this weekend, I'm not pulling over for anyone.' In another memorable flash of spirit, Webber turned on a reporter who had questioned his assertation that Alonso could still end up victorious. 'That's a ridiculous comment,' he thundered. 'Do you want me to come out and say that Sebastian is the only one who can win it? You're dreaming.' He was of course right, but you got the sense that all was not well in the relationships once again.

Heading into the Abu Dhabi GP, three races from the end of the season, Vettel had taken four consecutive victories. In the previous race in India, a disgruntled Alonso, who was second behind Vettel, sniped that the German was winning because he had a superior car. It is a common accusation in F1 that drivers only enjoy a spell of success because of the car they are driving. It is an easy way to trash your rival's achievements because there is simply no comeback given each team has produced a different car from the other. Would Alonso be winning every race if he were in a Red Bull, for instance? The simple answer is we don't know. The claim smacked of sour grapes and was another barb aimed at the team as they continued to excel: their success was clearly beginning to sting among the established manufacturers. Horner knew it and summed it up at the Abu Dhabi GP, saying: 'The fastest way to become unpopular in this paddock is to be successful. When you are slow, everybody likes you. When you are quick, you become a lot less popular. It is easy to knock someone who is having success. For some, it is uncomfortable the success that Sebastian and Red Bull have had. That's not our fault. He has not completed 100 Grands Prix yet, but he has won 26 per cent of them so far.'

The race in Abu Dhabi offered another marvel as Vettel battled from the back of the grid to finish on the podium. His performance at the Yas Marina Circuit smashed Alonso's theory that it was the car that was winning races, not Vettel.

In qualifying, Vettel had been the victim of an unfortunate technical mistake on the part of his team. After qualifying in third place, while on his way back to the pits, he was told to stop his car as it had been running low on fuel. F1's rules stipulate that a car must finish with a minimum of one litre left in the tank so the scrutineers can test the fuel to ensure it is legal. On this occasion, they were unable to retrieve enough to reach the required amount, which automatically triggered the sanction that demoted him from third to last place.

It was a slam-dunk penalty but, while acknowledging their error, Red Bull Racing set out to make it right for their driver, who risked losing a chunk of championship points to Alonso, or indeed Webber, through no fault of his own. The team made the smart decision to take his car out of *parc fermé* conditions, meaning they could now make changes to it – but this would mean that Vettel would be required to start the race from the pit lane, rather than on the grid, though still effectively in last place. To reflect this new situation, Red Bull changed his gear ratios, suspension and revised the aerodynamic package to optimise his race. Usually, a team would place the emphasis on balance, trying to make a car suitable for both qualifying and the race, so they find a compromise. However, given the penalty would see him start at the back of the field, the technical changes would afford him more grip and allow him to have a better shot at overtaking. In essence, the car was now optimised only for the race, now that qualifying was over – but the downside was he was not only starting in last place, but also starting in the pit lane, which meant he had a much slower opening lap.

Räikkönen was crowned the winner, but the story had been about Vettel swashbuckling his way through the field from last to third place on a track on which it is notoriously difficult to perform successful overtaking manoeuvres. When he was asked post-race if he had thought a podium was on, his answer provided a massive flex.

'It was difficult to predict the outcome but I was convinced I would have chances,' he said. 'The grid penalty was a big hit but every chance is an opportunity and I enjoyed it a lot. There was a chance for us to fuck it up, but we didn't.'

Horner in turn revealed how Vettel had remained mentally in control, despite the setback in qualifying. 'I went to see him in his room before the race to wish him good luck,' said Horner. 'He was in there playing a drum kit and said to me, "I'll see you on the podium." On Saturday night when we were in the briefing room and ready to slit our wrists, he had said it was not an issue and told us we could still do it.'

Red Bull Racing secured the constructors' championship title at the United States Grand Prix in Austin, Texas – the Circuit of the Americas being a new venue for F1. Although Webber retired from the race with an alternator failure, Vettel took second place, enough to wrap up the team's title. But it had been a slog – not in the physical sense, but the bureaucratic one that had seen the team hauled in front of the stewards more times than they cared to remember. Newey admitted the season had been tough as it seemed that each time he had unlocked an element with the car, it was immediately challenged by their rivals and subsequently outlawed by the FIA. In an interview with the BBC, Newey said that the victory had been the 'most tiring' of their three, adding that Austin had been 'very satisfying but a lot of hard work' to help the team recover after a slow start.

'Last year [the 2011 constructors' title] was obviously the easiest,' Newey said in the same article. 'To choose between constructors' and drivers' titles, I find it very difficult. To achieve the hat-trick is very special. [I was] lucky enough to achieve it at Williams and again here at Red Bull. It is a great tribute to everyone in the team.'

Vettel clinched his third drivers' title in dramatic fashion in Brazil, the final race of the 2012 season. He came into the race in São Paulo with a 13-point cushion over Ferrari's Alonso, meaning the Spanish driver needed at least a third-place finish to overtake him, assuming Vettel failed to score a point. Vettel had qualified in fourth and Webber in third but, in a tense start to the race, the two almost collided on the very first lap. In order to avoid his teammate, Vettel swerved and was caught in a collision with Williams' Bruno Senna, causing damage to his car and dropping him to last place. It was a complete disaster and if the race had finished like that, Alonso would have been crowned champion. As Vettel trundled round, quick-thinking Newey ordered Red Bull Racing's 'spy photographer' to get a shot of his car so they could assess the damage on the pit wall without requiring him to stop. Newey spotted that the crumpled bodywork had moved closer to the exhaust, meaning that it had not only impacted the performance of the car, but it was also now at risk of catching fire from the heat of the exhaust. Consequently, Red Bull racing were able to adjust his engine mapping so that the exhaust would be kept as cool as possible to prevent any risk of a fire. Vettel was able to nurse his car through the traffic to come home in sixth place, so Alonso's second was not enough to win the Ferrari man his third world crown. Sensationally, Vettel had achieved victory in the drivers' championship by three points and was now a triple world champion himself.

However, he had been forced to fight for it – and Webber's failure to help him had not gone unnoticed. It would have a monumental bearing on the following season.

CHAPTER 11

TO INFINITI AND BEYOND

– 2013 –

When a new title sponsor comes on board with an F1 team, the goal is obviously to get some exposure for the brand to increase global awareness. Japanese car brand Infiniti – the luxury division of Nissan – had already been a sponsor of Red Bull Racing for a couple of seasons but in 2013 they increased their commitment to become title sponsors of the team. It was the idea of Brazilian-born Carlos Ghosn, who became CEO of the Renault Nissan Alliance when it was established in 1999. It was a smart move to gain attention on the world stage – though it's fair to say that neither Ghosn, nor indeed anyone at the parent groups Renault or Nissan, would ever have expected to receive as much exposure as they did in the early stages of the season, when the simmering relationship between Webber and Vettel erupted. This time the fallout was massive.

The season got off to a fairly smooth start. Pre-season testing had gone relatively well, although another change to the rules had seen all the teams produce some of the ugliest F1 cars in decades due to their high noses and low front wings. The new front sections looked somewhat detached from the rest of the car, quickly earning them the moniker 'platypus noses'. Unveiled at the car launch in Milton Keynes, Vettel later named the RB9 'Hungry Heidi', after German model Heidi Klum. The RB9 had issues not only in terms of its looks, but also because Newey had halted its development during the previous season so the team could focus on improving the RB8 to allow them to secure both titles. By stopping the development of RB9 and switching focus to the RB8, Red Bull Racing would be starting on the back foot in 2013. The car would not have reached the ideal level of development that the team had hoped to achieve.

Personnel issues were, as ever, a matter of speculation, and there had been several changes afoot among their rivals ahead of the new season. Hamilton had stunned McLaren by moving to Mercedes and Pérez had replaced him, yet the latter was an unknown quantity as he had never driven for a leading team before. Horner was again quizzed about Webber's future after Marko had criticised the Australian's lack of consistency. 'I think that Helmut can be a little outspoken at times with his comments but he is entitled to his opinion,' Horner said around the time of the launch, 'but if we were not happy with Mark, we would not have signed him. We're very happy with Mark and we give both drivers equal opportunity. It's ultimately down to what they do on the circuit. For us, it doesn't matter which driver wins, as long as it is a driver in one of our cars. Both of these guys believe they are the best and the team will do the very best it can to support them.'

Over the winter, Horner himself had also signed a new contract extension with the team, despite being linked with a switch to Ferrari. He added: 'It was a natural extension for me and something that was logical. I came into F1 with Red Bull. Dietrich Mateschitz gave me the opportunity so it was a formality to extend our relationship. What we have achieved at Red Bull Racing is extremely special and my commitment has always been 100 per cent to the team.'

Despite the excitement of the new season, the opening race of 2013 at the Australian Grand Prix was forgettable: Vettel had taken pole but could not maintain the pace in the race, while Webber made a poor start, and they finished third and sixth respectively.

The Malaysian Grand Prix that followed, however, was the complete opposite. It was a race that proved to be the most memorable of the season and encapsulated the turbulent relationship between Vettel and Webber. What happened in Malaysia formed an irreconcilable split in the team that made the fallout in Turkey a couple of years earlier seem minor in comparison. The ramifications are still spoken about in the paddock today.

Webber was leading the race when the team radioed both drivers with the secret code 'multi 21'. Teams are allowed to communicate with the drivers but are mindful of rival teams eavesdropping on their conversations. They are often coy with the details or, as in this instance, use code that nobody outside the race team would understand. The instruction 'multi 21' meant that the cars would hold their position: car number two, Webber, would remain ahead of car number one, Vettel. A call of 'multi 12' would mean the opposite, with Vettel assuming the lead. It was clear to both what was being ordered by the team. However, on this occasion the instruction was not respected.

On lap 46, Vettel, who had failed to respond to calls for him to slow down, made his move on Webber, pushing his teammate close to the pit lane barrier. The two came within centimetres of touching wheels. Webber moved off the racing line to defend around turn two. But then Vettel got a good exit off turn three and by turn four he had better traction and took the lead. Over the radio, Horner interrupted their fight, saying, 'This is silly, Seb. Come on.' The two continued their battle but Vettel now had the lead and he would cross the line over four seconds ahead of his teammate.

The ramifications of his disobedience were huge and in the press room there was disbelief as journalists quickly recalled the details of what had happened in Turkey two years earlier. The atmosphere was terrible as the two drivers sat in the cool-down room ahead of the podium presentation, with Hamilton awkwardly joining them, having finished third. Webber was in such a rage that he did not want to go on the podium for his second-place trophy. He angrily confronted Vettel, saying, 'Multi 21, Seb! Multi 21!' That was the giveaway to the media that the secret code had been breached. If there were any doubts, Webber continued to dig his teammate deeper into the mire during his post-race interview, but also took a swipe at his perceived lack of support from the team: 'In the end, Seb made his own decisions today and will have protection and that's the way it goes.'

By the time the drivers had reached the FIA press conference after the podium presentations – which, incidentally, Webber did attend – Vettel's mood was noticeably different. He had initially seemed upset, almost embarrassed by his actions, yet in the second interview, he was calmer and seemed to almost shrug the incident off. He delivered a half-apology to Webber, saying: 'As you can see, I'm not entirely happy. I think I did a big mistake today. I think we should have stayed in the positions that we were.' He then added: 'I didn't ignore it on purpose but I messed up in that situation and obviously took the lead. I can see now he's upset, but I want to be honest at least and stick to the truth and apologise. I know that it doesn't really help his feelings right now . . . To sum it up, apologies to Mark.' Vettel later referred to himself as 'the black sheep right now' for going against the team orders. However, his attempt at an apology did not cut any ice with Webber.

The feud was gold for the travelling reporters who had made the long trip from Europe to Melbourne and then Malaysia for the opening two races of the season; they had been rewarded with plenty to get stuck into. Immediately after the race, Vettel headed back to visit the team's Milton Keynes HQ where he addressed the staff and explained his side of the story, while Webber revealed in his book *Aussie Grit: My Formula One Journey* that he received a direct call from Mateschitz, who was seeking an explanation as to what had happened because he feared it had damaged the Red Bull brand.

While the logical explanation for Vettel's disobedience centred on their bitter fallout following their collision in the 2010 Turkish Grand Prix, Horner says the roots for their meltdown in Malaysia could be traced back just two races, to the season finale in 2012 in Brazil where Webber had not assisted Vettel's start and ended up causing him to collide with Bruno Senna.

When we discuss the 2013 Malaysian GP over Zoom, Horner's face changes and he leans forward towards his laptop screen, revealing how he is still agitated by the race that drove such a cavernous wedge into his team. 'Multi 21', as he refers to it, 'had its foundations firmly in Brazil 2012, where Sebastian was up against Alonso for the title. He had qualified down the grid in fourth and was behind Mark. Before the race we talked with both drivers about our best chance to win the championship and I obviously asked Mark for his help that day. Unfortunately, he chose to take things into his own hands and squeeze Seb up against the wall off the start line, which then brought him into the pack and he got tagged by Senna. Anyway, he [Vettel] managed to come back and win the championship, but he didn't forget.

'Two races later in Malaysia, it was a wet start and then Mark got the crossover better [when it was time to move to the quicker slick tyres, rather than the grooved tyres used in the wet], which put him into the lead. We were sitting in a one-two position and I remember Adrian pushing me to lock the race down because he was concerned about reliability. So the order we had after the final pit stops was "multi 21", meaning car two [Webber's racing number] was ahead of car one [the number on Vettel's car]. The call went out to both drivers, but Seb was armed with a brand-new set of tyres and, with Brazil firmly in his head, he went out faster. Mark raced him hard but Seb passed him, against the instruction from the team to hold position.

'We had one very grumpy driver, and a whole bunch of controversy. I remember saying to Adrian, "You speak to the drivers in the room before they go on the podium just to defuse it and I will deal with the media." And it all kicked off! Sebastian was adamant in his mind that he wasn't going to give up a victory or the chance of victory, particularly after what had happened in Brazil. The relationship between the two of them was irretrievably broken at that point.'

Indeed, the relationship between Vettel and Webber was dissected in the media and the warring factions at Red Bull Racing were laid bare. Some questioned whether Vettel would face the wrath of Mateschitz – would he be fined or sanctioned in any way? Horner was again caught in the middle and also came in for some criticism himself, with some sections of the press questioning his leadership. And naturally it proved a tasty topic for rival teams, who seized the opportunity to take a dig at Vettel. Former McLaren team principal Martin Whitmarsh, who ran the team from 2008 until 2014, insisted a rift like that would never happen in his team. 'You cannot accept drivers not taking team orders,' he said. 'The team is bigger than any driver and they have got to respect that. It is a very serious matter if you tell a driver to do something and he doesn't do it and it could also be a breach of his contract.' Whitmarsh, of course, was entitled to his view, but it is worth noting that just one season before he was made team principal of McLaren, when he was the CEO of McLaren Racing, an inter-team fight between Hamilton and Alonso was so toxic that the Spanish driver severed his deal with the team after only one season and rejoined Renault.

Oliver Brown, writing in the *Daily Telegraph*, accused Vettel of 'dark duplicity' in an 'act of ruthlessness at best supremely ungallant, at worst morally questionable', which Brown suggested meant he was 'no ordinary competitor but a calculating marksman, far more of an heir presumptive to Ayrton Senna and Michael Schumacher than even his most strident advocates had imagined'.

Mateschitz poses with team manager Tony Purnell, during testing at the Circuit de Catalunya in November 2004.

Horner at the team's Milton Keynes HQ in January 2005. On his first day Horner recalls: 'I went upstairs to the office where there's a secretary in tears because she's just lost her old boss. I sat down at a desk and there were half-opened Christmas cards and a half-drunk cup of coffee.'

Darth Vader and storm troopers visit the Red Bull Energy Station prior to the Monaco Grand Prix in 2005. The PR stunt raised plenty of eyebrows in the F1 paddock and piqued the interest of one Adrian Newey.

Coulthard celebrates on the podium in a Superman cape after finishing third in the Monaco GP in 2006. Horner would later use the cape to protect his modesty when jumping into the swimming pool in the team's motorhome.

Coulthard, Newey, Horner, technical director Geoff Willis, head of engine development Rob White and Webber with the new Red Bull challenger for 2008: the RB4. It would prove to be Coulthard's final season in F1.

Newey on the grid before the Spanish Grand Prix in April 2008. Webber would finish fifth while Coulthard came twelfth. Vettel, driving for Toro Rosso, was eliminated on the first lap after a collision with Adrian Sutil.

Vettel and Scuderia Toro Rosso celebrate with Mateschitz, Team Principal Franz Tost and Dr Helmut Marko after winning the Italian GP in September 2008. The shock win would be the start of Vettel's glittering career in F1 and lead to his promotion to Red Bull Racing the following season.

Vettel is thrown in the air by teammates in the paddock after the win at the Autodromo Nazionale di Monza.

Team Principal Horner and designer Newey during practice for the Australian Grand Prix at the Albert Park Circuit in Melbourne, March 2009. The race would see a disappointing result for the team with Webber finishing 12th and Vettel 13th.

Vettel wins the Chinese Grand Prix 2009 ahead of teammate Webber. It was Red Bull Racing's first victory and pole position. Horner joined the two Red Bull drivers on the podium, note the broken trophy. It was only the 81st race the team had entered. Horner recalls: 'I just remember the feeling of getting on the aeroplane, still smelling of champagne, and just thinking that this one had been so special.'

Webber, Newey, Horner and Vettel are sprayed with champagne by teammates in front of the Energy Station at the British GP. Vettel was first and Webber second as the team recorded a one-two finish at Silverstone in June 2009.

Webber's first win came at the 2009 German Grand Prix where he was still suffering with a leg injury he picked up in a pre-season bike accident. The Aussie paid tribute to those who had supported him and added: 'And there are a few people that doubted me too, so hello to them as well!'

At the 2010 Monaco GP, Webber celebrates his win by jumping in the Red Bull Energy Station swimming pool. Vettel, who was second, also joins him in the water.

Newey gets a kiss from Horner in the team garage following the Abu Dhabi Grand Prix. Red Bull Racing are crowned world champions for the first time. 'In six years, Red Bull has come from a team that no one took seriously – that everyone thought was a party team – to the 2010 F1 constructors' champions,' said Horner.

Vettel is congratulated by Michael Schumacher after clinching his first F1 world title at the 2010 Abu Dhabi GP. He would later follow his idol's career by moving to Ferrari.

Vettel drinks champagne from his trophy after winning the Indian Grand Prix in 2011. The German started on pole, led every lap and set the fastest lap time on his way to victory in a clean sweep.

Brown's comments were ringing in everyone's ears when the press conference at the following race took place in China. It was held in the Red Bull Racing hospitality area, a modern, square building that sat on concrete stilts over a small lake – and the place was packed. Journalists and broadcasters squeezed in to hear what Vettel was going to say and they were not disappointed. The German, in contrast to his former apologetic demeanour at the press conference after the race in Malaysia, was this time bullish, and there was now no remorse for how he had behaved. Somewhat incredibly, Vettel even claimed that Webber never deserved to win the Malaysian Grand Prix in the first place.

Asked if he would do the same if he were in that position again, Vettel replied: 'I would probably do the same. It is not the end of the world. I love racing, I love working with the team. I cannot think of anything else that gives me that much pleasure. I don't know what the big deal is. I didn't mean to ignore the team order. I heard it but I didn't translate it the proper way, the way I should have. Had I understood the message, I would have thought about it, reflected on what the team wanted me to do, which was leave Mark in first place and me second. But having thought about it, I probably would have done the same thing. I was faster at the end, which is why I was able to overtake. On the one hand, I am the kind of guy that respects team decisions, but on the other hand, Mark was not the one that deserved it at the time.'

Wow. After the team and even Webber had promised to move on after the incident, here was Vettel reopening the wound, and this time he went even deeper. He continued: 'After all that happened in the past few years, Mark didn't deserve to win. Being completely honest, I have never had support from his side. I have got the support of the team and I think the team has supported us the same way. In terms of my relationship with Mark, I respect him a lot as a racing driver but I think there has been more than one occasion in the past where he could have helped the team. You could say it was payback, indirectly. In my opinion it is always best to be truthful. Maybe sometimes the truth is not what people want to see because controversy is more popular than the truth. I told you after the race what happened. I was racing, so as a racing driver I was fully focused on winning the race. I got a call on the radio, which I heard but I didn't understand at the time. I should have understood, which is why I apologised to the team. As a team member I didn't obey the team order. My intention was to win the race. I wanted to win and I succeeded.'

And still he continued, taking aim at the media for suggesting that he would face an internal reprimand for his behaviour. 'You could say I have undermined Christian,' he said, 'but I went to everyone straight after to explain what happened. The intention was not to undermine the decision of the team principal. In terms of a sanction or punishment? Maybe it is a bit of dreamland that you [the media] all live in. What do you expect to happen? We dealt with it internally. I apologised to the team; I took it very seriously.'

Vettel's outspoken comments were so incredible that my fellow reporters were turning to each other to ask whether they had misunderstood. They hadn't. It was a bizarre twist and completely unexpected, given the expectation that the incident would be played down to refocus on the race in Shanghai.

I asked Vettel in our interview about his relationship with Webber and whether following his retirement from F1 he had changed his stance from what he said at the time. Refreshingly, like Webber, he too is adamant that he still holds the same view and that it was simply born from their competitiveness. He also added that he now has a good relationship and respect for the Aussie.

'It's fair to say that with a bit of distance – that is, a couple of years later – I would still stand by what I said,' he says. 'I still think I would say the same things but it is mutual. You probably understand the other person better now and I have huge respect for him. I've seen how strong he is. I've had weekends where I just didn't have an answer [to beat him]. Overall, maybe I did have the upper hand, but I think we have a very good relationship now and I'm very thankful for that. Maybe at the time I didn't have the experience that he had and sometimes the broader view, but that doesn't excuse some of the things that happened. But I believe it was misunderstandings and I'm not surprised because we were both fighting for first place. It is how we were programmed when we grew up; to win. When you look at the design of the podium there is only one place at the top. Everything that happened I'm grateful for, because the big picture was I was able to learn from it a lot. Red Bull was giving both of us this incredible chance with a great car, a great team. It was a bit rough and it was probably a bit difficult to manage. I don't think Christian was in an easy position, or the rest of the team. But on the other hand, you'd probably always do the same thing again because you were fighting for victory.'

The race in China saw Vettel placed in fourth while Webber was forced to retire after only 16 laps when his wheel came off following a pit stop. He'd also suffered a problem in qualifying due to a faulty fuel rig that left him starting in the pit lane. In Bahrain, Vettel scored his second victory of the year and added a third in Montreal at the Canadian GP.

But then, at the next race, the British Grand Prix, Webber dropped a bombshell: he was quitting the team. Just 15 days earlier, Vettel had signed a new one-year extension to keep him at Red Bull Racing until 2015. Now, the team were facing a hole in their driver line-up after being told by Webber on the eve of the team's home race.

The timing was a defiant move. Webber only told Horner about his decision to end his 12-year F1 career in the briefest of conversations – just 20 minutes before the news of his defection was made public by his new team, Porsche, whom he was joining to race in their Le Mans sports-car project. Webber displayed some thick skin as he faced questions about the way he broke the news to his team, with Horner declaring he had 'taken matters into his own hands', adding, 'The guys back at the factory will be disappointed that they had to learn about it on the internet.'

Unrepentant, Webber said: 'It was a Porsche announcement. I informed Christian before the announcement, which contractually I should do, and that is what we did. It was about Porsche and Mark Webber. I think I helped the team today; they have to make some decisions for the future. I'm very much looking forward to this new challenge after my time in Formula One. I can hardly wait to pilot one of the fastest sports cars in the world.'

Reflecting on Webber's decision now, Horner is calm about the driver who would continue to be sponsored by Mateschitz as he moved to Porsche. 'Mark at that point had become quite tricky and distant to deal with,' says Horner. 'He didn't inform us that he was going to retire either. He just put out a statement on the Thursday before the British GP. I think he'd spoken to Dietrich a couple of hours before. There had been no indication he was going to retire but I think he knew the writing was on the wall. The relationship was so broken that we were unlikely to renew the contract for the following year, so he decided to take matters into his own hands at that point.

'I think Mark felt that the team was very much centred around Sebastian, but the reality is we had a situation that is similar today – the team will always respond best to the driver that is leading the championship.'

When Coulthard announced his retirement from F1 in 2008, he later admitted that he took the decision too early, but in my interview with Webber he had no such regrets: he still maintains the time was right for him to move on and join the Porsche project. He also makes the point that he had discussed the move with Mateschitz first, and says he still has messages in his phone of their conversations, which he holds as a dear memory to the late Mateschitz, who passed away in 2022.

'You know, some say it's because of Brazil,' he says with reference to the race the previous year. 'Seb felt that I could have been more cooperative with him, but once we checkmated the rest of the field and the race was shut down, we know what happened after that. How both cars finished that race I don't know. It was an absolute miracle that we weren't both in the fencing when you get the red mist coming down.

'I could have been competitive [if he had stayed in F1] but I would have missed the opportunity with Porsche and here I am nearly 10 years later still with Porsche. Red Bull came with me to Porsche, which was great. I spoke to Dietrich and said, "Do you want [to sponsor] the helmet or the drink bottle?" And he said both, so that was really nice.'

Vettel had another win in Germany followed by a third place in Hungary before the summer break. He came back with another win in Belgium, which was to be the first in an incredible nine-race winning streak – a record that would remain in place until 2023, when it was beaten by Verstappen. But ahead of the Italian GP, there was further news to digest: Red Bull Racing confirmed that Daniel Ricciardo had been chosen to replace Webber for 2014. It ended speculation that Red Bull Racing were considering Räikkönen, who was then driving for Lotus, instead opting for their young driver who had been performing well for Toro Rosso.

The email confirming the news landed on Monday 2 September at around 8.30pm. The timing was unusual from a European perspective but of course worked for an Australian audience, who were waking up to the news Webber was being replaced by his fellow countryman. Ricciardo responded by ending the Italian GP in seventh place for Toro Rosso, equalling his highest finish of the season, while Vettel won – although he was subjected to booing on the podium, in part because he was not a Ferrari driver and perhaps as a reaction to his feud with Webber. He won again in Singapore, Korea, Japan and India, the latter victory enough to clinch the constructors' title for Red Bull Racing, while Webber had another alternator failure and did not finish the race. Vettel's victory in India also secured his fourth straight drivers' championship. He pulled off some celebratory doughnuts on the straight after taking the chequered flag, sending wafts of tyre-smoke into the dusty air around the Buddh International Circuit, which ultimately triggered a £21,000 fine from the unhappy stewards who accused him of dangerous driving.

As he climbed from the cockpit as the victor, he sank to his knees to give thanks to his all-conquering RB9. He was still just 26 years and 116 days old. 'I am overwhelmed,' he said as he was interviewed immediately after. 'It is one of the best days of my life. I think back to when I started karting and F1 was so far away. I have to thank so many people who have taught me so much. Formula One is for the world's best drivers and it is fantastic to come out on top. The team is so strong and it's a pleasure to jump in the car. It was phenomenal and I can't ask any more. It was difficult for me, too, to receive the boos this season, even though I had done nothing wrong. But I overcame that and I'm proud to join the likes of [Alain] Prost, [Juan Manuel] Fangio and Michael [Schumacher],' he continued, referring to his four titles (Hamilton had not achieved his fourth by this point).

Newey commented on the success, too, saying, 'I guess some of the booing has been whipped up by his competitors. Some of it is about jealousy and some of it, in truth, is Malaysia. The bottom line is he is a great kid. Malaysia was a mistake but he has learned from it and that shouldn't distract from the true great he is.'

Vettel closed out the season with further wins in Abu Dhabi, Austin and Brazil, where Webber was second in his final F1 race. It brought the curtain down on a contrasting campaign to the previous year where Horner had been focused on fighting rival teams. In 2013, he was dealing with teammates at war. He'd now overseen a total of 47 wins in just 165 races under his reign and, reflecting now on that phenomenal end to a turbulent year, he admits it was tough, despite the on-track success. 'It's easier when you're dealing with the opposition than when you're dealing with a fighting family,' he says. 'There were quite strong opinions and you're having to manage that internally. The drivers are your two prime assets, but they're contractors and, you know, sometimes when they go a bit rogue it can make life quite complicated. You're having to deal with shareholders and sponsors and partners so sometimes when you're winning, the challenges are even greater than when you're losing.'

Incidentally, while Vettel was setting records in F1 for consecutive wins and for being the youngest four-times world champion, in the same year a young driver called Max Verstappen was also rewriting the record books. In his final year of karting, he won the World KZ Championship at Varennes-sur-Allier, France, to become the youngest winner of the title at just 15 years old. He had already wrapped up the other two categories he was competing in: the European KZ Championship and the European KF Championship. His rise had been meteoric: just three years earlier, in 2010 – the year Vettel celebrated his first F1 crown – he had won the junior karting championships, the WSK Euro Series and the WKS World Series. His next step would be to move to Formula Three. We would soon be hearing much more from this exciting young talent, but in the meantime the focus would be on personnel changes in the existing team.

CHAPTER 12

RED BULL RING'S RETURN
– 2014 –

All reigns in sport are cyclical. A championship victory celebrates a period of dominance, so winning four drivers' titles and four constructors' championships in a row marked a hugely impressive run for Red Bull Racing. The target is to keep that run going, but in Formula One, unlike in other sports where the regulations remain the same from year to year, the rulebook changes each season. These new directives can take the form of minor tweaks, such as a clarification to the bodywork like the hole in the cars' floor mentioned in Chapter 10, or the rear diffuser in 2010. But for 2014 the new rulebook saw some of the biggest changes in decades. Driven by a push to be cheaper and more efficient, the old traditional 2.4-litre V8 engines would be replaced by hybrid power units, which would now feature a 1.6-litre internal combustion engine that was fitted with a turbo, plus a two-stage electric battery that generated power from exhaust gases plus braking energy – rather like a hybrid road car.

It followed an initiative for F1 to invest in road-relevant technology with learnings that could be applied to mass-produced models by the manufacturers. The reason for the cost-cutting was sensible, as teams faced increased costs due to an expanding race calendar, with new races added in Austin, Texas, and Sochi, Russia, plus potential interest for a second race in the United States. This was in addition to returns for the Indian and Mexican Grands Prix. The problem, however, was the huge cost of developing the new power units (note the parlance, because an 'engine' only makes up one part of the hybrid system) – and for Red Bull Racing this was a particular challenge because some manufacturers, notably Mercedes, were already dedicating enormous resources to their vision.

Unusually for F1, it was no secret either. Mercedes had earlier thrown open the doors of their factory at Brixworth in Northamptonshire in the UK for a media day where they had shown off the work that had gone into creating their design. They were rightly proud: somewhat smug, even. By contrast, Renault were less forthcoming, the reasons for which would later become obvious. The new power unit raised a number of issues for their designers, who strived to emulate the curvature of the classic Coca-Cola bottle design due to its aerodynamic shape. A bulkier new engine with new ancillaries made the challenge more of a headache as the various F1 teams struggled to make it all fit – unless, of course, you were both a team and a manufacturer, such as Mercedes or Ferrari, where the design process of both chassis and power unit was more aligned and, in the case of the latter, with the engine and chassis department based on the same site. For Red Bull Racing, the situation remained that the engines were being manufactured in France and shipped to Milton Keynes to be fitted into the chassis.

As pre-season testing continued, Hamilton's decision to join Mercedes – initially lampooned – was now proving rather smart. He had been sold on Mercedes' vision not for 2013, but for 2014 and the new era of technology. It was quickly dubbed the turbo-hybrid era and had the potential to redefine the pecking order, not only due to the changing power requirements, but also the engines' reliability. The previous year, engines had to last a minimum of 2,000km before they were replaced. Now, however, they were required to last a minimum of 4,000km, so reliability was as important as speed. Any unscheduled change would trigger a grid penalty.

The other new element at Red Bull Racing was the promotion of Ricciardo from Toro Rosso, as announced the previous season. The Daniel Ricciardo you see on Netflix's *Drive to Survive* is exactly the Daniel Ricciardo you get in real life. I remember sharing an economy cabin section in 2012 on the flight from Australia to Malaysia when he was starting out in F1; he sat a few rows back and it was most unusual to see a driver travelling in economy class. At an interview we had in 2019 he replaced the 'H' for a 'C' in my surname and found it hilarious, and I felt obliged to humour him as if I'd never heard anyone say it before. He's full on – wonderfully quick on his day, and driven by an adolescent charm that is appealing but also disguises his ruthlessness.

Ricciardo was born in 1989 in Perth, Western Australia, to Italian-Australian parents. His dad, Giuseppe – known as Joe – moved to Australia from Ficarra, Sicily, when he was just seven. His mum, Grace, was born in Australia but her parents came from

Casignana on the Italian mainland. Ricciardo's Italian roots would always draw questions, understandably, from the Italian press, who were left bewildered by his decision to drop the second 'i' in the pronunciation of his surname.

Ricciardo's father had a passion for racing and was instrumental in encouraging his son to try karting at the age of nine. He won the Australian karting title in 2005 before switching to the Formula BMW Asia series in 2006, which was a single-seater category and a natural step up from karting. Still only 16, Ricciardo also competed in one event in the UK, racing in the Formula BMW UK series for two races at Snetterton, a well-known track on the lower formula, where he retired in the first race and finished eighth in the second. The following season, Ricciardo moved to Italy to compete in the Formula Renault Italia series, a feeder championship that would lead into Formula Three.

Like Webber before him, Ricciardo needed to move to Europe to test himself against a stronger field and in his first season in Italy he would face Red Bull-backed Jaime Alguersuari and Brendon Hartley, who were driving for the Epsilon Red Bull team and who would both later make it into F1 with Toro Rosso. His performance quickly caught the eye of Red Bull, who signed him up as part of their young driver programme in 2007. The sponsorship meant he was able to switch to the more competitive Formula Renault 2.0 West European Cup season and take in races at Le Mans, Barcelona and Spa.

Ricciardo impressed with eight wins in 14 races and for 2009 he moved to British Formula Three, where he won the championship at the first attempt driving for prestigious British team, Carlin. In 2010, he moved to Renault 3.5, the final rung of the ladder before breaking into F1, where he finished second in his debut season, only missing out on first place by two points. Ricciardo's progress had been rapid, but few expected him to reach F1 quite so quickly. He was signed by the now-defunct Spanish race team HRT and joined the grid halfway through the season as a replacement for Narain Karthikeyan. HRT were short of cash and had been propped up by Red Bull's investment in return for running their young drivers. They had also run Red Bull's youngsters Klien and Liuzzi when the team was known under its previous guise, Hispania Racing F1 Team, before it was rebranded as HRT and later folded in 2012. Ricciardo then spent two seasons at Toro Rosso, where he had finished in 18th and 14th place respectively in the drivers' championship, before his promotion to Red Bull in 2014.

Ricciardo's debut for Red Bull Racing was a memorable one. It came in his native Australia where he had impressed in practice before qualifying in second place. In Sunday's race, he would consolidate that position, crossing the line in second behind Rosberg, much to the delight of the home supporters. But as the crowd dispersed and made their way back to Melbourne city centre on the trams, news filtered through that Ricciardo's podium was being investigated by the FIA for an infringement. These post-race investigations can quickly dampen the spirit, and the mood in the Red Bull Racing hospitality building soon turned. There was a substantial delay, with mounting anticipation around what the FIA would conclude having scrutinised his car. Red Bull Racing's senior design team made their case to the stewards. It was now up to them to decide the outcome.

Shortly after midnight, the verdict was given that Red Bull Racing had breached the rules, which ultimately saw Ricciardo disqualified. It was a hammer blow and one that somewhat sums up the sport's unwelcome intricacies. After all, how can you leave a football match seeing your team win 3–0, only to wake up the next morning to find out they had been disqualified and the opposing team awarded a 3–0 victory instead? Of course, it is about obeying the rules, but in this instance it pertained to the confusing matter of the rate of fuel flow to the engine – a very niche issue, especially as the quantity of fuel is limited by weight, and this was found to be in accordance with the regulations. The quality of the fuel was also tested and found to be sufficient. Ultimately, Ricciardo was punished because the FIA declared that the sensors used to measure the fuel flow were non-conforming, despite providing no additional benefit to his engine's power. Given that it was the first race that required the completely new power unit regulations, Red Bull Racing might have been hoping for some leniency, but none was given.

For Vettel, things were even worse and gave a glimpse of the future difficulties he would face that season with the reliability and performance of the Renault power unit. A faulty sensor reading meant that Renault provided the wrong power unit setting for qualifying, resulting in him being down on power and qualifying way back in 12th. Think of it as turning the volume down on an amplifier. In the race, he lasted three laps before his power unit failed and he was forced out of the Australian GP. His bid to defend his title had got off to the worst possible start.

At the next race in Malaysia, things improved for Vettel, who came third, while this time Ricciardo was forced to retire following a bungled pit stop. He had been running in fourth place with 15 laps to go but when he made his pit stop he was sent back out without the front left wheel being tightened. He was pushed back into the garage by his mechanics, who fixed the issue. However, on lap 53 of 56 he was then forced to retire with a broken front wing. As a result of the unsafe release into the pit lane by his crew, the Australian was subsequently penalised with an additional ten-place grid penalty that he would serve at the next race in Bahrain. To his credit, in Bahrain he recovered to finish fourth, while Vettel was sixth.

It had already become clear, however, that Mercedes were getting significant benefit from their power unit, which was not only proving to be quick, but also incredibly reliable. Rosberg had won the opening race in Melbourne while Hamilton won in Malaysia, Bahrain, China and Spain. Red Bull were left reeling, and tensions between the team and Renault quickly escalated. Horner says he pressed for answers but it quickly became evident that his worst fears about the French car giant's lack of investment were beginning to come true.

'Mercedes started on the hybrid engine so early,' says Horner. 'We now know from some of the people who have since joined us from Mercedes that they had been working on the project for a number of years beforehand. Renault had an arrogance [because they knew] that they always had a great design. They had achieved success with the turbo engines they produced in the 1970s and 80s and they were confident that it would all be fine. I recall going to [former Renault boss] Carlos Ghosn's office on at least three occasions before the start to the season because we had heard the rumours about how much effort Mercedes were putting in. We knew from the Renault guys we were working closely with [to help the integration of the power unit] that they needed to step it up and that they needed to commit some more funding because we were going to be left behind. I remember going over to Paris with Adrian and Helmut and meeting in Ghosn's office but there was a reticence around fully committing to it in the way that Mercedes had.

'So Mercedes came out and hit the ground running but we could not do more than three laps. By the time we got to Australia for the opening race of the 2014 season, that was the furthest distance we had managed all winter. Sebastian retired but Daniel kept going and then got disqualified for something that today would be so minor. But it was very tricky because Mercedes were two years ahead of anybody else. They turned down their engines [power] so they could save on engine wear and preserve them for future races; they were so far ahead. We actually had a very good car that year but the engine was so bad. There was a lack of commitment from Renault, which meant that Adrian [Newey] became pretty disillusioned with F1.'

There were highlights, such as Ricciardo's win in Canada – his first in F1 – but only after Hamilton was forced to retire with a brake problem and Rosberg too experienced problems in a rare moment of fragility from Mercedes. 'I'm still in shock. This is ridiculous,' laughed Ricciardo after the race, exulting in his triumph, while Horner was quick to praise the start his driver had made to his Red Bull racing career. He had got the better of his teammate – the four-time world champion – in the early races too, beating him in Bahrain, China, Spain and Monaco. 'Amazing,' Horner said. 'The boy's driven brilliantly all year.'

Next up was a home meet for the Red Bull team. The Austrian Grand Prix at the Red Bull Ring returned to the F1 calendar in 2014, and there is something very special about it that defies logic. The hotels in the immediate area are largely unspectacular, as is the food. And those hotels and restaurants further away in Graz are a bit of a drive after a long day at the track. That said, the race is unique in that when you return home, you feel better than when you left. Maybe it is the Alpine air? Or the scenery? Or perhaps it's the Red Bull – because the town of Spielberg where the track is based is awash with it!

The circuit was once known as the Österreichring and hosted the Austrian Grand Prix for 18 consecutive years, from 1970 to 1987. The track was later shortened and renamed the A1-Ring and that too hosted the Austrian Grand Prix from 1997 to 2003 until it was no longer economically viable for the organisers to pay F1, or indeed Ecclestone, for the rights to host the event.

After losing the F1 contract, the circuit was sold to Mateschitz, who had ambitious plans to rebuild it. Red Bull drew up blueprints for a proposal which included expanding the circuit as well as building a racing school, a museum, a hotel and a hangar for some of Mateschitz's aircraft, at an estimated overall cost of around £485 million. However, the proposal faced opposition from local residents, who complained about the likely noise and pollution, and the plans were rejected. The redevelopment project was halted, but Mateschitz was reluctant to give up on his vision, and he set about forming radical plans to help reshape the local area. What became known as 'Projekt Spielberg' aimed to improve the local economy and surrounding infrastructure, with the long-term goal of bringing F1 back to the circuit.

Mateschitz's determination paid off and, eventually, the plans were approved. The circuit was renamed the Red Bull Ring and was reopened at a special Red Bull event in May 2011. The circuit chiefs, presumably encouraged by Mateschitz's wishes to see the circuit host Grand Prix races again, asked F1 about the prospect of rejoining the calendar in 2013, as a replacement for the failed plans for a New York Grand Prix, and finally got a slot for 2014.

It is not especially easy to get to Spielberg, a small town of 5,000 people in Styria, Austria, which sits in the valley of a mountain range. It is a two-hour drive from Vienna Airport, although this usually increases due to roadworks or the number of Verstappen fans towing their caravans to the Red Bull Ring from the Netherlands. In 2014, the smart thing to do was head over a day early in preparation for the inevitable traffic. However, not all of my colleagues did the same. Some decided to fly over on Thursday, the day of the press conference – arguably the most important day of the week for journalists, given the limited access to the drivers. So when they decided to post on social media about stopping off for apple strudel, there was little sympathy when they arrived at the Red Bull Ring late for duty, especially when they tried to claim their lateness was all just down to the traffic! The quality of the facility, however, soon cheered them. The press room remains the best on the F1 calendar, offering panoramic views of the track, excellent food and a limitless supply of Red Bull and coffee.

While it was a spectacular debut for the Red Bull Ring in its new guise, it was less memorable for the team. Vettel retired with an electronics issue and Ricciardo was placed an underwhelming eighth. Once again, Horner placed the blame firmly at Renault's door, indicating that Red Bull Racing were keen to explore their options for a new engine supplier for the 2016 season. The event had otherwise been a celebration of Red Bull but, when Horner spoke after the race, it was clear he was despondent due to the lack of progress. 'It's frustrating,' he said honestly. 'We've won all the races and championships with Renault, but the current situation just isn't improving. The reliability is unacceptable. The performance is unacceptable. It can't continue like this. It's not good for Renault and it's not good for Red Bull. Renault need to make a step to close that gap down with Mercedes. A team like Red Bull isn't short of choices and we want to make sure that we're competitive for the long term.'

Vettel's retirement from the race dropped him to fifth in the drivers' championship and it was clear he would have to come to terms with the fact that he was about to lose his F1 crown. Rumours quickly began to circulate that Vettel was unhappy with the situation at Red Bull Racing and it was easy to see why. The frustration with Renault had left him crestfallen. He was no longer winning races, although his teammate was. His head had dropped and, looking ahead, it was difficult to see any reason to be optimistic. Newey's interest in F1 had waned. He had become worn down by the continued battles with the FIA and their changes to the rulebook, seemingly designed to rein in his technical brilliance. Meanwhile, Horner was now embroiled in a very public war of words with Frenchman Cyril Abiteboul, managing director of Renault's F1 operation. Perhaps it was time for Vettel to leave what looked increasingly like a sinking ship?

At the Japanese Grand Prix in October, Vettel stunned Formula One with the news that he was leaving Red Bull Racing, telling Horner the night before that he would be activating a clause in his contract that enabled him to leave the team at the end of the 2014 season. The clause related to him not being in the top three of the drivers' championship at the end of September. It meant he was freely able to negotiate his way out of the deal for the 2015 season.

News broke on 4 October when the team released a brief statement. It read: 'Sebastian Vettel has advised us that he will be leaving Infiniti Red Bull Racing at the end of the 2014 season. We want to warmly thank Sebastian for the incredible role he has played at Infiniti Red Bull Racing for the last six years.' It added that Daniil Kvyat, the Russian driver who was at Toro Rosso, would be promoted in his place: 'As we wish Sebastian well in the next stage of his career, we also look to the future with excitement, as the vacancy makes way for the next generation of Red Bull racers. The Red Bull Junior programme has developed some proven talents in recent times, including Sebastian Vettel and Daniel Ricciardo, who has excelled in the RB10 and become a three-time Formula One race winner in his first season with the team. We're pleased to announce that Daniel will be joined in the team for 2015 by another rising star from the Junior Programme, Daniil Kvyat.' The statement appeared hurried – because it was – and the promotion of Kvyat seemed like a knee-jerk reaction.

Vettel himself was emotional, telling the press that he was not leaving the team because of Ricciardo, who had now also won in Hungary and Belgium to add to his victory in Canada. He was adamant that he was not shirking the challenge now presented by the Australian and that he remained on good terms with the team.

'Red Bull did nothing wrong and we are parting as friends,' he said, obviously having Webber's somewhat controversial departure in his mind. 'It has nothing to do with the results, even though they are not what we expected. I am loyal and I did not breach any contract. I am not running away from anything but there are times in life when you need something new and if there is an opportunity you have to grab it.'

It was clear Vettel had thought long and hard about his decision and it had pulled him in two. But where would he go? That was the missing piece of this jigsaw. There had been speculation but for the time being there was no news from Ferrari – who still had Alonso and Räikkönen in their team. Horner was certain. 'Obviously Ferrari have made him a very attractive offer,' he said in the Suzuka paddock, which was buzzing with the news. Horner's comments swung the spotlight onto the Italian team, who, remember, still had two drivers under contract, ultimately forcing their hand. His instinct was later proved correct, but for the time being, nothing was confirmed.

'I know Sebastian very well and we spend a lot of time together and you can see that he has had a bit on his mind recently,' Horner continued. 'Inevitably a decision like this you don't take lightly but last night he sat down with us and informed us. So all I can do is wish him the very, very best for the future. He will still be close to our hearts at Red Bull, but on 1 January he will be a competitor. If somebody's heart is not there, it doesn't matter what you have on a piece of paper. It has to be right for both sides. He has reached a stage in his career where he fancied a new challenge. That is his prerogative and, like in any relationship, if somebody's heart is not in it then it is time to move on.'

As we discuss his departure from Red Bull Racing, Vettel says the engine issues had changed everything that season. 'It was very difficult because it felt like only a couple of weeks earlier – but it was obviously months or even a year or two – when I was extending the contract with Red Bull and thinking, "I don't know if I ever want to leave this team because I'm happy here." But it was a bit of a surprise how quickly things changed. The bigger picture was the rules changing in 2014 and it was very clear that we were so far back with the Renault powertrain. We went to the first test [in 2014] and we had so many problems and the outlook was not great. Mercedes still had so much more potential; the engine was so good. How they didn't win every single race that season I don't know. It did something to me. It confused me. I lost the belief that the team could turn it around quickly.'

He also explained how it was not the first time he had held talks with Ferrari and how it was Michael Schumacher who first instigated the meeting with then Ferrari boss Stefano Domenicali. 'I spoke to Ferrari some years before,' he says. 'It's funny, I spoke to Stefano in 2008 and he offered me "an option". I was like, "What do you mean?" I was extremely honoured and I remember Michael was involved and he helped set up a meeting. I asked them what they meant by option, and they said, "If we want, we can have you." And I asked, "And if you don't . . . ?" I could not say yes to that. Then we spoke again some years later and they were rolling out the red carpet, saying they want to reinvent the brand and take me on board and telling me how much they were going to invest. At the same time, I realised that F1 was now an engine formula. Your chassis might be very good but if your engine is not there, then it's not going to happen. So I had a change of heart, and then, speaking with Michael, it just brought up all these childhood memories and dreams. It was all the emotion. It was a big, big decision and I was on a new journey.'

Ferrari would not confirm Vettel's place in their team for 2015 until 20 November after they had confirmed Alonso's departure. Only then was Vettel able to speak about the switch. 'When I was a kid, Michael Schumacher in the red car was my greatest idol and now it's an incredible honour to finally get the chance to drive a Ferrari. I already got a small taste of what the Ferrari spirit means when I took my first win at Monza in 2008 [with Toro Rosso], with an engine from the Prancing Horse built in Maranello. The Scuderia [a term used for a racing team in Italian] has a great tradition in this sport and I am extremely motivated to help the team get back to the top. I will put my heart and soul into making it happen.'

Reflecting on Vettel's departure now, Horner says he had an inkling that he would have had his head turned: 'The situation was different with Sebastian compared to how it was with Mark. Sebastian had a breakpoint in his contract around September time. And Daniel had had the upper hand all year: he won three races to Sebastian's zero. Sebastian could see that Renault's commitment wasn't there and meanwhile he was being wooed by Ferrari. They came in with a big offer and he felt it was time to step away from Renault.

'Around the Singapore Grand Prix, the race before Japan, I could tell that something was going on. And then when we got to Japan, he asked to see me in my hotel room on Thursday night, and he said, "I just want to say that I've signed a contract with Ferrari, and that's what I'm gonna do." He exercised that trigger point in his contract because he wasn't in the top three of the championship and it gave him a route out. I think, with hindsight, we should have taken more time to consider who his replacement should have been, rather than just taking Daniil [Kvyat]. He had been showing some promise, but, in reality, it was way too soon.'

By a strange quirk of fate, at the same race at which Vettel had announced his intentions to leave the team, Verstappen would be handed his first opportunity in F1. The 17-year-old had won eight races in the European Formula Three Championship and had been rewarded with a place at Toro Rosso for the following year. There had already been a growing interest in the teen, who became the youngest driver in the sport's history when he took to the track in Suzuka for the first practice session of the Japanese Grand Prix on the Friday. He'd warmed up for his first taste of F1 by playing a computer game, running simulations of the Suzuka track on a PlayStation, yet he defied his lack of on-track F1 experience by posting a time that was quick enough for 12th place in the timesheets, despite suffering a mechanical failure six minutes from the end of the session. He was remarkably calm, a character trait we would come to know well over the course of time, and he spoke with maturity and confidence. 'I'm not focused on the age,' he said. 'It doesn't matter to me. If you are ready for it and you have prepared well, age is just a number. Sebastian started when he was 19 and look at him now. Some people can make it and some cannot.'

Vettel was one who had certainly made it, and it had been a glorious six years with Red Bull Racing. Looking back on his time with the team, I asked Vettel to pick out his highlight. He picked three: Red Bull Racing's first race win in China in 2009, his first title in 2010 that he clinched in Abu Dhabi, and the season finale also in Abu Dhabi in 2013 following a nine-race winning streak. 'China was massive,' he says over our video call. 'The first win for Red Bull. It was a massive step because in 2008 I had finished ahead of Red Bull in the constructors' championship driving for Toro Rosso, which they weren't happy about. When Australia came around, we were third quickest in practice and I thought, "Yeah, we're with the big boys now." It is not like now where if they're not in the top five there is something wrong. This was Jaguar who had never achieved anything like this. We were just growing. It was like things were starting to happen. This was the first time we are getting somewhere and it was massive. The whole team spirit was great. I think that was the best experience to be part of that. Winning Abu Dhabi in 2010 the first championship was big. And then that final run we had in 2013 was amazing. It probably sounds a bit sad, but I did enjoy everything [more] beforehand, whereas when you're on a winning streak you don't put your attention on the enjoyment because you are so focused. But in 2013, the championship was sealed and it was a bit more relaxed. We wanted to keep winning but we had a blast every Sunday. That was great because you could enjoy it. Normally you sort of rush back and everyone is trying to get back home, but that end of season was a bit different. We celebrated and had a big party; it was a great time with the team. I was very present and I am grateful for that.'

CHAPTER 13

LIFE AFTER SEB
– 2015 –

Vettel's departure was not the only loss felt by Red Bull Racing over the winter. In December 2014, their Milton Keynes factory was targeted by thieves, who stole more than 60 trophies. The incident happened at 1.30am on Saturday 6th, when six men used a silver 4 x 4 to smash open the doors to the reception area where all the team's trophies are proudly displayed. The men made off with the silverware, leaving the team exasperated and upset. Horner said at the time that the trophies 'took years of hard work to accumulate', making the point that 'their intrinsic value is low; they would be of little benefit to those outside of the team and, in addition to that, many of the trophies on display were replicas'.

A few days later, around 20 of the trophies were discovered some 70 miles away in a lake near Sandhurst in Berkshire, after being spotted by a member of the public. Horner was relieved that some of the trophies had been recovered but was still incredulous that someone would try to take them in the first place, given they would have been too hot to sell on. The upshot was that once the doors were repaired in reception, a couple of giant bollards were installed outside the building to prevent a repeat incident. The sprawling site at Milton Keynes now has greater security and the trophy cabinet, which has tripled in size, is full again.

'It was the hardest year in our history,' says Horner as we speak about the 2015 season over a video phone call. He is in his office at the team's factory, where there are a number of mini crash helmets on display behind his desk. 'Adrian had lost interest and several members of staff were being chased by other teams. Dietrich was questioning Red Bull's involvement in Formula One. He was pissed off that we had no room to be competitive, so it was a tough year.'

The writing was on the wall from the outset. The team came up with a creative idea for a camouflage design to be used during the winter tests. The livery was similar to that used on pre-production road cars to protect them from prying eyes. Such techniques in the past had included using masking tape or vinyl sheets to create swirly black and white patterns. Red Bull had opted for a black and white design on the RB11 and it certainly created a stir within the media as the team teased the launch livery ahead of testing in Jerez. At the time it was rare for teams to go to the effort of coming up with a special livery for testing; it takes considerable time to get approval and for many the effort seemed unnecessary. But Red Bull Racing were always keen to do something different and the new swirly black and white look went down well with the assembled press, ensuring that all the mainstream sports media carried the images of the car – it was yet another branding masterclass from the team. However, the results from testing left Red Bull Racing wanting to disappear rather like the camouflage had intended. The team completed the second fewest laps of any of their competitors, a miserly total of 359. Only McLaren, who were using Honda's new engines, had performed worse with just 177 laps under their belts.

Perhaps even more of a concern was the lap times. From the running in Barcelona, the venue for the final eight days of testing, it was clear that Mercedes were again the quickest car, with Rosberg and Hamilton topping the timesheets. The best lap time from a Red Bull driver was 12th, set by Ricciardo, while Kvyat's best was only good enough for 17th. Interestingly, Verstappen's quickest lap on his debut for Toro Rosso had him placed above Ricciardo in 11th spot. Carlos Sainz Jr, in the other Toro Rosso, was eighth. Red Bull Racing had their work cut out and they knew it.

All eyes were on the new driver who had been hurriedly brought in to take Vettel's place. Daniil Kvyat is Russia's most success-ful F1 driver to date. He was born in 1994 to parents Vyacheslav and Zulfiya in the Bashkortostan region of southwest Russia. His dad worked for Russian oil company Bashneft at the local refinery, first as a mechanic before working his way up to become a financial director. Daniil started karting around the time his family moved to Moscow in 2000 when he was six. He had some early success in the Russian championships but, like Webber and Ricciardo before him, he needed to move in order to progress further.

The Kvyats relocated from Moscow to Rome when Daniil was just 11 years old to enable him to pursue his career. He joined an Italian school and on weekends he would race karts. His breakthrough came in 2008 when he signed a contract with Zanardi, a karting team that was headed up by Dino Chiesa, who had overseen the junior careers of many successful racers including Hamilton and Rosberg. Kvyat, who was then 14, only had one top-ten championship finish before he decided to swap teams and join Morsicani Racing, competing in the same class, the KF3 junior category. Kvyat thrived under new manager Angelo Morsicani, finishing third two years in a row in the CIK-FIA Karting European Championship, the premier karting series. He also won several high-profile competitions, such as the Bridgestone Cup European Final in Lonato and the Silver Cup in La Conca.

His performances caught the eye of Red Bull, who were impressed not only by his speed but also his attitude – he was incredibly determined and hard-working – along with Sainz, whom he had been competing against. Both drivers were offered a test in the summer of 2009 before being offered contracts to join the young driver programme, which would provide them with the financial backing and management structure to progress with their careers in exchange for sponsorship of their respective teams. If they showed promise, they could be promoted either to the Red Bull Junior Team, or bypass that and go straight into Toro Rosso, depending on their results.

Red Bull would keep Kvyat incredibly busy in preparation for his progression to F1, often placing him in different categories so that he would become a more rounded driver, learning skills on different tracks and driving different styles of racing cars. This would not only keep him sharp but also ultimately determine whether he had the full potential to progress in the Red Bull programme. In 2011 alone – when, let's remember, he was still only 17 – he flew around the world and competed in a dizzying 52 races, taking 27 podiums.

After a stint in the Renault feeder series, Red Bull had seen enough and moved him to GP3, placing him at Arden in 2013. A late surge with wins in Spa, Monza and Abu Dhabi saw him clinch the championship at the first attempt. Kvyat finished the season with his first taste of F1, driving for Toro Rosso during the opening practice sessions for the United States and Brazilian F1 Grands Prix weekends. It was reward for his progression and one final hurdle for him to overcome to see how he performed on the biggest stage of all. He proved his ability and was subsequently promoted to Toro Rosso in 2014, where he finished his debut season in 15th place in the championship after scoring points in five of the 19 races. In truth, his debut in F1 had largely gone unnoticed, which was ultimately a good sign, for it meant he was not doing badly, and neither was he causing accidents and drawing attention to himself.

In the opening race in Melbourne, however, Kvyat's Red Bull Racing career got off to the worst possible start. Actually, it didn't even start. He broke down on the way to the grid. Ricciardo did finish the race, but was classified in sixth and behind a Williams and Sauber, two cars that had been at the back of the grid for a number of seasons but were now benefiting from Mercedes and Ferrari power units respectively. Hamilton won and Rosberg was second – but the Brit was an incredible 34 seconds ahead of third-placed Vettel on his Ferrari debut. Ricciardo even apologised to the Australian fans for what he called 'a boring race' while Marko predicted Mercedes domination would make the whole season 'dull'. Both views were echoed by Horner, who also labelled the Renault power unit in the back of the Red Bull car 'undrivable' and added: 'The highlight for me was Arnie [Schwarzenegger] on the podium.' The actor-turned-politician had presented the winner's trophy to Hamilton.

Horner would later speak to the press at length to explain his concerns at how the season was shaping up after just one race. He even called on the FIA, the governing body who had been so hellbent on reining in his team's technical advantage in previous seasons, to adopt the same approach to Mercedes. 'On today's evidence, we are set for a two-horse race at every Grand Prix this season,' he said. 'When we were winning – and we were never winning with the advantage that Mercedes has – double diffusers were banned, exhausts were moved, flexible bodywork was banned, engine mapping was changed mid-season – anything was done to pull us back. And it was also done to McLaren and Williams in other years. Is it healthy to have a situation like this? The FIA, within the rules, have an equalisation mechanism and that needs to be looked at. Take nothing from Mercedes; they have done a super job. They have a good car, a fantastic engine and two very good drivers. The problem is that the gap is so big that you end up with three-tier racing and that is not healthy for Formula One. I fear the interest will wane.' It was a fair point: little had been changed in the regulations to reel in Mercedes' huge advantage in terms of their engine power in the same way Red Bull Racing had been forced to make changes to the design of their car to effectively slow them down.

Horner's words hit a nerve with the Mercedes chief, Toto Wolff. The Austrian had had an average racing career before entering F1 as a shareholder with the Williams team. He joined Mercedes in January 2013 to become an executive director and later brokered a deal for 30 per cent ownership of the F1 team. Working alongside compatriot Niki Lauda, Wolff had guided Mercedes to the title in 2014, although his critics were keen to point out that the team had already been set up by the previous management, including Ross Brawn, who of course led Brawn GP's Jenson Button to the title in 2009.

Horner and Wolff had rarely seen eye to eye and the flashpoint in Melbourne is just an example of how tensions simmered between the two within the competitive and sometimes ruthless environment of F1. Wolff did not hold back in Melbourne in his response to Horner's comments. 'If you come into Formula One,' he thundered, 'try to beat each other and perform at the highest level and then you need equalisation after the first race – you cry out after the *first race* – that's not how we've done things in the past. I think: "Just get your fucking head down, work hard and try to sort it out."' Wolff was urged by his press man to qualify the swearing and quickly added: 'I didn't mean the f-word in relation to him,' meaning Horner.

Another journalist asked Wolff about his team being drawn into a political row in the same way that Red Bull Racing had in the past, with other teams protesting about the legality of their car design. 'It is always a political season,' he said. 'It was last year and it is this year. There is this wall in Jerusalem that you can stand in front of and complain. Maybe the guys should go there.' Wolff's outburst and the mental image created by his reference to the Wailing Wall were unprecedented and, while many in the room nodded their heads in agreement, it was interesting to see how the two team leaders were now going head to head.

The source of Horner's frustration was obvious. It all boiled down to the lack of progress that had been made with the Renault power unit. Becoming a works team in 2009, when Renault increased their level of support to fully back Red Bull Racing rather than treat them as a customer, was supposed to have heralded a new relationship between the two parties. The waters had quickly become muddied, however. As was the case in the previous seasons, Renault were still not investing at the same rate as Mercedes and Ferrari, or indeed Honda, who arrived at the hybrid project later than the other three. While Red Bull Racing were effectively getting their power units free of charge by virtue of the title sponsorship deal with Infiniti, struck in 2013 and worth an estimated $30 million, the deal was obviously confusing, for it was now advertising a Nissan brand rather than a Renault one.

Horner was furious in Melbourne and continued to point the finger at the production of the power units in France. 'It's been a tough weekend,' he said. 'The engine is quite undrivable. You can see and hear that. There is a lot to be done. It's worse than in testing. It's a spiralling effect. They need to have a vision for a fix and quickly. You can see that Ferrari have made a good step and Renault appear to have made a retrograde step. Until they get to the bottom of the issues, it is going to be difficult to address it and understand. It is frustrating that we are further back than we were in Abu Dhabi [for the 2014 season's finale] in both power and driveability. After this weekend it's important that we regroup with Renault, because we are obviously in a bit of a mess at the moment. It has been a shitty day for us.'

Horner and Red Bull Racing's patience continued to be tested as the season continued: in April, Kvyat radioed the team that he was 'on fire' when he had a Renault power unit failure in China, sending his car up in smoke. A fourth-place finish in Monaco for the Russian and a fifth for Ricciardo afforded the team some smiles the following month. However, the track was an outlier as it is the least power-demanding on the calendar, given the number of slow corners and lack of places where drivers can reach top speed. Put simply, Monaco was the one circuit where the team were not hamstrung by the lack of power.

It is a similar story at the Hungaroring on the outskirts of Budapest in Hungary, which is characterised by medium-speed corners and a lack of overtaking points, suiting the aerodynamic properties and limited power of the Red Bull car. Kvyat was an impressive second and Ricciardo third, following his retirement at the previous race, the British Grand Prix. Interestingly, Vettel won the race in Hungary and Verstappen was fourth in his Toro Rosso, making it a Red Bull Junior one, two, three and four.

Ricciardo was second in Singapore – again a track with similar characteristics to Monaco that does not rely so heavily on power – but in general the team were simply not in a position to compete with Ferrari or Mercedes, and they now slipped behind Williams to fourth place in the constructors' championship. It was at this point that the relationship between Renault and Red Bull Racing reached a new low. It was a remarkable story. The fairytale rise from backmarkers to world champions had been undone in a few seasons and the team's future was left in doubt. Horner no longer had warring drivers to worry about, or even the FIA. This time his fight was to save the team and the thousand staff it employed. Horner saw no option but to cut ties with Renault and that meant terminating the Infiniti title sponsorship. However, it left the team in the rather unusual position of having no power unit to go racing with in 2016.

From the outside, it looked like a huge failure on Horner's behalf that he had triggered the exit but he had to try something to ensure his team would be competitive again. Renault had powered them to glory in all their championship victories between 2010 and 2013, but now the French car brand was rather publicly shamed as frustrations ran high. Renault boss Abiteboul made the point, 'When we [Renault] were winning championships with Red Bull, no one was talking about us.' Now they were making headlines, but for the wrong reasons. As a result, not only were Red Bull Racing seeking a split, but Renault had also had enough of all the negative press and sought their own option to re-enter F1 as their own team, five years after pulling out.

With Mateschitz's support, Horner looked at developing Red Bull Racing's own engine division, seeking a collaboration with British engineering company Ilmor, although this became complicated due to their ownership by Mercedes-Benz. Mateschitz later met with Mercedes non-executive chairman Niki Lauda, hoping that his fellow countryman would persuade Mercedes to supply Red Bull Racing with engines. Lauda was sympathetic to Red Bull Racing's situation, but he was not able to persuade Wolff, who was dead against the idea of Mercedes' power unit division supplying the team's biggest rival, even if it was a lucrative deal for Mercedes.

With bridges burned at Renault and Mercedes unwilling to supply Red Bull Racing with power units, the only team Horner could turn to now were Ferrari. Remember, they had already once cut ties with Ferrari at the end of 2006 to start their partnership with Renault. Also, Ferrari's hybrid power units were not in the same league as Mercedes. Sure, they were an improvement on Renault's offering, but not by much, for they still had reliability and performance issues. But they were willing to allow Red Bull Racing to become a customer again. Ferrari president Sergio Marchionne declared that offer in June

2015 – only he stopped short of saying which power unit they would supply. It was a wonderful game of brinkmanship. Ferrari were capable of delivering, but they also knew they were Red Bull Racing's only option. Would the Italian team offer their potential new customer a new power unit, or would it be last year's specification? Also, how much would the deal now cost Red Bull Racing given that their options were limited to just one choice? A further element that the team had to consider was Ferrari's interest in Verstappen, who was beginning to shine with a number of finishes inside the top ten. He was under contract with Red Bull Racing until 2017. Could he be a bargaining chip that would be included in the deal?

Tempers were frayed and it reached a point where the sport was about to lose one of its biggest teams by virtue of a reluctance for the engine-makers to broker a deal. Ultimately, Horner's attempts to find a company willing to come in and help them failed. The Ferrari deal came to an end after concerns about whether Red Bull Racing would get equal quality and technical support, as it would be likely that Ferrari's works team would receive the latest updated parts first, rather than their customers, while Mercedes remained adamant that they would not supply Red Bull Racing. With a dwindling list of options, Red Bull Racing made a last-roll-of-the-dice attempt to encourage Volkswagen to bring their Audi brand to F1. However, the German car giant was at that time engulfed in the emissions scandal, also known as 'Dieselgate', where it had been revealed that some of the cars sold between 2009 and 2015 had been deployed with software to illegally reduce emissions readings during engine tests. The company was braced for a legal battle and had set aside huge monetary reserves to cover their potential costs. Entering the F1 power unit race was simply not a high priority for VW at that time.

Rumours circulated that Red Bull would quit F1 as a consequence. The news came from a website called *Speedweek*, which published an article under the headline: 'Formula One withdrawal takes shape'. Although not a Red Bull publication, it has a history of following the team closely. The article claimed: 'Red Bull does not want to have customer engines that have 30 to 40 horsepower less and can be manipulated by the constructor in case of the customer team endangering the works team' – in other words, they did not want to be hamstrung by an engine supplier if, say, they were more competitive than the actual works team. Even the softly spoken Newey was vocal about the situation, which now involved F1 supremo Bernie Ecclestone and FIA President Jean Todt, saying: 'We're possibly going to be forced out of Formula One – Mercedes and Ferrari have refused to supply us out of fear. Red Bull should not be put in a position where they're only there to make up the numbers. They [Mercedes and Ferrari] are concerned we would beat them with their own engine. Within the regulations, the engines can be balanced somewhat so that there's less of a performance disparity than there is at the moment, but the FIA has been unwilling to do this. We need to get back to the position where all teams have access to an engine which is there or thereabouts – if it's a couple of per cent behind then OK, but when it's 10 per cent behind it's too big a gap.'

It was a bad look for F1 and there was a very public meeting in October between Horner and Ecclestone at the US GP in Austin, with Wolff also playing a fleeting part as he popped in and out of the Red

Bull Racing hospitality unit in the paddock. There was a real sense that the meeting was the last-chance saloon for the team to secure an engine deal. Reflecting on that meeting now, Horner – who had formed a close friendship with Ecclestone – says: 'F1 actually wanted us to be in a competitive position. Bernie tried very hard to get us a Honda engine at that point, but [McLaren boss] Ron Dennis had a veto that he exercised and so we were stuck with no options. That was really frustrating. I ended up having to go back to Renault to broker a deal to become one of their customers, but because of all the mudslinging, the engine could not be badged as Renault, so we could not criticise them.'

At the final race of the year in Abu Dhabi, Horner confirmed that the team's participation in 2016 was secure and they had managed to renegotiate with Renault. It was far from ideal but better than the other option of shutting down. Effectively, despite the poisonous relationship and with neither side really wanting to work with each other, Red Bull Racing had pushed back on their original contract with Renault, which still had time to run, believed to be another two seasons. Together they managed to thrash out terms that satisfied both parties, though the full terms of the agreement would not become known until the New Year.

The disappointing season had concluded with Ricciardo in sixth place in Abu Dhabi while Kvyat was tenth, taking the final point available. It meant that the Russian, despite his inexperience, had beaten his Australian teammate in the drivers' championship by a slender three points. Kvyat was placed seventh and Ricciardo eighth, while Red Bull Racing sank to fourth in the constructors' championship – a whopping 516 points behind winners Mercedes. All round, it was a season to forget.

CHAPTER 14

MAX MAKES HIS MARK

– 2016 –

The 2016 Formula One season would contain a seminal moment in the form of Max Verstappen's debut for Red Bull Racing. However, the story behind his promotion is unusual and serves as a timely reminder of the ruthlessness of the sport.

The winter had seen the media's thirst for Red Bull Racing news quenched by the reprised Renault power unit deal. Somewhat confusingly, to differentiate it from the Renault-built, supplied and purchased power unit, it would be known as a TAG Heuer – named after the luxury watch maker. TAG Heuer had recently split from long-term partner McLaren and was a new addition to the growing list of sponsors on the latest Red Bull Racing car, which was officially titled Red Bull Racing-Tag Heuer RB12. The arrangement was unusual, although not unique. The Swiss company had done a similar deal with McLaren when they rebranded Porsche-built engines in the 1980s.

Red Bull Racing's threats to quit F1 had been silenced – for now. But there was still some disillusionment with the wider situation within F1 and the team's inability to find a competitive engine supplier. Ecclestone had openly criticised the state of the sport: he said it was 'the worst it's ever been', before adding, 'I wouldn't spend my money to take my family to watch a race. No way.' Understandably, Mercedes' Lauda had taken issue with Ecclestone's comments as he felt the Brit was inferring that Mercedes' success had caused the sport to become dull. Lauda was clear that from his perspective, F1 was entering a new era and people just needed to embrace it. 'Everything is just starting to get going,' said the Austrian. 'Everyone is very positive – and he has to do this and destroy everything. I don't understand why he does it.'

Ecclestone's opinion was not exactly shared by Horner, but it was not contradicted either. Horner's issue was not with the sport per se, but in particular with the power unit situation. 'Until the engine rules are sorted out, we are at a disadvantage and we can't hide that,' he said. 'Ferrari and Mercedes are engaged in a power struggle with the people who control the sport – and we are caught in the middle. We know that Mercedes and Ferrari do not want to supply us with competitive engines and there is nothing we can do about it, which means we have to do the best with what we have. Until that changes, nothing changes. But everyone has to realise that sport is entertainment and to have entertainment, you have to have competition.'

Winter testing had shown a slight improvement in reliability with the new TAG-branded engine, although Toro Rosso's lap times using the previous-season spec Ferrari power units were actually quicker. However, the discontent within the team was still a cause for concern for Horner, who worried about the enthusiasm of their most crucial component: its chief designer, Newey. Disillusioned with F1,

Newey hankered over other design projects, so the opportunity for him to work with Aston Martin on an ultimate road car came at the right time. It was a strange dichotomy for Horner: he needed his prize asset to work with his F1 team, but he could not afford for him to grow discontented with the sport and pack it all in.

Consequently, Newey split his time across projects with Red Bull Advanced Technologies, a division of the business for projects that don't fall into their F1 operation. It has since worked with hypercars, hydrogen-powered racing cars, bikes, boats and balloons, creating the world's first floating skatepark, 2,000 feet in the sky. Although the project was not formed specifically for Newey, it would have the benefit of keeping him pacified and would allow him to flex his creative wings in areas where he felt he was being stifled in F1. Newey would go on to design the AM-RB 001 for Aston Martin – better known as the Valkyrie – which had the goal of being 'faster around Silverstone than a current Formula One car'. Production numbers of the road car were limited to just 150 and the price set at $3.5 million.

At the season-opening race in Melbourne the pace of the Toro Rosso was again better than Red Bull Racing during the early practice sessions, as Verstappen and Sainz impressed in the sister team. In the race, lightning struck twice for Kvyat as he was unable to start the Australian Grand Prix for the second consecutive year: this time an electrical failure on the way to the grid denied him the chance to take part in the race. Ricciardo defied expectations to come home in fourth place after starting in eighth place on the grid. In the Toro Rosso, Sainz was ninth and Verstappen tenth. At the next race in Bahrain, Kvyat had further bad luck in qualifying, as he was quickly knocked out of the new elimination qualifying format that F1 was trying. In a change to the original three qualifying segments, now a clock would tick down and every 90 seconds the slowest driver was eliminated. The format was ridiculously complicated and heavily criticised. Kvyat was one of the first to be eliminated and qualified in 15th. In the race, on the opening lap he made contact with Force India's Nico Hülkenberg before fighting back to seventh place, one spot behind Verstappen, while Ricciardo was fourth.

At the Chinese Grand Prix, the third race of the year, Kvyat was involved in a flashpoint that would have a significant impact on his racing career. The Russian, who had made such a rotten start to the year, finished third to take an unlikely podium, but during his race he was involved in an accident with Vettel, who in turn drove into his Ferrari teammate, Räikkönen. Vettel was furious that he had been squeezed on track by Kvyat and labelled him 'a torpedo' and 'a madman'. 'You ask what happened at the start?' said an agitated Vettel to Kvyat in the cool-down room after the race. 'If I didn't go to the left, you'd have crashed into us and we'd all three go out. You came like a torpedo.' Kvyat retorted that he was just racing hard, to which Vettel replied: 'If I'd kept going on the same line, we'd have crashed; you were lucky this time.' It was incredibly condescending, but provided an alluring moniker for headline writers and very quickly Kvyat became known as 'the Torpedo'. Interestingly, there was little weight given to Vettel's accusations, with even Ferrari boss Maurizio Arrivabene saying afterwards: 'Pointing the finger at somebody is not correct. I think that Seb or Kimi, they would do the same in Kvyat's position. This is racing. It's not a monopoly.'

Incredibly, the two drivers would collide again on the opening lap of the next race, the Russian Grand Prix, sparking an incendiary reaction from Vettel. The Russian driver was pumped up for his home race but missed his braking point on two occasions, with Vettel on the receiving end both times. First, Kvyat drove into the rear of the Ferrari, breaking off bodywork and causing Vettel to have a puncture. Then he went into the rear of Vettel's car a second time, punting the German into the barriers, breaking his front wing and suspension and putting him out of the race. There was some ambiguity over the coming together in China, but this was a slam-dunk mistake from Kvyat, who was penalised by the race stewards with a ten-second time penalty, which he had to serve when he came into the pits. Vettel fumed over the Ferrari team's radio, turning the airwaves blue with expletives. He was bitterly upset and demanded an apology from Kvyat, whose torpedo nickname was becoming more and more fitting. Kvyat apologised and explained that he had simply been caught out, saying, 'When people brake in front of you, unfortunately sometimes there is no time to react. I had no time to react to Seb's braking. All the mess came from me. It's not great but sometimes these things happen from lap one. It's probably not the nicest lap one in my career, I will learn from it and should be all fine next time.' Only it wasn't.

Kvyat was hauled into Red Bull's HQ after the Russian Grand Prix, and Marko made it clear that he was unimpressed with his driver. The Austrian labelled him 'over-motivated' and accused him of not only ending Vettel's race but also compromising the race for Ricciardo, who had been caught up in the resulting melee and suffered some damage on his way to a lowly 11th-place finish. Marko also revealed that Vettel had spoken with Horner, telling him to have a word with Kvyat – quite an extraordinary moment for F1, as drivers at rival teams, no matter how close, rarely resort to such tactics.

What followed was one of the most ruthless moments in Red Bull Racing's short history. On 5 May, Kvyat was relegated from the team in favour of Verstappen. Just two races prior, he had scored a podium and had been seventh in the drivers' championship. He had also beaten his more experienced teammate in his debut season for the team. But none of that counted for anything now: Kvyat was dropped back to Toro Rosso in place of Verstappen, who was just 18 years old. It was a hammer blow for Kvyat, who was left 'devastated' by the demotion according to Pyry Salmela, the performance coach who had been by his side and had helped him prepare for his time in F1.

Salmela started working with Kvyat at the end of 2013 when the Russian driver – then aged 19 – had joined from GP3. Both men were newbies to the sport. Salmela had been introduced to Red Bull by fellow Finn Antti Vierula, who trains the Finnish driver Valtteri Bottas. He has since worked with a number of F1 racers, including Red Bull drivers Pierre Gasly and Liam Lawson. Both Salmela and Vierula previously worked for the famed Hintsa Performance Institute, who have a strong history of working with F1 drivers, including Hamilton. Their website boasts that the company has helped drivers win 17 Formula One world titles.

Salmela recalls the moment the 22-year-old Kvyat was dumped, when we speak over the phone in between the Qatar and United States Grand Prix races in October 2023. 'It was obviously heartbreaking,' he says, 'and I think it took him time to process and put a plan in place to move forward. People also forget that, just before, he had had a podium in China. Now, looking at the context, you can understand how there was a rising star coming up very fast in Verstappen and they wanted to bring him up to F1 – and that has been proven to be a pretty successful journey! I have never seen anyone like Max; he's since proven to be one in a million. But I sometimes feel a bit sorry for Daniil, because people forget that actually there were some pretty good moments for him, and he was a talented driver. However, there were external elements that were going around that were affecting the big picture,' he says with reference to the power unit problems with Renault, which had limited Kvyat's ability to show how quick he could be.

He continues: 'I have to say, if I am honest, Daniil was from my perspective, physiologically, the most talented driver that I ever trained. His response to training was insane. The amount he improved in such a short time was something I barely ever see happening. He was always quite slim but people never knew how athletic he had become. He was dedicated to putting in all the time required. He was a really competitive person, which of course is one of the key characteristics that you see among the top drivers. Outside of the car, I don't know how people perceive him, but my perception is of an extremely good-hearted person.'

Salmela also points out that the scenario faced by Red Bull Racing was new for the team. 'Sebastian was so regimented, dedicated, and he knew how to lead a team,' he says. 'If you have been in Formula One for only a year, you probably won't have that leadership experience. It shows too that you are judged as being only as good as your last race. That should not be the case. Honestly, people really do forget how good Daniil actually was in his first year in a car that is not as competitive as it is today.'

Verstappen was by now well known to the F1 media, who had watched him with interest from his first run in an F1 car at the 2014 Japanese GP where he took part in practice, aged only 17 years and three days. When he made his debut the following season for Toro Rosso, still aged 17, reports noted that his father would need to drive him to the F1 tracks because he was too young to get a road licence in many countries. On his 18th birthday – a year after being granted the FIA Super Licence needed to compete in Grands Prix – Verstappen wrote on his website, 'It's great to be 18 and to have a driving licence. I have to say it's a relief to pass the test. If I want to go somewhere on my own, at least now I'm able to jump in my Renault Clio RS and go. That sense of liberty feels great.'

Verstappen was born on 30 September 1997 in Hasselt, Belgium. His father was former F1 driver Jos Verstappen, who competed between 1994 and 2003 and drove for a number of different teams, achieving two podiums in 106 starts; his mother, Sophie Kumpen, was also a successful karter and competed against Horner in the 1989 Junior World Kart Championship. Curiously, Jos Verstappen's own website contains an account of his son's arrival, with some mildly amusing meticulous F1-style information. 'This afternoon Jos and Sophie became the proud parents of a healthy son,' claims the site. 'His name is Max and he weighs 3265 grams. Max Emilian, as is his full name, is 48.5cm long. Sophie delivered Max at 13.20 without any complications. The delivery lasted for 40 minutes. Max had chosen the right moment to come out. Now Jos and Sophie can enjoy some time with Max before Jos has to leave for Japan. If Max has inherited the racing talents of both his parents a new F1 driver for the year 2020 has been born today.' In fact he'd made the step up to F1 four years earlier than predicted!

Although born in Belgium, Verstappen chose to have a Dutch racing licence, as growing up he spent more time in the Netherlands due to his karting career. He lived on the Dutch border and said he always felt more Dutch. He steamrollered his way through the junior karting categories, having started racing at four and competing since he was seven years old. When he was a child, he accompanied his dad at the racetrack while his father raced in F1. Jos was a Dutch karting champion but, despite making his breakthrough to F1, he never achieved the success his talent had warranted. He was also notoriously hard on his son's racing career. At a world championship karting event in 2012, during which Max had crashed into another racer when he was looking nailed-on for a win, Jos had driven his teenage son home in the van as normal – but when they stopped at a petrol station, he was still so furious that he told Max to get out and drove off, leaving his son at the garage. Jos later said he knew that Verstappen's mum was travelling behind and knew she'd pick him up, but nonetheless, you get the picture.

Verstappen dropped out of school when he was 15; he had fallen behind with his education as a result of his days spent competing across Europe. At the same age he would have his first conversation with Marko about joining Red Bull Racing's young driver programme. His father's funds, plus any sponsorship that had been drummed up by his manager, Raymond Vermeulen – who had also acted as Jos's manager – had been spent, so having sponsorship from Red Bull would allow him to continue his career. 'I usually talk to a driver for about 20 minutes to get a picture of his personality and the whole story, but with Max I sat for an hour and a half,' Marko told German newspaper *Bild* in an interview in 2016. 'He was a young body, but with a mind that was certainty three to five years ahead. Now his development has slowed, levelled off, and his age and maturity have come together. I saw what maturity he had and how much he had learned in his karting time, and with what commitment he approached his racing.'

Ferrari and Lotus had expressed an interest in signing Verstappen but, like Mercedes, who already had both Hamilton and Rosberg signed up, it was not clear how Verstappen's career would be able to progress with the other teams, as they did not have a spare seat available for him. It would be a huge gamble to put in an untested rookie over an established driver. Red Bull's situation was different, for they had access to four seats on the grid and could offer Verstappen a chance, as indicated by his debut opportunity to drive in first practice in the Japanese GP. He joined the Red Bull Racing programme in 2014 and that allowed him to compete in the FIA Formula Three series, where he finished the season in third place. The following year he was in F1 with Toro Rosso.

'Max has proven to be an outstanding young talent,' Horner said in a statement released on the Thursday ahead of the Spanish Grand Prix in 2016, confirming his promotion to Red Bull Racing. 'His performance at Toro Rosso has been impressive so far and we are pleased to give him the opportunity to drive for Red Bull Racing. Dany [Kvyat] will be able to continue his development at Toro Rosso, in a team that he is familiar with, giving him the chance to regain his form and show his potential.' The swap was noted by Jenson Button, with the McLaren driver upset at Kvyat's demotion. The 2009 world champion tweeted: 'What about the podium in the previous race?' Kvyat was understandably asked about his reaction to the decision and said: 'There was no real explanation, to be honest. If the bosses want something to happen they just make it happen.'

Horner looks back on the switch now with the gift of hindsight, but at the time it was not so obvious as to why the decision was made to swap the drivers. 'We were really struggling with Daniil, who could not adapt to the new car, particularly the braking philosophy when we moved to a new supplier,' says Horner. 'He had a big shunt in Russia. Red Bull are in a unique position where it has four drivers under contract and you can move them about [unlike Mercedes]. There was a lot of interest growing in Max and it gave us the opportunity to extend our relationship with him by putting him into the A-team, as it were. We had kept a close eye on him and he had come into the factory and done some work on the simulator. All the tell-tale signs were there that this kid had serious talent.'

Serious talent indeed, but nobody could have predicted what happened next. On his debut for Red Bull Racing, Verstappen won the Spanish Grand Prix. It was an astonishing story and one of those moments when as a journalist you realise you are witnessing something special.

The precursor to Verstappen's maiden win was a collision between Hamilton and Rosberg, which was akin to the Vettel–Webber incident in Turkey 2010. Just as that had ripped the team apart, so too did the first-lap incident between the two Mercedes drivers, and their relationship would never be the same again. With the two taken out of the equation, the F1 community breathed a sigh of relief as it meant there would be a different winner for the first time in 2016. The fact it was Verstappen, having never driven the Red Bull Racing car in a race, or indeed the TAG-branded engine, was remarkable.

The team had decided to split their race strategy for their two drivers, meaning that one would make two pit stops and the other would make three. In theory, Ricciardo's strategy of three stops was the quicker option. He had the preference, having qualified ahead of Verstappen in third place while the Dutchman qualified in fourth on the grid. In theory, it would allow the Aussie fresher tyres at the end of the race where he would be able to make up positions, whereas Verstappen would need to defend much more on his older rubber. However, Verstappen managed to drag out the life of his tyres to finish ahead of Räikkönen and Vettel, while Ricciardo was fourth. At 18 years and 228 days, Verstappen had become the youngest driver to score a podium finish and the youngest ever to lead a lap of a Formula One race, breaking the previous records that were all held by Sebastian Vettel. In the process he also became the first Dutchman to win a Grand Prix, prompting Dutch TV commentator Olav Mol to shout a number of expletives and burst into tears after he crossed the finish line.

I take Horner back to the moment in Barcelona where everything changed for Verstappen. 'He was on the pace from the very first lap,' says Horner with some certainty. 'He just got on with it. He pushed Daniel really hard in qualifying but they both lined up third and fourth, and we had out-qualified the Ferraris and were just behind the Mercedes. We were there to pick up the pieces and, to be honest with you, we felt that it was the three-stop strategy with

Daniel that was going to be the faster race and that we would take more of a risk with Max. But the way he managed the tyres was outstanding and, under massive pressure from Kimi [Räikkönen], he did what he needed to do to win the race. It was unbelievable.'

So how did they celebrate? After all, this was the party team. 'We celebrated in the normal way,' says Horner somewhat disappointingly, before laughing as he then remembered: 'We had a big team photo; we had not won since Spa 2014. It was my daughter's birthday and Bernie [Ecclestone] had been given a cake by the promoter of the Barcelona race and it had a bow on it. She was 13 or something and he took off the "Barcelona" bit and got his wife Fabiana to write "Happy Birthday" on it. He came down to our hospitality and gave her this cake and invited everyone to have a piece of this cake. And then when we cut into it, it was bloody polystyrene!' Horner shows me a picture of the cake on his phone and adds: 'Typical Bernie, you know, he got a false fucking birthday cake!'

One person not in the mood for much celebration was Ricciardo, who said in the post-race media interviews that he was 'bitter' about the strategy decision that led him to lose out to Verstappen. He had led the first 28 laps of the race but his three pit stops meant he ended up finishing fourth. He said: 'I'm a bit devastated. A big part of me is happy the team are on winning form but it's hard to celebrate. To not be on the podium sucks. I will pull the guys aside to ask them what the deal was today. I don't want to come across as a bad sportsman. Whatever happened on track, Max crossed the line first. Sure, it is every man for himself and I'm bitter – not at Max; he did what he had to do – but I'm bitter at the situation.'

He would have some more frustration with the team at the next race, finishing second in Monaco when he had started on pole. On lap 32, Ricciardo stopped for fresh tyres as his team responded to an earlier stop by Hamilton, who was in second place and challenging Ricciardo for the lead. However, the Red Bull team were caught out. Ricciardo's mechanics were not prepared and he was forced to sit in the pit lane waiting for the correct tyres. The extra time cost him dearly and he was leapfrogged by Hamilton, who won the race as a result of Ricciardo's slow stop. 'Two weekends in a row I've been screwed now. It sucks. It hurts,' he said afterwards. Verstappen, meanwhile, had come off his high in Spain with a bump and failed to finish after running into the barriers.

Ricciardo would, however, taste victory in 2016, winning the Malaysian GP with Verstappen coming second, as the team recorded their first one-two finish in the hybrid-power-unit era. The race caused controversy, but not in the way you'd imagine. Nine men, dubbed the 'Budgie Nine', were arrested for stripping to their tight-fitting 'budgie-smuggler' underwear, which was covered in the Malaysian flag. The stunt – along with drinking beer from their shoes, a fad that had become known as a 'shoey' – had upset the authorities, who considered it 'intentional insult' and a possible breach of the peace. The men were later released after being charged for causing a public nuisance.

In the penultimate race of the year in Brazil, Verstappen delivered a performance that was outstanding. It was the type of drive that garnered an unusual moment of universal respect from journalists. The heavy rain made conditions treacherous but Verstappen defied the odds to come home in third place. There was one standout moment, when he pressed the throttle pedal on his Red Bull, sending it into a twitch as it slipped on the wet surface. Somehow, he managed to keep it out of the concrete wall and battled back from 16th place with just 16 laps to go. Where others might have wilted, he excelled, and was undeterred by his near-miss.

For the second time that season, it was something magical to witness first-hand. After the race, Horner said: 'We witnessed something very special. It stands out to me like Ayrton Senna in Monaco and other great drives in history.' He wasn't wrong. Verstappen closed out the season with a fourth-place finish in Abu Dhabi, with Ricciardo fifth. The Aussie had taken third in the drivers' championship behind Rosberg and Hamilton, while Verstappen was fifth. Red Bull Racing were second in the constructors' championship and there was renewed optimism after some difficult seasons that they were again heading in the right direction.

CHAPTER 15

THE CHANGING FACE OF F1

– 2017 –

Two big changes happened over the winter before the 2017 season kicked off, one of which would have a monumental impact on the future of the sport. The first was Rosberg's shock retirement from F1. Although this did not directly impact the Red Bull Racing team, it did provide everyone involved in the sport with a timely reminder of what it takes to win a world championship. Rosberg had dedicated himself solely to the task of beating teammate Hamilton to the title, cutting himself off from his family as a result. It had taken so much out of him that he was not prepared to do it again, so he decided to quit the sport as the champion, going out at the top. He has since returned to work as a TV pundit but his break from the sport was totally understandable given the ferociousness of his inter-team battle with Hamilton.

Rosberg's sudden departure left Mercedes in a hole as to who would replace him. Rather like Vettel's bombshell in 2014, such unexpected changes can cause plenty of problems, with consideration needed to be given to the potential new driver's dynamic with his teammate, the ability to fit in within the wider culture of a new team or indeed whether the car design suits. Each driver has a particular driving style and teams try to tailor themselves around them. Whoever came in would need to adapt to Rosberg's preferred set-up on everything from seat positioning to braking. Mercedes picked Valtteri Bottas from Williams; he already had ties to Toto Wolff, as the Austrian had acted as his manager at various intervals in his F1 career.

The other change would influence the whole of F1. Liberty Media, an American company founded by billionaire John Malone, completed their purchase of the rights to Formula One for an estimated $8 billion (£6.4 billion) and with it came the end of Ecclestone's reign as F1 supremo. Liberty Media had already purchased a share of the Formula One Group at the tail-end of 2016 for $4.4 billion (£3.3 billion) but faced scrutiny from the financial regulators before it cleared the final two stages and reached approval. The takeover was announced on 23 January 2017 and saw the return of Ross Brawn as managing director, while former Ferrari team principal Stefano Domenicali joined as the new chief executive of F1. Chase Carey, a media executive who had previously worked for News Corp, 21st Century Fox and Sky plc and was close to Malone, would become the chairman of the newly formed group.

The initial reaction was centred on Ecclestone's departure from F1. The 86-year-old had run the sport for nearly 40 years and felt as though he had been 'forced out', having overseen the purchase from the sport's previous owners, Delta Topco, a Jersey-based company owned primarily by investment companies CVC Capital Partners, Waddell & Reed, and LBI Group. Ecclestone and a number of other investment companies also had a stake in the company. To ensure the transition was smooth, given his historic control of F1, Ecclestone was offered the role of chairman emeritus and would act as an advisor to the board. On paper it was a more senior position, though in an interview with German publication *Auto Motor und Sport*, Ecclestone makes it clear he did not see it that way and said: 'I was dismissed. This is official. I no longer run the company. My position has been taken by Chase Carey.'

Ecclestone had been the sport's kingpin for decades and single-handedly transformed F1 by maximising lucrative TV deals and commercial agreements. In the process he became one of the richest people in the UK. He was born on 28 October 1930 in St Peter South Elmham, a village in the north of Suffolk, England, his family relocating to Bexleyheath, southeast London, shortly before the outbreak of the Second World War. Ecclestone left school at 16 to work as an assistant in the chemical laboratory at the local gasworks, while in his free time he worked on motorbikes, starting a business selling second-hand parts before forming his own dealership.

He tried racing, entering a 500cc race at Brands Hatch in 1949, and had moderate success before quitting to focus on his growing business. In 1957 he returned to racing, this time as a manager for driver Stuart Lewis-Evans, purchasing two cars from an F1 team that had folded. He even tried to qualify for the 1958 Monaco Grand Prix himself, without success. Ecclestone turned his back on racing again the same year, following a tragic accident for Lewis-Evans, who succumbed to the injuries he suffered in the Moroccan Grand Prix. However, he was persuaded to return to motorsport management for Austrian racer Jochen Rindt, also becoming part-owner in the driver's Lotus Formula Two team. Tragedy struck again when Rindt died following a smash in Monza, leaving Ecclestone bereft. This time, however, he would not turn his back on racing. Instead, he brokered a deal to buy the Brabham F1 team in 1971. The team did not become competitive until 1974, when their fortunes changed thanks to the promotion of talented car designer Gordon Murray.

Around the same time, Ecclestone formed the Formula One Constructors Association (FOCA) with fellow team bosses Sir Frank Williams, Colin Chapman, Teddy Mayer, Ken Tyrrell and Max Mosley. Ecclestone saw the potential to raise revenues from the sport's television rights, selling them to different territories, long before the pay-per-view model had been established. He was at the fulcrum of the teams' financial interests, which were brought together in the 1981 Concorde Agreement that tied F1 teams in with the governing body and dealt with the distribution of prize money and profits. All the while, his own F1 team achieved mixed success, though its drivers included Niki Lauda and Nelson Piquet, who would go on to become world champions. In 1988, Ecclestone sold the Brabham team to Swiss businessman Joachim Lüthi, making close to a $5 million return on his investment.

Despite no longer owning a team, Ecclestone continued to run FOCA and also established Formula One Promotions and Administration (FOPA) to manage TV rights for the teams. FOPA would later become abbreviated to the more understandable Formula One Management, or FOM as it is still called in the paddock. FOPA would oversee the sale of the TV contracts and receive the fees that the promoter would pay for the rights to host their Grand Prix, and consequently was responsible for paying the prize money to the teams. Ultimately, Ecclestone would be rewarded for the deals he brokered, and in turn be the hand that fed the teams, cementing his place as the controlling force in the sport. Ecclestone's business model attracted significant investment. Key battles between Ayrton Senna and Frenchman Alain Prost saw F1 attract global audiences. The sport was thriving, as was Ecclestone.

In 1996, Ecclestone transferred ownership of his F1 companies to SLEC Holdings with the intention of floating the business on the stock market, with his now ex-wife Slavica in control. However, the plan drew the gaze of the European Commission, who started investigating the sport's dealings with International Sportsworld Communicators. The company was owned by Ecclestone, who in 1996 had signed a 14-year agreement with the FIA for exclusive broadcasting rights back to his own company. They would be responsible for providing the live broadcast feed which would be taken by TV companies in different countries. The practice remains the same today, with much of the broadcast put together at Biggin Hill.

Despite the investigation, subsequent investment in SLEC followed, with banks Bayerische Landesbank (BayernLB), Lehman Brothers and JPMorgan Chase all buying in. Ecclestone's position was again called into question in 2004 as the three banks threatened legal action in a bid to win more control over how F1 was governed. However, the banks all finally backed down amid a concern that a breakaway racing series that would rival F1 could leave them with nothing of value. Ecclestone's ability to convince the F1 teams to commit to a new Concorde Agreement in 2004, thus negating the threat of a breakaway championship, in return for a healthier share of the profits, drew him a stay of execution. His powerful ability to prevail in adversity had again come to the fore.

In November 2005, he oversaw a change of ownership when CVC Capital Partners announced plans to purchase shares in SLEC. The following month it would acquire the F1 shares held by JPMorgan Chase. The deal took three months to receive the green light from the European Commission, with Ecclestone reinvesting for a 13.8 per cent stake in the business through holding company Alpha Prema. Ecclestone would now effectively run F1 for CVC, driving the sport forwards with a series of lucrative deals for races in the Middle East and Russia.

The calendar continued to grow with the return of the US Grand Prix in Austin, races in Azerbaijan and growing interest from other countries. F1 also piqued the interest of Liberty Media, who quickly saw the potential in a sport that, until they took over, had no marketing department and limited social media presence. While Ecclestone had tied the sport up to lucrative TV deals, Liberty Media saw the potential to open it up to the masses and, crucially, a younger audience. Ecclestone had famously snubbed the younger demographic, once saying they were not the intended audience as they would not be able to afford to buy the Rolex watch brand that F1 was helping to advertise. In a wide-ranging interview with *Campaign Asia-Pacific* magazine in 2014, he said:

'Young kids will see the Rolex brand but are they going to go and buy one? They can't afford it. Or our other sponsor UBS – these kids don't care about banking. They haven't got enough money to put in the bloody banks anyway. That's what I think . . . I don't know why people want to get to the so-called "young generation". Why do they want to do that? Is it to sell them something? Most of these kids haven't got any money. I'd rather get to the 70-year-old guy who's got plenty of cash.'

Ecclestone was always good for an outrageous quote. He was known for his chauvinistic comments towards women, once suggesting that 'women should be dressed in white like all the other domestic appliances'. And he attracted more criticism in 2022 after saying he would 'take a bullet' for his friend, the Russian president Vladimir Putin. Did he mean any of it? It is hard to say; he always liked to give good copy. Around the time of Liberty Media's takeover, he took myself and a group of journalists out for a burger with his wife Fabiana – a memory that came flooding back to me in October 2023, when he was convicted of tax fraud and given a suspended sentence, and after the hearing he went to the nearby Borough Market with Fabiana to buy some doughnuts.

Horner lamented Ecclestone's departure from the F1 coalface as we discuss the turbulent start to 2017. 'Bernie had run it for 40 years and it was his business. He controlled everything and now Liberty Media had given complete control to Chase Carey. Bernie had never had a boss in his life, so it was never going to work. I think those of us who were close to him tried to explain to him what was going on and could see what was coming. I think by the time Bernie had offered him a shoebox of an office in his offices at Prince's Gate, Chase had recognised that [this relationship] was going to be a tricky one. I couldn't see how they could coexist. Effectively they gave Bernie a title [that of chairman emeritus], but he said if he was so high up, he'd be invisible!'

Horner recalls a time when Ecclestone and Carey were still sussing each other out. 'Bernie offered me a lift to a Formula One Commission meeting in Geneva,' he says. 'We get to Biggin Hill [the aerodrome where much of F1's operations are based in southeast London]. Chase and Bernie had hardly talked on the way there. When we arrived at the airport, Chase had forgotten his passport, because if you're in the US, you fly around from state to state and don't need one. I just remember Bernie saying, "Oh well, never mind. We'll see you when we come back," and he just left him. That was kind of awkward. You could see what Liberty Media wanted to do: embracing digital media, and just opening up the sport and trying to engage a younger audience. But Bernie had done such a great job and had been so good to us, he was a personal friend, so it was hard to see it come to a close the way it did.'

On track and heading into the new season, Verstappen had become a major talking point in the media. His performance in the wet in Brazil had won over many, and it was now clear just why Red Bull Racing had rated him so highly. He was still only 19, but the support was growing, especially in his homeland. Already the orange-clad Dutch fans were prominent at the Belgian and Austrian GPs, and he was due to perform a demo run in his F1 car in Zandvoort, which would later become home to the Dutch Grand Prix. It felt like he had the whole nation behind him, and there was no doubt that the elevation in his profile was having an impact on Ricciardo, especially after the latter suffered a run of poor luck due to reliability issues. With Rosberg and Hamilton's rivalry over, the press looked with keen interest at the dynamic between the two Red Bull racers and questioned who would come out on top over a season-long battle.

Meanwhile, one relationship that was to remain fractious was Red Bull Racing's with Renault, especially after an underwhelming winter test where, despite more regulation changes pertaining to aerodynamics, they were still hamstrung by the output of their TAG-branded power unit. Hamilton, therefore, remained the clear favourite to take the drivers' crown from his retired teammate for Mercedes.

In the Australian GP, Ricciardo made a disastrous start to the season. He started from the pit lane after crashing in qualifying. In the race his car suffered an engine failure on lap 29 of the 58-lap race. 'Car is done,' he said over the team's radio, before adding, 'let's get the fuck out of here!' In the next race in China, Ricciardo finished behind Verstappen, who came third, again drawing plaudits. Verstappen had suffered his own engine problem in qualifying that meant he started the race down in 16th place, but he made up nine places by the end of the opening lap. He passed Ricciardo on lap 11 and defied the odds for a podium. It was a performance in similar conditions to the race in Brazil the previous year, where he narrowly missed the barriers and produced a miraculous save to keep his car on the track and pointing in the right direction. Verstappen was now being compared to the likes of Senna, and it was difficult to disagree.

However, occasional positive results aside, reliability woes continued to hamper Red Bull Racing's overall progress on track. Verstappen retired in Bahrain with a brake issue while brakes also caused Ricciardo's retirement in Russia. In the Spanish GP, Ricciardo took third but Verstappen retired after a first-lap accident. The Dutchman retired again in Canada with an electrical fault, while Ricciardo took another podium place. The frustration was beginning to show and rival teams started circling, making tentative investigations into the respective driver contract situations. If they were unhappy, could they be persuaded to jump ship? Horner was quick to warn off any potential suitors, saying they both had long-term deals with no break clauses like the one Vettel had activated. It was marvellous brinkmanship all round, as the rumour mill prompted his clarification. Whether the rival teams believed it or not was a different matter.

There were more ups and downs over the course of the season. Ricciardo won the Azerbaijan GP, while Verstappen retired after losing oil pressure. In Austria, Ricciardo was third again, while Verstappen crashed out, and the two would suffer their first coming together in the Hungarian Grand Prix. Tempers boiled over as they made contact on the opening lap. Verstappen had gone wide at turn one and, as he attempted to stay ahead of Ricciardo at the next corner, he locked his brakes and crashed into his colleague, ripping open the bodywork of his Red Bull. The Australian spun on the leaking fluid before grinding to a halt, blasting on the team's radio: 'Was that who I think it was?'

'Yes,' his Red Bull team replied.

'Fucking sore loser,' Ricciardo responded. He raised his middle finger at Verstappen as he sailed past on his second lap while Ricciardo remained stranded.

In the press conference after, Ricciardo was still scathing: 'There was no room to pass. Bottas was in front and I was on the outside, so there was no room. I don't think Max likes it when a teammate gets in front. You've got the whole race to try and repair the mistake but the pass was never on. It wasn't even a pass; it was a very poor mistake.

There isn't an excuse for it. He tried to go round the outside at turn one and, all of a sudden, what was a good start is a bad start. He sees me go past and thinks, "I've got to fix this," and then we crashed.'

Verstappen, who survived the incident without damage to his car, finished fifth before apologising to Ricciardo and his team. Somewhat embarrassingly, it had happened in front of Mateschitz, who was making a rare appearance at a race. Horner told the press how he had reminded his drivers of their duties to bring the cars home in front of the team's owner. He said: 'We discussed the first lap, and I said to both of them, "You are starting next to each other so please give each other enough room, and remember that Dietrich is here this afternoon, too." Both drivers nodded in agreement, but as soon as the red light goes out, a lot of that goes out of the window. It was inevitable they were going to crash at some stage, but the most important thing is how the individuals have dealt with it. Max has been mature enough to hold his hand up and admit that he made a mistake. There was no intent in it. It was just frustrating.'

Just past the midway point of the season, and with relations with Renault at an all-time low due to all the retirements, Red Bull Racing announced a partnership for 2018 that would see the team rebranded as Aston Martin Red Bull Racing, with the British car designer potentially coming in as a future power unit supplier. Relationships between the companies had grown through the supercar project and it was a step that would signal a further departure from the Renault brand. The news coincided with an upturn in results, for Verstappen at least, as he took victories in Malaysia and Mexico, while he was second in Japan. He had now become F1's most-wanted man, with Ferrari and Mercedes keen to prise him away from Red Bull. His future was a hot topic within the media, particularly as interest in the title race fizzled out with Hamilton in good form and Vettel's challenge wilting. Verstappen's options were endlessly dissected and he was linked to stories suggesting the moves would see him quadruple his pay to at least £20 million a year.

All contract talk was killed on 21 October, when Red Bull Racing confirmed that Verstappen had signed a new deal with the team, believed to be a one-year extension to his current deal but with highly improved financial terms. The 20-year-old was signed up until the end of 2020 as Red Bull Racing made their intent clear that they wanted to retain him for the long-term future. In the press releases that accompanied the news, Verstappen cited Red Bull's backing for him as a young driver as a factor in his decision to remain with the team, saying the team 'have always backed me and share my ambition'. Although perhaps they did not appreciate it fully at the time, this was a major coup for Red Bull Racing, who had secured the services of the highly rated driver at a time when they were not as competitive as they would have liked. Verstappen was painfully aware of how the team were hamstrung by their power unit deficit to Mercedes but he had seen something to make him want to commit.

With one piece of the jigsaw in place for 2018, the team then turned their attention to activating their right to sign up Ricciardo for another season. At 28, he was still young and, like Verstappen, he had been linked with a move to Mercedes or Ferrari, while McLaren too were a strong option. Red Bull Racing had made it clear they wanted the Aussie to remain with the team. However, it had become evident by now that Verstappen was seen as the future, not Ricciardo.

CHAPTER 16

TURBULENT TIMES
– 2018 –

Red Bull Racing headed into the 2018 season in a positive mood. Verstappen had signed a new long-term deal and Ricciardo had been retained for another season. The team had been buoyed by the results in the tail-end of the 2017 campaign and they hoped to benefit from the host of new aerodynamic rules coming in for 2018.

The main focal point was the introduction of the halo, the cockpit canopy that sat over a driver's head and protected them from flying debris should they strike another vehicle or crash barrier. It was capable of withstanding a load of over 12 tonnes. While its introduction was logical, there had been plenty of opposition from drivers, who did not like the aesthetics and felt it would limit their visibility. Meanwhile, purists did not like the idea of closing up the cockpit, as they did not feel it was in keeping with the spirit of F1 racing and suspected it was moving towards a design more associated with the US-based Indycar series. However, the halo was born out of two recent tragedies. The first involved Frenchman

Jules Bianchi, who succumbed to his injuries in 2015 after having struck a recovery vehicle that was being used to move another car at the Japanese GP the previous year. Then there was British driver Justin Wilson, who was fatally struck by debris while competing in an Indycar race in 2015. The halo has since proved to be a worthy addition and has saved lives or prevented serious injury on several occasions, most notably Romain Grosjean's fiery smash in Bahrain in 2020.

Red Bull Racing launched the RB14 in February, a week before pre-season testing in Barcelona. The very fact that they had not waited until the last moment – in fact they were the third team to launch but the first of the 'big teams', taking in Ferrari and Mercedes – implied that they had been ahead of schedule with the concept and development of their new car. Added weight was given to this theory when the team adopted a new test livery. Had they faced time restrictions in getting ready for the new campaign, it is likely that the design team would have pushed back on the marketing ideas. The fact they were going to all this effort added up to a show of confidence. The black and white swirls we first saw on the RB11 in 2015 would not make a return; instead the RB14 was presented in a dark blue and black livery with the sponsors' logos in white, including the new Aston Martin branding on the rear wing.

Reliability, however, was still a major unknown. The previous year the team had suffered 13 retirements: one more and they would have outnumbered podium finishes. So there was naturally a concern that Renault had again failed to make significant progress to improve that situation. The other concern was whether Ricciardo would be prepared to put up with another season of stop–start performance. Over the winter he had made noises implying that it was imperative for him to be in a competitive car.

A lot of focus in the pre-season had been on Toro Rosso, who, with the Renault relationship in tatters, had struck a deal with Honda, following McLaren's decision to terminate their deal with the Japanese company. Should things go well, then Red Bull Racing could look at following suit. However, given McLaren's notable struggles with the Honda power unit, it remained cause for concern.

The engine conundrum had clearly left Red Bull Racing in a difficult position. Fundamentally, the car design was good but the team felt hamstrung by the power unit and, with Mercedes unwilling to budge on their stance, Horner was out of options. 'We put it to Honda, who had been dumped by McLaren,' says Horner when we discuss the turbulent 2018 season. 'They were going to go to Sauber and at the last moment we managed to persuade them: "Don't go to Sauber, go to Toro Rosso, because if you are any good by June, and you've got as much power as Renault or more, we will switch, too."'

However, the team's constantly changing fortunes that season would make it a tough decision. A steady opening race in Melbourne saw Ricciardo take fourth place while Verstappen was sixth. By contrast, in the Bahrain Grand Prix that followed, both cars were out of the race by the fourth lap. Ricciardo's car shut down with an electrical failure and Verstappen lost drive as his car powered down. Incredibly, despite their reliability woes, it was the first time in eight years that both Red Bull Racing drivers had retired from a race and it was the team's first race since the 2016 Russian GP – where Kvyat had collided with Vettel – at which they would fail to score a single point.

Moreover, in the laps prior to his retirement, Verstappen tangled with Hamilton, earning himself a puncture in the process. Hamilton, who just a few weeks earlier had predicted that the Dutchman was a threat to his championship, was quick to condemn the 20-year-old. It was the first time that Hamilton had been so vocal about Verstappen and it provides the earliest example of a fault line in their relationship. On watching their contact back in the cool-down room after the race, Hamilton labelled Verstappen a 'dickhead', albeit muttering it under his breath.

Meanwhile, Horner tried to apportion blame on both drivers. Unsurprisingly, Hamilton was not in agreement. In the post-race media session, he took a pot-shot at both Verstappen and Horner: 'They are not getting the results they should. Max should have finished a decent race, because he's good enough to do that. I think to myself if [former McLaren teammate] Fernando [Alonso] was in that car today he would have finished a decent race and got points for Red Bull. I just hope Max is learning through whatever situation he's going through. I went through that stuff when I was a young guy, so I know how it is.'

With Hamilton's words still ringing in his ears, Verstappen would again land himself in controversy at the next race in China. This time, on lap 43 he punted Vettel off the track, and both drivers spun. For his part in causing the accident Verstappen was handed a ten-second penalty and would finish the race in fifth place. By contrast, Ricciardo recorded his first victory of the season, an unprecedented result given his sixth-place start on the grid. It was a swashbuckling drive which benefited from some quick thinking from the team, who called him in for a pit stop when the two Toro Rosso drivers collided on track, while Ferrari and Mercedes failed to respond to the situation. It enabled the Aussie to have fresh rubber in the final few laps, allowing him to push his car harder and pull off some overtaking moves to pass the cars ahead.

Interestingly, the post-race news agenda was pulled in two directions. Ricciardo's stellar performance and his magnificent quote of 'sometimes you just have to lick the stamp and send it' lit up the wires. Meanwhile, Verstappen made himself an easy target for blame in the same way Kvyat had a few years earlier. And his rivals were queueing up to take shots. 'I don't need to say anything here,' said Vettel, who finished eighth, as he pointed the blame squarely at Verstappen in a radio interview. In a separate interview, Lauda, Mercedes' non-executive chairman, added: 'It was completely Max's fault. When you compete in more races you should get more clever – especially when you want to win or challenge for the championship – but he is going the other way. He needs to sort himself out. Nobody can help him.'

Verstappen was in real danger of sinking under a barrage of criticism. His blood-and-thunder driving style, which had won so many plaudits in his breakthrough season with Red Bull Racing, was now making him a magnet for attention for the wrong reasons. All he needed was a clean race weekend and a solid haul of points. Unfortunately, he got the complete opposite at the Azerbaijan Grand Prix, the fourth race of the season.

Coming into the race, Horner had played down Verstappen's recent accidents as a run of bad luck, pointing out how Vettel, too, had made mistakes in his early career. However, his attempts to calm the increasingly pervasive narrative of Verstappen's tempestuousness were all undone in a handful of laps around the Baku City Circuit. The Red Bull teammates traded positions over laps 27 and 28, causing Horner's foot to wag in anxiety – a common sight during race day – as he sat watching on the pit wall. Ricciardo then regained fourth place from the Dutchman on lap 35 in a game of cat-and-mouse. Just five laps later they were both out of the race after colliding with each other at turn one. Verstappen had overtaken Ricciardo in the pits and made a late defensive block on the Australian, causing the cars to make contact. Horner was furious. The team's priority has always been to bring both cars home. An incident where they had taken each other out of the race was unacceptable.

Both drivers were summoned to the team's Milton Keynes factory to apologise to staff for their errors in judgement, with Horner reading the riot act after the race: 'They both recognise they have screwed up and they will be apologising to all the members of the team. They are in the doghouse. They have been reminded of that. They are highly paid individuals and they have to act with the team's interest in mind, not their own. Both drivers should have enough of a brain to avoid such an accident. We will take measures to guarantee it won't happen again.'

Verstappen's words afterwards, however, were noticeably different in tone to Vettel's apologetic comments following his early mistakes. Unrepentant, Verstappen simply said: 'We lost a lot of points unnecessarily. We don't need to speak about who is at fault because we are representing a team. This has happened before; you learn from it and we have to make sure it doesn't happen again. We will talk about it and see what happens.'

In order to prevail in Formula One, you need to have a thick skin, for it is a competitive environment. It was once labelled 'the Piranha Club' allegedly by Ron Dennis, who made the quip when

Eddie Jordan lost Michael Schumacher's contract to Flavio Briatore in 1991, reflecting the ferocious nature of the attacks and the prevalence of competitors out to knife their rivals in the back. The sport remains just as ruthless today. But the thick hide displayed by 20-year-old Verstappen was something else. He seemed impervious to the criticism. When asked about his experience heading back to the factory after his rather public telling-off, he joked: 'It was good. It was actually very sunny as well, so that helps.' Was humour the right tactic rather than humility? Probably not, but he stuck with it. Ahead of the Spanish Grand Prix, where he would go on to finish third, he was asked if he would have done anything different in the race in Baku with the benefit of hindsight. 'No,' he said, 'I think we will crash in every single race,' he replied with a laugh. 'You need everyone to crash with your teammates.' It was difficult to tell if he was being naive, funny or really did not give a damn, which is probably the correct assessment.

The race in Spain would only prove to be a brief hiatus from the controversy. At the Monaco Grand Prix, Verstappen again crashed, this time in practice, which resulted in him starting the race from the back of the grid. Verstappen lost control of his RB14 in the closing minutes of the final practice session at the famous swimming-pool section of the track, ripping off his front wing. However, the damage was more substantial than first feared and required extensive repair work, including a new gearbox, which triggered a grid penalty. As the team were unable to fix the damage in time, he did not get the chance to race in qualifying and instead had to start from the pit lane. He also received another dressing-down from Horner following what was now a fifth major error in six rounds.

It is difficult to imagine now, but at the time it was clear that Horner's patience was wearing thin. 'Max needs to learn from it and stop making these errors,' said an exasperated Horner in Monaco. Perhaps the telling-off in Baku had not actually sunk in? What would have added to Horner's exasperation, though, would have been seeing Ricciardo win in Monaco in what was yet another maverick performance. He nursed his car home with only six gears, rather than the full eight, for all but 18 of the 78 laps. *And* with badly worn tyres. *And* with a faulty engine that was down on power. It was another heroic victory from the popular, perma-grinning winner.

But the attention from the media was clearly getting under Verstappen's skin. At the press conference before the Canadian Grand Prix, Verstappen's attempts to deflect the criticism backfired when he lashed out at one too many questions from the media about his recent performances. 'I'm getting really tired of all the questions,' he said. 'If I get any more I might headbutt someone!' He was noticeably agitated and the outburst was unwarranted and not funny. It only served to increase the focus on his attitude to the growing pressure he was experiencing. He was also defiant about his approach to racing. He did not want to dial down on the aggression that had helped him reach the pinnacle of motorsport. The reaction inevitably attracted yet more attention in the form of 'Mad Max' headlines. Once again, he had allowed himself to become an easy target for criticism.

Fired up, he responded by setting the quickest lap times in practice and earning a solid third place on the podium, finishing one spot ahead of Ricciardo in a race that is otherwise remembered for the model Winnie Harlow waving the chequered flag too early, so the results were taken from the 68th lap, rather than the full distance of 70.

While contending with his young driver's battles with the press, Horner had also identified the Canadian Grand Prix in June as the point at which the team needed to make a call on which engine they would use the following season. Persist with the Renault reliability problems, or roll the dice and go with Honda? 'Montreal was the crunch point,' Horner says as we look back at the breakdown in the relationship with Renault. 'We said to Renault, "If you haven't made a significant step, we're out." By the time we got to Montreal, there was nothing to choose between the two engines. However, the commitment and investment Honda were making behind the scenes was just so much greater than what Renault were doing. Honda's factory in Sakura was just miles beyond that of Viry.'

Red Bull Racing confirmed the news they were switching to Honda ahead of Renault's home race in France. The timing felt apt; even if the reason they pulled the trigger at that point was to allow the team the best chance to integrate with Honda, it was still a smack in the face to the French company. The move would allow Red Bull Racing to strengthen the partnership Honda had with Toro Rosso. And with Honda's UK F1 operation conveniently based in Milton Keynes, there was already some synergy, which had clearly been lacking during Honda's time with McLaren.

The Austrian Grand Prix would prove to be another test of Verstappen's character. It would have been easy for a driver without the same mental toughness to suffocate under the barrage of questions he was facing, all dwelling on the mistakes rather than the highlights. He had ridden a wave of positive press during his breakthrough season, but this was an altogether different environment. However, Verstappen did not waver. Straight to the point, he said in his press conference ahead of the race that his critics were only taking pot-shots at him because they were 'jealous', blaming the 'keyboard warriors' who criticised his driving style on social media. He was in a bullish mood – and could afford to be after negotiating trouble-free races in Canada and France, finishing third and second respectively. He would also go one better in Austria, taking the victory as he capitalised on a rare double DNF from the Mercedes duo of Hamilton and Bottas, who both suffered mechanical failures. It was Verstappen's first win since the 2017 Malaysia GP and served to dissipate the frenzied attacks on his character.

The Austrian Grand Prix would also become significant for the team's other driver, in what would prove to be a period of twisting loyalties and back-and-forth deliberations for Ricciardo, ultimately culminating in his decision to quit the team. The origins of his decision can be traced back to the previous season when Red Bull Racing had rewarded Verstappen with a new long-term deal. It did not take a genius to figure out that Verstappen was the rising star of the team, even if he had subsequently faced criticism from the media. Ricciardo, like Webber before him, was fearful that he was no longer enjoying equal status – not with regard to equipment, as had been the case for Webber, but more in regard to long-term support. Glenn Beavis, who was acting as Ricciardo's manager at the time, had been perturbed by some off-the-cuff comments from Marko at the Monaco Grand Prix: 'I want to win the title with Daniel in 2018, and then win it with Max in 2019 and 2020.' While said with good intentions, Marko's comments had marked Ricciardo out as the short-term option for the team. Verstappen was the future. In addition, like his fellow countryman Webber, Ricciardo had only been offered a rolling deal each season, and that had invited the likes of McLaren and Ferrari to make tentative approaches. It was no surprise that his head had been turned.

If Ricciardo had any lingering doubts whether there was a disparity in the team, his suspicions seemed to be confirmed following his collision with Verstappen in Baku at the Azerbaijan GP. The initial narrative was that Verstappen was to blame. However, the lack of punishment served on his teammate would only have fuelled Ricciardo's belief that Verstappen was being treated differently. Horner had notably defended the Dutchman in the wake of the criticism and it was easy to see how the situation fed into a negative – albeit unproven – narrative that the team had rallied behind Verstappen at the expense of his teammate. The relationship became strained, with those working in the Ricciardo camp becoming increasingly at odds with Red Bull.

Then, at the Austrian Grand Prix, Ricciardo met with Mateschitz – a rare opportunity to get some clarity on his position within the team. What happened next remains unknown to anyone but the two gentlemen having the discussion. Commenting on Ricciardo's career for ESPN's F1 site, journalist Nate Saunders wrote: 'Red Bull's version is that Mateschitz offered a contract which was exactly the same as Verstappen's in all areas, in a bid to end any suggestion of favouritism. Red Bull maintain that is the deal they offered. Ricciardo's camp always denied that was the case. It has been suggested to ESPN by several well-placed sources that he would have signed that deal if those terms had been offered.' Saunders goes on to say that the outcome of the meeting, which culminated in a hand-shake, is also up for debate. 'A misunderstanding appears to have occurred at that meeting, too,' he wrote. 'After their chat, the two men shook hands. Ricciardo was appreciative of the talk with Mateschitz but it had not swayed him either way; his mind was still not made up. To Mateschitz, given what he had felt to be the nature of their conversation, the handshake which followed was confirmation he was going to stay with Red Bull.'

Horner clearly believed that a deal had been reached. When we discuss Ricciardo's departure, he explains how the Australian broke the news to him over the phone – and how he initially thought it was a joke. 'I got Dietrich to speak with him in Austria at the Grand Prix and there was a deal agreed between the two,' he says with certainty. 'And then I think he was very badly advised, because the contract was all drawn up. Initially it was a two-year deal and it became a one-year deal, which we accepted, and we said we would give him an out if the Honda engine was not delivering.

'I remember, I was driving up the M40 just before the summer break and there was a tyre test in Budapest so he wasn't available to sign the contract on the Monday. On the Tuesday he was driving our F1 car during the Pirelli test and then he was going straight to LA. He rang me having just got off the plane in Los Angeles and you could smell something was not quite right, because there was a contract right there and you've only got to sign the bloody thing. He'd spent three days coming up with excuses and then he rang me and said, "Look, I'm not going to re-sign, I'm going to go to another team." Now, if that team had been Mercedes or Ferrari, I could understand that, but when he said the team was Renault, I honestly thought it was a Daniel wind-up because 98 per cent of our problems that year had been because of Renault fuck-ups! He'd won Monaco that year with an engine that had failed. All the retirements were just horrendous. He had to tell me three times before I actually believed what he was saying, but Cyril [Abiteboul, Renault's boss] had convinced him that it was all going to be hunky-dory the following year, and he'd be the number one and they would pay him a lot of money.'

The suggestion was that Ricciardo had signed the Renault contract on the flight to LA. Horner was not the only one left trying to digest the news. McLaren's Zak Brown, who was said to be another suitor, was also apparently baffled, as were the media. 'It was probably one of the most difficult decisions to take in my career so far. But I thought that it was time for me to take on a fresh and new challenge,' said Ricciardo in the quotes to accompany the press release, which also confirmed that the French driver Pierre Gasly would be promoted from Toro Rosso for the following season. Ricciardo wanted to try somewhere else and, for reasons unknown, Renault felt like the right destination for him. Then, after revealing his news to Red Bull Racing, his form tumbled. At the Belgian GP he crashed out. In Italy he did not finish due to a clutch failure. In Austin he had another DNF due to a battery failure. And in Mexico, he had a hydraulic failure. It was a miserable end to his first stint at Red Bull Racing.

By contrast, Verstappen made a strong end to the campaign with podiums in his final five races, including a victory in Mexico that meant he finished the season in fourth place in the drivers' championship, while Ricciardo was sixth. Whether it was intentional or not, Verstappen was now the de facto team leader at just 21 years old.

CHAPTER 17

THE HONDA GAMBLE

– 2019 –

The start of the 2019 season was a pivotal time for Red Bull Racing, as they ushered in a new era using Honda power units. For such an important switch, they had Verstappen, 21, spearheading their team with five wins to his name, alongside Pierre Gasly, 23, who had competed in just 26 F1 races.

It was a huge contrast to McLaren's approach in 2015 when they started their partnership with Honda engines. The move by the Woking team was based on a belief that they would not be in a position to fight for world championships as a customer buying their engines from a supplier. They needed the full support of an engine maker, almost in the same way as being a works team. Their strategy for their drivers was interesting. McLaren decided to demote Kevin Magnussen to test driver and pair two-time world champion Alonso alongside Jenson Button. That move made a lot of sense at the time. On paper at least, their vast experience would allow McLaren to benefit from the detailed technical feedback required by Honda for them to make progress and catch up with the other power unit manufacturers.

But after a slow start and well-documented reliability problems, relationships suffered. At the 2015 Japanese Grand Prix, it was too much for Alonso when he was overtaken by a Toro Rosso. Exasperated by the lack of horsepower from his power unit, he snapped over the team's radio, shouting to his race engineer: 'GP2 engine, aghhhhh!' The outburst implied that Honda's engine was so down on performance that it should have only been used in the lower race categories; to rub salt in Honda's wound, Alonso made this comment publicly on Honda's home turf. It was a move he would later regret when the conversation, which was private with his race engineer, was played out on the world television feed for everyone to hear.

Here it is important to remember that Japanese work culture has many layers, which perhaps McLaren struggled to understand. Breakdowns in communication were common. For example, it is one thing to ask whether Honda could produce an engine capable of achieving 1,000 horsepower. Sure they could, so the answer was technically 'yes'. But it is quite another thing to ask them, 'When can you produce an engine capable of achieving 1,000 horsepower?' Red Bull Racing were keen to learn from McLaren's mistakes and consequently they had a much closer relationship with Honda's technical plant in Sakura, plus they also benefited from the fact that Honda's facility in Milton Keynes was conveniently located near Red Bull Racing's HQ – and was eventually assimilated with some of its staff into the Red Bull campus.

Pre-season testing had been encouraging, with no major reliability issues. However, it would be a season of experimentation and almost a given that the team would become hamstrung by grid penalties later in the year for unscheduled changes with their power unit, as Honda introduced new parts with improved power and reliability. Mercedes and Ferrari would have the stronger, completed package but, on his day, Verstappen had proven he had the skill to challenge for victories. On the eve of the new season, Hamilton was very much the favourite to retain his title; however, the 34-year-old identified Verstappen as the next in line to take his world crown. Before the season-opener in Melbourne, he said he expected more of a challenge from Verstappen – which ultimately he welcomed. 'Red Bull have got a great car,' he said honestly, and then, somewhat ironically given what was to come later, added: 'They were very strong at the end of the year and they've got a new engine now, too. Will it be able to compete with ours? They will have to improve on their reliability, which has been a big downfall for them. But I hope so, because it would be epic if Red Bull could mix it with us a bit more week in and week out.'

Confusingly, and somewhat frustratingly from a media perspective, Red Bull Racing and Mercedes launched their season's challengers on the same day, 13 February. Among the larger teams at least, season launches have traditionally been an opportunity to showcase their new car with their sponsorship partners and stakeholders, getting some media coverage for those brands who pay for their logos to be on the cars. Under Liberty Media's ownership, however, the car launches have been a way to engage with a younger audience, with an event more tailored to the social media influencers. The focus is now on engaging those watching on their phones, with live unveils of the new livery, whereas in the past it was more about impressing the journalists and conducting interview sessions with the drivers and team bosses. Nowadays, it is very much a visual offering.

Another big change for the new season occurred around the same time as the 2019 launches, when *Drive to Survive* aired for the first time on Netflix. The fly-on-the-wall TV show had been shot during the 2018 season and edited over the winter. It burst onto the screens and opened the sport up to a new audience. It is no under-statement to say the show was the most important thing to happen to Formula One under Liberty Media's ownership. As members of the media, my fellow F1 reporters and I had agreed to be fair game in the production, which led to the slightly odd situation of us going about our business, asking the questions, only to find that we were being featured on the TV show some months later. In my case I found this out after being told by Mercedes boss Wolff that there was an exchange between us from a press conference, which I had forgot-ten until it was broadcast on the show.

None of us expected it to be such a hit. Chris Medland, a colleague and good friend of mine, appeared in the first series of the show as a talking head and was brought in as an expert to guide the producers through the ins and outs of the sport. 'At first there was quite a lot of scepticism about what Netflix would do for F1,' he says as we discuss the impact the series made. 'Many in the paddock expected it would be redundant given how long after the event the series would come out. My job was just to help the producers under-stand the sport a little bit more, explaining the basics on camera but also answering any questions for them. That meant a lot more input than just the filming days – of which for me there were around seven or eight across the year, while there was days and days of footage to edit on location. There were a few occasions where they'd be looking for a specific storyline to go down and I'd push back if I felt it wasn't accurate. But the first season worked very well at providing a basic understanding for new fans, which I think is what helped it reach far beyond anyone with an F1 interest.'

Season one of *Drive to Survive* centred heavily on Ricciardo and his relationship with Red Bull Racing. It gave key drivers and team principals distinct roles, with a particular narrative. For instance, Guenther Steiner, by now at Haas, is jovial; Horner flips between being the goodie and bad guy; Ricciardo is presented as a lovable figure. It is compelling theatrics and gets to the heart of F1, which is part sport, part business and part entertainment.

It was very obvious that the series leaned into Ricciardo's character, his split from the team and also Red Bull Racing's deteriorating relationship with Renault. Series one, episode four, is called 'The Art of War' and is the pick of the bunch for that season's offering, providing a mix of drama and fly-on-the-wall footage. There are barbs between Horner and Renault's managing director Cyril Abiteboul, while Ricciardo is the star of the show, his comical facade dropping when he explains his decision to join Renault and leave Red Bull Racing. Then there is tension as he reunites with Red Bull Racing following his announcement that he's off at the end of the season. It all makes for compelling TV.

Red Bull Racing threw its doors open to the series and embraced the early filming days, accounting for why they were so heavily featured in its first season, while the other big teams wanted to maintain a distance, opting to see how well it was received first. It was a bold move to allow full access to a TV crew, especially with limited power to oversee the final edit. However, Verstappen would eventually grow frustrated with the series and went as far as to say he did not want to be part of it. In 2021, he said at the US GP how he understood the series was being used as a promotional tool but said, 'As a driver, I don't like being part of it. They faked a few rivalries which don't really exist.'

At the 2019 season launch, Red Bull Racing distributed some images of the RB15, while a few miles down the road at Silverstone, Mercedes were putting their challenger through its paces on a designated filming day. F1 rules put a limit on testing, but teams also have an allocation of time for filming to capture video and pictures for their own use, which provides an extra opportunity to ensure everything works as expected. The news of the day came from Horner, who declared that Verstappen was the man to beat: 'Sebastian had a messy year, last year. Max was the second-highest points scorer to Lewis. And I think he's probably the driver they fear most.'

Most significant was Horner's assertion that Verstappen had matured and that he had learned from his mistakes the previous season. He added: 'Max has evolved so much, entering his fourth full season of Formula One. I think he is much more rounded with experience. Individually he's got all the tools and skill to take the fight to Lewis, Sebastian or whoever may be the challenge this year.'

However, before the first race of the year could get underway, the F1 community was cast into mourning following the death of Charlie Whiting, the FIA's most senior figure. Whiting was 66 and died of a pulmonary embolism on Thursday 14 March in Melbourne, where he was due to officiate at that weekend's season-opening Australian GP. Whiting had commanded the respect of both drivers and team bosses. The FIA president at the time, Jean Todt, called him 'a central and inimitable figure who embodied the ethics and spirit' of F1.

Whiting had worked in F1 since 1977 in a number of roles before joining the FIA in 1988, where he pioneered and championed a number of safety improvements to circuits and race cars. His tragic passing left a huge hole as he had served as the F1 race director and liaison between the F1 teams and the FIA, meaning he was the go-to man for teams to check the regulations and also acted as the referee who oversaw each F1 race. Michael Masi, who had worked as race director of Australia's V8 Supercars series, had joined the FIA as deputy race director for Formula Two and Formula Three just a few weeks before. The objective would have been for him to take some of the responsibilities of the lower racing categories off Whiting, while also benefiting from Whiting's experience working in F1. However, Whiting's passing meant that Masi was suddenly promoted to the role without really having any experience of working in F1. In an interview with *Motorsport* magazine in 2019, Masi would later admit he was thrown in 'at the deep end' as he was forced to get up to speed instantly in the Australian GP. He would later shoot to prominence for the wrong reasons with his handling of the Abu Dhabi Grand Prix in 2021.

The season got off to an unexpectedly good start, for Verstappen at least, with a podium finish in Melbourne, while Gasly finished out of the points in 11th place. It was Honda's first podium since Rubens Barrichello was third in the 2008 British Grand Prix driving for the Honda team, but Verstappen was quick to play down expectations, saying, 'Starting the season with a podium in Australia is really positive but Melbourne is not a typical circuit so we can't get carried away.' Mercedes boss Toto Wolff, however, had seen enough to brand Red Bull Racing a 'threat' to his team in the title race.

Verstappen followed up his third place with three consecutive fourth-place finishes before taking another podium, again third place, this time in Barcelona. This left him third in the drivers' championship, but still 46 points behind the leader Hamilton. As expected, it was tougher for Gasly, who had a retirement in Azerbaijan and had finished sixth on two occasions in China and Spain before he scored a fifth place in Monaco, albeit behind Verstappen, who was fourth, as the track again proved to be an outlier in that it was a good one for Red Bull Racing. It could have been even better for Verstappen had it not been for a five-second penalty for an unsafe release from his pit stop into the path of Bottas, with the Finn forced into the pit wall by the emerging Red Bull man. Verstappen, who had pressed Hamilton for the win but was unable to find a way past, was demoted from second to fourth once the penalty had been applied.

The race, however, was more widely remembered as a memorial to the late Niki Lauda, who had passed away shortly before the weekend after a period of ill health. The Austrian, who famously returned to racing just days after suffering a horrific fiery smash in 1976, had also overseen the early days of Jaguar Racing, where he was offered the role of team principal halfway through the 2001 season before leaving at the end of 2002. Lauda had recently undergone a double lung transplant and had had two kidney transplants in previous years.

Verstappen recorded his first win of the year at the Red Bull Ring in Austria – but he was made to wait for almost three hours for it to be confirmed. For such a fast-paced sport, some of the decision-making is an incredibly slow process. The investigation centred on an overtaking move on Leclerc on lap 69 of 71 for the lead. It was an aggressive move from Verstappen and Leclerc let his feelings be known over the team's radio. However, Verstappen was officially exonerated. Horner summed it up: 'If those things are not allowed in racing, then what's the point of being in Formula One? It would have been incomprehensible to have changed the podium. It was tough racing but Max was slightly ahead of Charles.'

There is a strange atmosphere in the press room in those hours spent waiting for an FIA decision. It isn't so much the delay to the final classified result, but more the looming threat of anti-climax if an interesting victory is taken away. On that day the feeling was particularly acute. Between their two drivers, Mercedes had won all eight races of the season so far, with the French GP before the race in Austria a total procession for Hamilton. Seeing a different winner on the podium certainly reinvigorated the sport after a spell of such dominance.

Verstappen would win again in Germany, just two races on from his success in Austria. The victory was especially memorable as it was Mercedes' home race and was supposed to be a celebration for Red Bull Racing's rivals. It was held on 28 July at Hockenheim and the German car manufacturer had adopted the title sponsorship, so the race was officially called the Mercedes-Benz Grosser Preis von Deutschland. The company was celebrating their 125th year of competing in motorsport, and their 200th start in F1. To toast the double landmark, the team adopted a special one-off, historic livery and the team's drivers and staff all wore period-inspired outfits from the 1930s. All a bit of fun when you are winning, but after a wretched weekend for Mercedes – with Bottas crashing out and Hamilton finishing ninth – it was too easy to accuse them of taking their eye off the ball.

Verstappen excelled in the tricky conditions; at one point he went into a 360-degree spin but managed to hold it from crashing out. Also, one factor that is frequently overlooked in F1 is the role the team plays in pit stops. Getting the four wheels changed in the quickest time possible without a mistake can make a huge difference to a driver's track position. So, while other teams were slipping up and making errors in the changeable conditions, Red Bull Racing's mechanics pulled off the fastest-ever F1 pit stop time of 1.88 seconds when Verstappen pitted on lap 46. He ended up finishing 7.33 seconds ahead of Vettel, who was second; Kvyat was third in his Toro Rosso.

Verstappen's two wins in close proximity meant he shot back up the news agenda. The narrative followed a familiar pattern: questions about his future, despite the long-term contract with Red Bull Racing, plus debate on whether he could take the fight to Hamilton. Horner fuelled the speculation at the British Grand Prix when he backed his driver to beat reigning world champion Hamilton if they were both placed in equal machinery. It was a tantalising prospect but ultimately one which would be hard to actualise. Neither team would be willing to allow their drivers into each other's car, and stripping the idea back to a straight go-kart race was equally unlikely to get the green light from their respective bosses. That meant the debate was played out in the media, which Verstappen was still keen to avoid. His relationship with the press had not changed from when he was snapping back at all the criticism. Verstappen preferred not to get into F1 politics; he simply wanted to win races – an attitude we would come to see more and more. Ahead of the Hungarian Grand Prix, he was asked how he felt about public opinion holding him in higher regard than Hamilton, who of course had the better car and was winning week after week. It was widely argued that while the design of the Red Bull Racing car was good, Mercedes still had the horsepower advantage with their unit. Verstappen claimed to not be bothered by the comparison. 'I don't say anything about this and I don't care,' he said in the press conference. 'For me, the most important thing is to perform on track. I made a big jump into Formula One and I made mistakes when I started. I am still getting better. I am only 21 and you learn how to become better through experience.' While he was unable to get another win in Hungary, Verstappen did take his maiden pole position and was placed second behind Hamilton, with the two enjoying a good battle for position, until the Brit benefited from some fresher tyres late in the race, allowing him to overtake the Dutchman.

After the Hungarian Grand Prix, Red Bull decided to promote 23-year-old Thai-British driver Alexander Albon alongside Verstappen, at the expense of Gasly. Albon and Gasly had clashed on track in the German Grand Prix when the Red Bull Racing driver tried to pass the Toro Rosso car. Albon had defended his position and pulled to the right and Gasly had run into the back of his car, damaging his own front wing and causing a puncture that sent him skidding off track. The Frenchman had no hiding place at the Hungarian GP when he was lapped by Verstappen. Horner now admits that, similar to the earlier Kvyat situation, they perhaps promoted Gasly too soon to the A-team, while Albon was showing a maturity and speed at Toro Rosso having gone from last to tenth at the Chinese Grand Prix and taking sixth from 17th on the grid in Germany. 'It was difficult,' Horner says as we discuss Gasly's short 12-race stint within the team. 'It was probably too much too soon for him, and being Max's teammate by this stage certainly wasn't going to be easy. Pierre was struggling. He was lapped in the Austrian Grand Prix and then he was lapped again by Max in Budapest and the writing was on the wall. We needed to do something because it was almost not fair on him. The only real option we had was to take Alex, who had shown real promise at that point in the Toro Rosso, and promote him.'

Albon made a good start, finishing fifth in the Belgian Grand Prix on his first race for the senior team, while Verstappen's time at Spa came to an abrupt end with a first-lap accident that sent him out of the race. Albon scored points in eight of the last nine races, missing out only in Brazil, a race that was won by Verstappen with a commanding drive from pole position. Albon should have been on the podium too in São Paulo but was spun off by Hamilton on the penultimate lap. The stewards issued Hamilton with a five-second time penalty for causing the collision, dropping him off the podium to seventh – all of which was no use to Albon, who was left down in 14th in the classified results. Nonetheless, it proved to be a strong end to the season, especially with Verstappen taking a win, a second and a third place in the final three races.

At the final race in Abu Dhabi, it was a good time to catch up with Verstappen as he assessed the season and laid out his plans for the future. He had cut out the mistakes and not been afraid to stir it up with Hamilton on track and in the media. With Vettel's career taking a nosedive and with Bottas offering no real threat to Hamilton, all eyes were on whether Verstappen could take the fight to the Mercedes man and end his domination. After brilliant wins in Austria, Germany and Brazil, we reflected in the paddock and when the conversation came around to Hamilton, Verstappen said: 'I'm not afraid of Lewis at all. Otherwise, it would be better to stay at home. If I was not here to win, it makes no sense being here, because then your whole attitude is wrong. It is good to have drivers like Lewis around you. He is a six-time world champion and won a lot of races, but I want to be in his position. I want people to think it boring that I am winning every weekend.' It was a telling quote that would of course come true.

CHAPTER 18

PUT ON HOLD
– 2020 –

The year started with the news that Verstappen, who was still only 22, had agreed a new and improved contract with Red Bull Racing that stretched until the end of the 2023 season. In essence it was a contract extension but one that had caught the paddock by surprise, for he already had a deal in place. However, the new terms quelled talk and speculation about the Dutchman being lured to Mercedes, should Hamilton decide to join Ferrari, as had been heavily suggested in the media. Verstappen's manager Raymond Vermeulen negotiated a competitive financial package that would have no doubt tested Red Bull's resolve to secure the service of the highest-rated driver on the grid. But the new contract was a win for all parties. It would fend off any interest from rival teams, while the progress the team was making with Honda and their power units appeared to satisfy Verstappen that he could be a serious contender for the title in due course.

In the run-up to the new campaign, Horner was predicting big things for his young driver, again drawing comparisons between Verstappen and reigning champion Hamilton, as well as Ferrari's Leclerc. In a press briefing ahead of the new season, Horner praised Verstappen's wheel-to-wheel race craft, adding, 'The only person I have seen Lewis make mistakes around is Max. Max is the coming man and Lewis is 35. It is inevitable in any sport that there is a new generation coming. In F1, you have Max and Charles Leclerc at Ferrari and it is all set for a thrilling year . . . Max is the most in-form driver in F1. Lewis is the world champion. We will have to see who is best at the end of the year. If we can give Max the tools, then he will deliver.'

It was indeed shaping up to be a memorable year – but not in a way that anyone could have predicted. What followed was a complete paralysis of the world as the Covid-19 pandemic hit, stopping F1 as it lined up ready to race in Australia. There is a photo of the cramped press conference held in Albert Park, Melbourne, on the Friday, the day the Australian Grand Prix weekend was due to start, where Liberty Media's Chase Carey declared the race was being suspended. I remember being gripped by a fear that the global lockdown would see me separated from my family on the other side of the world and I hurriedly phoned the travel department to seek an urgent flight home before borders were closed. As a journalist you are at the heart of the news story and the thrill of reporting on it remains such a buzz, but in situations like these you are left worrying about the impact it will have on your family life.

The warning signs of the pandemic had been clear to anyone who had been working closely on F1 news long before it was reported by the mass media. I remember writing a story in the New Year about how the Chinese Grand Prix was in doubt due to the spread of the coronavirus in the country and potential sanctions imposed by the government. The race was indeed eventually postponed on 12 February, with F1 seeking an alternative date in the year to host it, as they looked to maintain a record 22-race calendar. However, at the pre-season testing, fears continued to grow about the transmission of the virus. A Chinese colleague, who displayed no symptoms whatsoever, was asked not to visit a particular team's hospitality unit, as uncertainty and distrust spread in the absence of any reliable information or guidance. Staff dared not cough or sneeze through fear of being questioned about their health.

Nonetheless, the season ahead was progressing as planned. My flights to Melbourne, via Hong Kong, had been booked well in advance. Many teams who were travelling the same route had rescheduled, due to the territory's obvious link with China. Among the drivers, the line, 'We trust the FIA to make the right decision,' continued to echo around the press conference room each time they were asked about their views on whether they were happy to be pressing ahead against a backdrop of uncertainty.

The flight to Melbourne was extremely strange and left me feeling strained. Heathrow Airport was unusually quiet and, as I boarded the 11-hour flight to Hong Kong, my heart skipped a beat when I saw the flight attendants wearing full PPE: plastic aprons, rubber gloves and face masks. I had been to Asia many times, so the sight of someone wearing a face mask due to pollution or a cold was not uncommon, but this was the first time I had experienced it among all the staff on board a flight. It made me wonder if I was doing the right thing, putting myself in jeopardy for a motor race. The arrival in Hong Kong was equally surreal. Like much of Asia, it had responded to the pandemic much quicker than Europe and the rest of the world. The usually bustling airport was a ghost town with only one or two restaurants open as a few souls wandered quietly through the terminals.

Conversely, the arrival in Melbourne was a step back to normality. The warm, bright sunshine was welcome and restored a sense that perhaps being in Australia for the season-opener was the right thing to do. That said, there had been no clear guidelines given by the FIA, so at a Red Bull Racing event in Melbourne, the team took it upon themselves to practise social distancing before the phrase was more widely used.

A PR stunt saw Verstappen and Albon riding on motorised cool boxes around Station Pier near the Albert Park Circuit. Both drivers were in high spirits and it was all good fun to kick off the season ahead of the following day's media commitments. The Thursday media day went ahead as planned, with drivers reluctant to speak about F1's decision to press ahead in the face of a global emergency. All apart from Hamilton, who uttered the immortal line 'cash is king' when asked why he thought F1 was in Australia. It was one of the many standout moments from that unforgettable part of the season. Another came later when news broke that McLaren were withdrawing from the Australian Grand Prix after a team member had tested positive for Covid, just as a group of us journalists were about to kick off our usual post-work evening football match. Naturally we all returned hurriedly to our laptops to cover the story.

What happened next was intriguing. Horner called a meeting with the team bosses at the Crown Hotel in Melbourne and suggested they invite F1's managing director, Ross Brawn. He came, along with the FIA's race director, Michael Masi, to discuss what they would do in the wake of McLaren's decision to withdraw from the race. Meanwhile, the message from the promoter was clear: they wanted the race to go ahead. Neither F1 nor the promoter were willing to pull the plug. However, the final decision depended on the outcome of a vote with the team bosses.

In the meantime, local radio bulletins were saying that fans should attend, but the news emerging from the teams was different and the race now appeared to be in doubt. The conflicting stories made it incredibly hard to decipher fact from rumour, and from a personal perspective I was keen to have clarity so I could get earlier return flights booked if need be, fearing the country was about to be placed into a total lockdown. During this time, there was no official comment from the FIA, F1 or the teams as the decision still hadn't been made.

There were three main factors. Firstly, there was the question of whether the FIA and F1 felt the as yet largely unknown virus was a danger to life, and whether they would allow the race to go ahead with or without fans. The second issue was whether teams would side with McLaren and withdraw as a show of support. A championship round without all the participants would not necessarily feel like a full round. And the third issue – perhaps, if being cynical, the trickiest to navigate – was who would pay for the event if it were cancelled? F1 wanted the revenue from the promoter; the promoter wanted to host F1 to raise revenue – so if one side cancelled, would they be in breach of contract?

The most uncomfortable of victories as Vettel defies team orders not to overtake Webber on his way to victory in the 2013 Malaysian GP. The 'multi 21' rift blew a hole in the two drivers' relationship.

Vettel clinched the title with victory in the 2013 Indian Grand Prix and celebrated by performing donuts in his RB9, for which he was later fined $21,000. It would prove to be the last of his four drivers' championship titles.

Ricciardo celebrates his first F1 win in Canada. It comes as Mercedes' Lewis Hamilton and Nico Rosberg suffer a rare off day and the Aussie pounced to take full advantage. 'I'm still in shock,' he says after the race. 'This is ridiculous!'

The Red Bull Ring reopened in 2014 as the Austrian GP returned to the F1 calendar. It was a long-term goal for Mateschitz to see his home race back on the schedule.

Vettel poses next to the Red Bull Racing trophy cabinet on 2 December 2014. A few days later, 60 trophies would be stolen in a smash-and-grab raid. The majority would be discovered floating in a lake some 70 miles away in Berkshire.

A Red Bull one, two and three? Vettel celebrates for Ferrari on the podium next to Ricciardo and Kvyat after winning at the Hungaroring in 2015. Three Red Bull juniors alongside Verstappen, who came fourth.

Verstappen wins on his debut for Red Bull Racing in the 2016 Spanish Grand Prix. Horner recalls how the Dutchman was 'on the pace from the very first lap' and how Ecclestone had left him with a polystyrene birthday cake!

Ricciardo celebrates his win at the Malaysian GP in 2016 by initiating the shoey celebrations. Horner toasts the victory by drinking from the Aussie's race boot while Verstappen joins them on the podium after finishing the race in second place.

Ricciardo takes the plunge in Monaco 2018 after a hard-earned victory with only six gears *and* a faulty engine.

Gasly and Verstappen pose in one-off James Bond-inspired race suits during a photo shoot at Silverstone in 2019 to celebrate the team's title sponsorship with Aston Martin.

Fun in the sun. Albon and Verstappen ride motorised cool boxes in Melbourne 2020. The race at Albert Park would be cancelled just a few days later due to the Covid pandemic.

An iconic moment of 2021 as Verstappen's car lands on top of Hamilton's during the 2021 Italian Grand Prix. It is the second time during the season they collide as they fight for the title. Both drivers escape unharmed but while Verstappen walks away, Hamilton tries in vain to put his Mercedes in gear and get back into the race.

All eyes on the prize. The thrilling 22-race season in 2021 came down to the final race in Abu Dhabi with Verstappen and Hamilton level on 369.5 points. I had produced an eight-page pull-out in the *Sun* if Hamilton was to win a record eighth world title – it never got to see the light of day after a dramatic final few laps.

Verstappen wins his second world crown at the 2022 Japanese GP – home of engine-suppliers, Honda. He expresses his shock at winning the title, believing that only half-points would have been offered due to the rain-hit race only lasting 28 laps. He is surprised to learn in the cool-down room that he had in fact been awarded full points due to a change in the rules for that season.

Red Bull Racing pay tribute to the late Mateschitz by wearing jeans ahead of the 2023 United States GP in Austin, Texas. It marked a year since the Red Bull founder passed away. Despite his enormous wealth, he was always seen wearing jeans.

Verstappen wins the 2023 Abu Dhabi Grand Prix, his 19th victory of the season where he led over 1,000 laps, scored 575 points, achieved the most consecutive victories in F1 (10) and took the most podiums in a season (21). He was also the only driver to finish every race in the 2023 season.

A decision between all the parties was required. Horner was adamant that the race should have gone ahead as planned and says today that he sticks by that view. However, as he explains in our interview, not all the team bosses were aligned and the vote was split. 'I had convinced some of the teams and said, "Come on, guys, let's at least run on Friday and if any more cases come up, we can re-evaluate it in 24 hours' time," ' he says. 'For the sake of one positive test, there's 400,000 people here and we've come all the way to Australia, are we really going to pack everything up and go home and go through all the airports where there is a risk of catching Covid anyway?'

As Horner explained in his column on the team's website, the decision initially hung in the balance. 'Ross called the FIA president, Jean Todt, who said he would go with the majority,' he wrote, 'so it was down to Ross as he had the final vote. He said he agreed with my suggestion, to do further tests and evaluate the situation in 24 hours, and he also wanted to get the event rolling. My feeling was that if the government and medical authorities felt it was safe for the race to go ahead, then as a race team we were prepared to race. But, soon after the meeting had ended, I had a telephone call from Ross at around 3am, who said we had a bit of a problem because Mercedes had changed their position. It also meant they would not supply engines to their customers. It turned the situation on its head and the eventual outcome changed. As a result, there was little choice for F1 but to cancel the event.'

The Australian Grand Prix was cancelled in a very public press conference in Albert Park on the Friday, while fans were literally still queuing at the gates to get into the circuit. A joint statement from F1, the FIA and the Australian Grand Prix said: 'Following the confirmation that a member of the McLaren Racing Team has tested positive for Covid-19 and the team's decision to withdraw from the Australian Grand Prix, Formula One and the FIA convened a meeting of the other nine team principals on Thursday evening. Those discussions concluded with a majority view of the teams that the race should not go ahead. Formula One and the FIA, with the full support of the Australian Grand Prix Corporation (AGPC), have therefore taken the decision that all Formula One activity for the Australian Grand Prix is cancelled.'

As the world was plunged into uncertainty, one of the great untold stories of the pandemic was the way that F1 teams responded to help out. Dubbed 'Project Pit Lane', volunteers at Red Bull Racing aligned with other teams to produce ventilators for the UK's National Health Service. It took just three weeks to produce a working prototype, astounding people working in the medical profession. Interestingly, the project, which was not eventually taken up by the NHS, saw staff from Renault work alongside those from Red Bull Racing in a cohesive effort for the first time since the teams parted ways.

Later that summer, as the first wave of the pandemic abated, thoughts turned to restarting the sport. Eventually, with strict testing and travel protocols in place, Formula One went ahead with the difficult task of returning to action under new Covid-safe conditions at the start of July, with two races held at the Red Bull Ring. The circuit had worked closely with F1 to ensure that the sport returned safely, albeit without fans able to spectate in person. Teams would be subjected to regular tests and any positive Covid results would see staff isolated in bubbles to prevent further spread.

The race in Austria was a successful return for the sport but not for the Red Bull team. Verstappen, who was going for his third straight win at the team's home circuit, was forced to retire after 11 laps with an electrical fault, while Albon's race was also cut short because of an electrical issue three laps from the end, but only after being hit by Hamilton's Mercedes. Horner had dinner with Albon after the race and admitted his driver was feeling down about the result but motivated about the car and the team's performance, which were both strategically sharp.

From the media's perspective, the focus was on a spat between Red Bull Racing and Mercedes. Horner's team had protested over the FIA's failure to punish Hamilton during qualifying where he appeared to ignore some waved yellow warning flags telling him to slow down. Red Bull Racing sought clarification from the rule-book and presented new evidence in the form of a video that showed Hamilton failing to slow. Just 41 minutes before the race was due to start, Hamilton was issued a three-place grid penalty, dropping him from second to fifth and promoting Verstappen to the front row and Albon to fourth. Toto Wolff delivered some fighting talk to the media afterwards, saying 'the gloves are off' in Mercedes' battle with Red Bull Racing. Horner hit back, saying it was just sour grapes. 'Rivalry between the drivers and between the teams is what competition is all about, so long as it is respectful,' he said. It was a classic example of the simmering rivalry between the two bosses that was to continue as the season progressed.

In the second race in Austria, this time titled the Styrian Grand Prix after the region where the track is located, Verstappen was third and Albon fourth in a much-improved result for the team. Verstappen continued the good progress with second places in Hungary and the British Grand Prix but he would go even better in the second race at Silverstone – a one-off event named the F1's 70th Anniversary Grand Prix that was held a week after the British GP. Verstappen's victory was a faultless performance and at the end he was comfortable enough to enjoy some banter with his race engineer about staying hydrated and sanitising his hands. Just a few laps earlier the same engineer had urged him to slow down to preserve the life in his tyres, to which Verstappen quipped back: 'Mate, this is the only chance of being close to the Mercedes – I'm not just sitting behind like a grandma!' The win was one of two he would achieve that season, the other coming in Abu Dhabi where he would finish the campaign with 11 podiums from the 17 rounds of the championship. The victory in Abu Dhabi was a display of dominance, as Verstappen not only won the race, but also led every lap from pole position and laid down a very important marker for the following season.

As for Albon, while he was unable to match Verstappen's achievements, he had a solid season, although he might have had mixed feelings witnessing Gasly win in Monza for Red Bull Racing's B team. This was the former Toro Rosso, now renamed AlphaTauri to promote Red Bull's clothing range by the same name. In the following race at Mugello in Tuscany, Albon must have been relieved to score his first podium, earning praise from Horner over the team's radio after crossing the finish line. The reply from the mild-mannered racer was remarkably endearing: 'Thanks, everyone. Thanks for everything. Thanks for sticking with me.'

Albon would also take third place in the Bahrain Grand Prix, behind Verstappen, who was second. It was a race, however, remembered for a different reason – a first-lap crash for Haas driver Romain Grosjean, who had clipped Kvyat's AlphaTauri car and ricocheted into the barriers at 119mph. The force of the impact saw his car pierce the crash barriers, ripping the car in two before it caught fire. Grosjean was alive thanks to the protection from the halo cockpit canopy, which stopped his helmet absorbing the force of the impact. However, the Frenchman found himself trapped while his Haas was engulfed in flames. He was stuck for 28 seconds, stunned and confused, before – incredibly – he managed to climb from the wreckage, squeeze through a gap in the fence and pull himself clear of the flames. He was treated for burns by the medical-car driver Alan van der Merwe and doctor Ian Roberts. The result itself was forgotten, paling into insignificance compared to the miraculous escape everybody had just witnessed.

Before the end of the season, somewhat inexplicably and unexpectedly, Honda dropped the bombshell that they would leave F1 at the end of the 2021 season. The timing was baffling – the announcement came just when they were winning again and receiving the positive uptick in reputation, after investing heavily in the project since their return to F1 in 2015, then toiling through the criticism and negativity during the McLaren years.

However, the decision was made high-up at Honda, after an assessment of their F1 operation concluded that it did not fit in with the company's plans. The sport was still heavily associated with the petrol-fuelled internal combustion engine, whereas Honda's vision was to focus on carbon-free technology. This of course put Red Bull Racing and AlphaTauri back on the hunt for a new engine supplier. It felt like they were back at square one all over again. The frosty relationship with Wolff – and with Lauda sadly having passed – meant Mercedes' engines were not an option. The Renault relationship was also toast, leaving only Ferrari as a viable option. The Italian team supplied Alfa Romeo and Haas but their power unit was proving uncompetitive. Horner had his work cut out trying to find a new supplier, while also assuring Verstappen and his advisors that all was in hand.

Shortly before Christmas, there was another surprising piece of news to digest when Red Bull Racing confirmed the signing of Sergio Pérez, in a move that would see Albon demoted to test and reserve driver for both Red Bull and AlphaTauri. The Mexican had finished the season strongly and ended fourth in the drivers' championship standings. He had also won the penultimate race of the season, the Sakhir Grand Prix in Bahrain, driving for Racing Point. Pérez, 30, was being let go from his old team to make way for Vettel, who was arriving from Ferrari, as Racing Point rebranded to become Aston Martin for the 2021 season.

Horner was keen to point out that Albon was still being retained by the team, but the prospect of pairing Pérez with Verstappen was too irresistible to ignore. 'Alex [Albon] is a valued member of the team and we thought long and hard about this decision,' he said. 'Having taken our time to evaluate all the relevant data and performances we have decided that Sergio is the right driver to partner Max for 2021 and look forward to welcoming him to Red Bull Racing. Alex remains an important part of our team as test and reserve driver with a key focus on 2022 development, and we would like to thank him for his hard work and contribution.' There was no doubt that Albon, 24, was progressing, but the simple truth was that he was unable to keep up with Verstappen, who had cemented his position as one of the best drivers on the grid. Sadly for Albon, despite his earlier gratitude to his team for sticking with him, it was Horner's job to make a tough call to ensure they had the best chance of future success. It was yet another round of musical chairs in the driving seats of Red Bull Racing, and a decision that would prove to be critical in the coming season.

CHAPTER 19

MAX IS WORLD CHAMPION

– 2021 –

'The pace of the Mercedes is just too strong. Max is driving his heart out there but we're going to need a miracle in these last ten laps to turn it around . . .'

Christian Horner's words from the pit wall to TV commentators, calling for divine intervention in the final throes of the Abu Dhabi Grand Prix, have since been immortalised. The whole of the 2021 season came down to the last few laps of the race around the Yas Marina Circuit. The pulsating battle between Hamilton and Verstappen had been gripping fans all season, spilling out into cross-team rivalry between Red Bull Racing and Mercedes and their respective bosses, at a level of intensity not previously experienced in modern F1. It was all captured by the Netflix cameras, but actually the final edit only scratched the surface of the drama. With a handful of laps to go, Nicholas Latifi crashed his Williams and the subsequent safety car period saw the race flipped on its head, culminating in Verstappen overtaking Hamilton in dramatic and, admittedly, controversial circumstances, to win his maiden world title.

The year ended in scenes of high drama but it had an explosive start too. Before the season had even kicked off, Horner had again touted his driver as the best on the grid. He pointed out that Hamilton's absence due to Covid from the penultimate race in 2020 had given reserve driver George Russell an opportunity to nearly win in his first race for Mercedes, proving the Silver Arrow car was superior. 'Max is the best, yes,' said Horner before a wheel had turned that season. 'Russell's performance at Mercedes confirmed that for me. Max and Lewis stand out, but while we absolutely should not be blind to all that Hamilton has achieved, he does have access to a good package at Mercedes, while Max has to get more and more out of his car. You can see that by the fact that a driver from Williams [Russell] qualified directly on the front row of the grid and almost won the race. If someone had to get into Max's car if he had coronavirus, they would never reach his level of performance.' Furthermore, Horner listed his star driver as Mercedes' key target should Hamilton decide to retire. Meanwhile, Verstappen promised to take the fight to Hamilton each weekend, while looking to form a strong partnership with Pérez, whose development would be key to Red Bull Racing's success. The fuse had been lit and in Bahrain, the first race of the season, it was time to stand well back.

Verstappen was quickest in all three practice sessions at the Bahrain International Circuit and had qualified on pole for the fourth time in his career. In the race, Verstappen was on a different pit-stop strategy to Hamilton, which set it up for a perfect finale. Hamilton would pit early for hard, durable tyres but this would mean he would have limited grip in the latter stages of the race, whereas Red Bull decided to leave Verstappen out on track longer, allowing him to have fresher tyres with more grip in the final few laps.

During the race, both drivers were warned about exceeding track limits, going wide at turn four and gaining an advantage, a rule that the stewards were now keen to enforce, despite the drivers having initially been told it would not be an offence. Both drivers were left questioning new F1 race director Masi's instructions from the race control room, as Masi had allowed the manoeuvre to go unpunished during practice. 'How is that legal? I thought we weren't allowed to do that,' asked Verstappen as his team told him Hamilton had been going wide at turn four, contradicting Masi's instructions. Hamilton, meanwhile, was on to his team saying: 'I thought there were no track limits,' as they tried to warn him about the new rules.

In the final few laps, Verstappen used the advantage of his superior tyre life to gain on Hamilton before launching his attack, but he ran wide of turn four to get the move done. He was now leading the race – but his lead was brief as he was subsequently told to relinquish the place to Hamilton as he had gone off track. He had one final attempt in a desperate bid to pass, but his tyres were shot and Hamilton clung on to take the win. In the fallout, Wolff said, 'At the end, the racing gods were on our side' – an ironic choice of words given what was to happen in Abu Dhabi – while Horner pointed out the inconsistency of changing track limits rules mid-race, saying it 'shouldn't be shaded grey', and calling for clear decision-making from the FIA stewards. As for Hamilton, he summed up his fight with Verstappen for the win perfectly. Having largely been untroubled since Rosberg's retirement, he said: 'Twenty-two more races this season?! Holy crap. I'll be grey by the end of it.'

The scores were reversed in the second race of the season in Imola, Italy, where Hamilton had entered the weekend being quizzed about his toughest rival on track, which he credited as Vettel. He did, however, point out that Verstappen 'doesn't have the background that Seb has but he obviously has a chance of being a future champion and whether that is now or later depends on the job that I do'. The media interpreted that as a snub for Verstappen, but the reality, at this stage of the pair's careers, was that Hamilton had not had much competition from Verstappen until now. Hamilton took pole ahead of Pérez and Verstappen. But the Dutchman made the much better start while Hamilton faltered and crashed, resulting in him mounting a late recovery for second while Verstappen took the 12th win of his career.

Hamilton would win in Portugal while Verstappen was second as they traded positions in all three of the opening races. Heading into the Spanish GP, which was won by Hamilton with Verstappen again second, the Mercedes driver summed up their relationship, insisting they would keep their fighting clean. 'The pressure is immense between us all and there's a huge amount of respect. Max has been pulling absolutely everything out of the Red Bull and giving us a great run for our money, so it's going to be like this for the rest of the season – and exciting. It is very, very hard but fair and that's what makes great racing. We will continue to keep it clean and keep it on the edge.' However, by the Monaco Grand Prix, tensions were upped a notch when Mercedes started questioning the legality of Red Bull Racing's car design. Wolff's suspicions had been aroused when Hamilton reported an unusual amount of flex shown by the rear wing of Verstappen's car when travelling behind him in Barcelona. F1's rules stipulate that a car's bodywork cannot move beyond certain parameters based on aerodynamic force. Wolff's threat to protest annoyed Red Bull Racing, who maintained they had nothing to hide at the showpiece race – which, incidentally, was won by Verstappen.

The needling between the two teams continued to play out in the media, while the results on track were extremely close. Ahead of the Azerbaijan GP, Verstappen said he couldn't be bothered to play 'mind games' with Hamilton, preferring to 'do his talking on the track'. Hamilton snapped back and accused Verstappen of 'feeling that he has a lot to prove', as the championship battle heated up.

The race itself was remembered for a dangerous tyre blowout for Verstappen, which snapped his car into a wall at over 200mph. In the aftermath, tyre suppliers Pirelli said the blow-out was caused by a 'circumferential break on the inner sidewall' but added that 'the prescribed starting parameters (minimum pressure and maximum blanket temperature) had been followed'. That said, a new set of protocols were introduced at the next race in France. However, it drew a cryptic response from Hamilton. 'Whenever there's a failure, they [the FIA] put the pressures up [in the form of stipulation in the regulations], so that tells you something,' he said, without explicitly revealing his feelings and stopping short of saying what he felt had gone wrong. 'We didn't have a problem. Pirelli have done a great job with tyres.'

Verstappen won again in France, causing Hamilton to start questioning the updated Honda engine. He made remarks about the 'straight-line speed' but Wolff had seen nothing to suggest foul play.

It prompted an amusing remark from Horner ahead of the Austrian GP: 'I think Toto has answered it very well and maybe he should explain it to his driver. I listen with interest sometimes to the theories Lewis has, which are some way from reality.' Hamilton's inquisitiveness could be forgiven. He was seeking some solace after Verstappen consolidated a three-race winning run that had left him trailing by 32 points after the Austrian GP. Tensions were then taken to a new level at the British Grand Prix at Silverstone, a race that would change the course of the season.

An explosive first-lap collision between the championship leaders resulted in Verstappen being flown to hospital for medical checks. If there were any lingering doubts about the ferociousness of the rivalry between the two, they were now dispelled. In the previous races, it had been Hamilton who had yielded to Verstappen. But in his home race, cheered on by a capacity crowd for the first time since the pandemic, Hamilton was not going to back out of a duel with the Dutchman. Verstappen was leading as Hamilton pulled out of his slipstream to try to overtake the Red Bull and the two collided at the 180mph Copse corner. Hamilton's Mercedes made contact with the rear of Verstappen's car, stripping the tyre from the rim of the rear-right wheel, sending him sliding sideways into the tyre barrier in a huge impact. Hamilton's ambitious move was punished by the stewards, who served him with a ten-second penalty for causing the accident, but he still managed to win the race before celebrating on the pit wall with the thousands of fans who had climbed onto the track after the race.

Horner, and later Verstappen too, took umbrage with Hamilton's celebrations, claiming it was 'disrespectful' and 'unsportsman-like' given that neither he, nor Mercedes, knew the severity of

Verstappen's condition as he was in hospital. In the post-race media interviews, Horner labelled Hamilton's victory as 'hollow' after the 51g accident. 'What I'm most angry about is the lack of judgement, or the misjudgement and desperation. Thankfully we got away with it today but had that been any worse, a ten-second penalty would have looked pretty meaningless.' Marko added that Hamilton's 'reckless behaviour should be punished with a suspension'.

Of course, there was also the view from the other side, with Wolff saying, 'It always takes two to tango.' He added: 'It was hard racing, and hard racing sometimes, if none of them gives in, ends in collisions.'

Horner is still agitated by the result at Silverstone when we discuss it some two years later. 'An air of desperation had set in from Mercedes. Max was 32 points ahead in the championship and I think Lewis knew that if he didn't stop the rot, then it was going to be too big a gap and I think that's why he was overzealous into the corner. It was a massive accident; we had a driver who had been injured and airlifted to hospital, and Lewis and Mercedes were jumping up and down and crowd-surfing. I just found it disrespectful to a competitor.'

At the following race in Hungary, there was more drama as Verstappen limped home in ninth place after Mercedes' Bottas made a mistake on the opening lap. He misjudged his braking point and clattered into Verstappen, ripping the Red Bull car apart. The resulting accident also took Pérez out of the race.

Then, at the rain-lashed Belgian Grand Prix held on on 29 August, the race was prematurely ended during the third lap due to a heavy downpour. Both laps one and two took place behind the safety car, so there was no overtaking and Verstappen, who started on pole, was rewarded with a win ahead of Russell and Hamilton, who had started in second and third place respectively. Masi's controversial decision not to start the race earlier was a bone of contention, for there were breaks in the weather. His reluctance to race, combined with a failure to clear the standing water on the surface, meant that, in accordance with the sporting regulations, the final result was taken from the end of lap one, with half points given to drivers who finished in the top 10 positions as less than 75 per cent of the 44-lap race distance had been completed. It resulted in Verstappen taking 12.5 points while Hamilton scored just 7.5 – a deficit that would prove crucial at the season finale.

And at the Italian Grand Prix in September, there was yet *another* huge impact that would drive a further wedge between Verstappen and Hamilton. The flashpoint happened on lap 26 after both drivers had suffered slow pit stops, putting them on a collision course with each other. Hamilton and Verstappen were side by side going into turn one at Monza. There was no room for Verstappen, who, like Hamilton at Silverstone, refused to surrender his position. The two banged wheels and Verstappen was launched off the kerb and landed his Red Bull car on top of Hamilton's Mercedes. The grandstands erupted, as too did the press room. Compared to this, the contact at Silverstone had been inconsequential: this was more akin to the famous Ayrton Senna and Alain Prost collision at the Japanese GP in 1989. (That crash forced Prost to retire, allowing Senna to take the chequered flag. However, he was immediately disqualified for missing the chicane after the incident. Despite appealing the decision, he was given a suspended six-month ban for causing the collision.)

Verstappen climbed from his cockpit and walked away while Hamilton tried in vain to put his car into reverse so that he could make his way back onto the track. Both were summoned to the stewards, where Verstappen would be the one who was predominantly held at fault for causing the accident and slapped with a three-place grid penalty for the following race in Russia. Hamilton had claimed that Verstappen 'knew he was going over the kerb, but he still did it' while Wolff labelled Verstappen's actions a 'tactical foul'. Hamilton later hailed the halo cockpit device for protecting him from Verstappen's car, saying, 'I feel very, very fortunate today. Thank God for the halo. That did ultimately save me. I've never been hit on the head by a car before, and it's quite a shock for me.'

Verstappen countered that Hamilton left him no room to manoeuvre his car. 'If he'd left me just a car width we would have raced out of turn two anyway,' he said, 'and I think he would have probably still been in front. But he just kept on pushing me wider until there was nowhere to go.' Brawn provided a wry note: 'I hope the championship is won on the track – not in the barriers or the stewards' room.'

Hamilton won in Russia, where Verstappen was quizzed about his relationship with his rival, who had previously been explaining what it was like fighting for your first F1 title and how the pressure builds. Verstappen's response was somewhat surly: 'Yeah, I'm so nervous I can barely sleep. It's so horrible to fight for a title. I really hate it. Those comments just show he really doesn't know me. Which is fine. I also don't need to know him.'

Verstappen then won the next two races in Austin and Mexico City, as the pair traded blows like heavyweight boxers. There was also some enjoyable verbal sparring off track between Horner and Wolff. Wolff had suggested the Red Bull chief was like a 'protagonist' in a pantomime, to which Horner had replied: 'Toto likes to throw in a comment here or there. I am fine with that. It is pantomime season coming up anyway. I was quite flattered, actually, to be called the protagonist. You also need an antagonist to have a protagonist and one could say that Toto fills that role pretty well if it were a pantomime. Maybe the pantomime dame role might suit him.'

At the Brazilian GP, Hamilton was called to the stewards, who wanted to inspect the rear wing of his Mercedes, which they suspected of breaching the rules. The part was later removed from his car and he was prevented from qualifying and forced to start from the back of the grid in the sprint qualifying race that F1 had been trialling. F1 had decided to spice up the programme for F1 weekends by introducing shorter 30-minute races, offering points for the top eight finishers, with eight points going to the first-placed driver, down to one point for the finisher in eighth place. The concept would give spectators more racing action to view. However, like Sunday's traditional Grand Prix races, drivers still needed to qualify for the sprint race itself, using the traditional format of three qualifying sessions with five cars eliminated in Q1, five in Q2, before a top-ten shootout for first place in Q3. The controversy did not end there as Verstappen was fined €50,000 for touching and examining the rear wing on Hamilton's car, a breach of the *parc fermé* rules that say F1 cars must not be touched once a driver has exited the car after the race, pending scrutiny by officials.

At the Qatar Grand Prix, it was Horner's turn to be in trouble with the stewards. Horner felt aggrieved that a marshal had incorrectly waved a yellow warning flag, ordering drivers to slow down. Verstappen had missed it, meaning he was subsequently dealt a five-place grid penalty. Horner was unimpressed by the decision to penalise his driver and said: 'I think it's just a rogue marshal that's stuck a flag out and he's not been instructed to by the FIA.' The comment to Sky F1 earned the Red Bull Racing boss a warning from the governing body.

The two drivers clashed on track for a third time at the Saudi Arabian Grand Prix, the penultimate race of the season. The flashpoint occurred when Hamilton, who won the race, accused Verstappen of brake-testing him. Hamilton was attempting to overtake Verstappen for the lead on lap 37, but the Dutch driver suddenly braked hard, causing Hamilton to run into the back of his Red Bull at high speed. He subsequently slammed Verstappen over his team's radio, shouting, 'Fucking crazy! It was just dangerous driving.' Hamilton later declared: 'The rules haven't been clear from the stewards . . . I know I can't overtake someone off track and [that I therefore have to] keep the position. That's well known between all us drivers. But that doesn't apply to one of us. He is over the limit, for sure.' Hamilton clearly felt Verstappen had acted dangerously, adding: 'I have avoided collisions on so many occasions with the guy. But you live to fight another day, which I did.'

Verstappen drew a line under the incident, saying, 'A lot of things happened that I don't agree with but I don't think we need to talk about it. He had the run and I braked late and I got a little bit offline. We both missed the corner and it's not fair that I got a penalty.'

All these theatrics had not gone unnoticed in the paddock. The 1997 F1 champion Jacques Villeneuve accused the championship fight of turning into a 'Hollywood show' – in other words, he wanted it to be a straight battle on track and not over-dramatic like a film. 'I just hope we have a nice clean race in Abu Dhabi,' he said. 'And may the best man win – and not anything Hollywood. We already got our Hollywood hits this year.' How ironic given what was to come.

Somewhat incredibly, Verstappen and Hamilton arrived at the final race of the season in Abu Dhabi level-pegging on points. The previous three races in Qatar, São Paulo and Saudi Arabia had provided the stages for an astonishing fightback from Hamilton, who had won all three, with Verstappen finishing second each time. Now it was a straight shootout: whoever finished higher in the final race would win the title. Despite Villeneuve's protests, this set-up was about as Hollywood as it gets.

In the build-up to Abu Dhabi, the news agenda was focused on whether the two drivers would keep their racing clean, after having clashed so many times on track that season. The spotlight was also on the FIA stewards, and whether they would be reminding the two title contenders beforehand about their responsibilities as F1 drivers to set an example to racers in the lower categories. Drivers always meet with the stewards before each F1 weekend, normally on the Friday night, and this time the focus was very much on Masi's handling of the simmering relationship between Hamilton and Verstappen and whether he would remind them to keep it clean.

Meanwhile, the trash talk continued. When asked if his opinion of Hamilton and Mercedes had changed over the course of their battle, Verstappen was blunt in the press conference, saying, 'Yes, very much so. And not in a positive way.' As the tension mounted ahead of the race, the press room and the paddock were filled with a sense of foreboding that the outcome of the championship, after some brilliant and thrilling racing, would end in controversy.

Verstappen qualified on pole and Hamilton lined up on the grid in second place, but the Brit quickly overtook the Red Bull driver at the start. Verstappen battled back and by the sixth corner was vying for first place when Hamilton ran wide of turn seven, rather than take the corner within the lines. Hamilton claimed that he was forced wide and rejoined the track some 10 metres further up. Red Bull Racing's pit wall made it clear to the stewards in race control that they felt Hamilton should have been made to give the place back to Verstappen, but the appeal failed, allowing Hamilton to keep hold of first place.

During Verstappen and Hamilton's first pit stops, Pérez stayed on track and took the lead, doing a tremendous defensive job of slowing Hamilton down. Despite having fresher tyres, the Mercedes man could not find a way around the Mexican, allowing Verstappen to slice Hamilton's lead from 11 seconds to just under 1.5 seconds. Then, on lap 53, the race was turned on its head when backmarker Nicholas Latifi crashed his Williams into the barriers after making a mistake. Now, it seemed, the slightest error of judgement from the Canadian had plunged the outcome of the whole season into jeopardy. The journalists were on the edge of their seats in anticipation as to what would happen. Would the race be stopped? Would this epic season now finish behind the safety car? What an anti-climax after such a brilliant battle! The excitement was huge and, from a personal perspective, all I could think of was the eight-page pull-out I had produced for the *Sun*, which was being printed in anticipation of Hamilton winning a record eighth world title. In the event, the drama was to continue in ways none of us could have predicted. The fallout went as follows:

Lap 54: The stewards deployed the safety car and Red Bull Racing seized the opportunity to pit Verstappen for fresh tyres. Mercedes were caught in the confusion and decided to keep Hamilton out on old tyres. 'That's unbelievable, man,' Hamilton said over his team radio, knowing he had lost the tyre advantage.

Lap 55: The attention then turned to Masi's handling of the clear-up operation to remove Latifi's car. As the laps ticked down, the high-drama season looked to be ending behind a safety car. The pressure started to build on Masi from both Mercedes and Red Bull Racing at the pit wall. The first message received from race control was that all the lapped cars would not be allowed to overtake the safety car. It would take too long for each car to pass the leaders and get to the back of the pack while the remaining laps behind the safety car ticked down. Put simply, by the time all the lapped cars were in position again, the race distance would have been reached and the race would have finished behind the safety car.

Lap 56: Horner questioned Masi about the five lapped cars between leader Hamilton and second-placed Verstappen. Horner made it clear that he felt the five lapped cars that had not stopped for fresh tyres, unlike Verstappen, should be allowed to overtake Hamilton and join the back of the pack to form the correct running order. The Red Bull Racing team manager director Jonathan Wheatley also had a discussion with Masi where he emphasised the point Horner had made. Wheatley said he urged the race director to tell them to pass Hamilton and the safety car and join the rest of the field, to which Masi, sounding panicked, replied: 'Understood, just give me a second.' Wheatley then added: '. . . And then we've got a motor race on our hands.'

Lap 57: Masi decided to rule that only the five cars that were in between the duo were now allowed to un-lap themselves and overtake both Hamilton and the safety car, effectively moving out of the way. In doing so, it made it a straight fight between Verstappen and Hamilton for the title, a one-lap shootout – only the Red Bull driver had a fresh set of tyres, which was a huge advantage. Wolff was exasperated and radioed Masi, saying: 'Michael . . . Michael, this isn't right. Michael, that is so not right. That is so not right.' The safety car was called in at the end of lap 57.

Lap 58: With the safety car called in, the race resumed for one single remaining lap. The whole outcome of the season had been boiled down to this one, final lap in the last race of the year. The tension at the track was unbelievable. Horner was glued to the screen in the pit wall, gripped with tension as he watched Verstappen make his move on Hamilton at turn five. The Mercedes man put up a defence but had no answer to Verstappen's superior grip. The Dutchman powered past and, despite a late challenge from Hamilton at turn nine, Verstappen crossed the line in first place, winning the title, screaming down the team's radio in disbelief. The Red Bull Racing garage erupted with celebrations, and Horner's emotion came pouring out over the radio as he congratulated his driver.

Red Bull Racing's jubilation was in stark contrast to the anger erupting in the Mercedes garage. Wolff clearly felt that the result was unfair. He was upset by Masi's intervention to remove those five cars that would have acted as a buffer between Verstappen and his driver. His team had been caught out by their strategy to not pit Hamilton earlier, but there was an inevitable question mark over Masi's response given the radio exchange he had had with the Red Bull pit wall.

Should Masi have allowed the five cars to unlap themselves? What about the other cars that had been lapped? Despite not being in the way of the two main protagonists, should they too have not been subject to the same rules? If all lapped cars were told to unlap themselves, by the time it would have taken them all to move out of the way there would not have been enough laps left to restart the race and Hamilton would have been crowned champion. Wolff called on Masi to roll back the result to the previous lap in a desperate attempt to see his driver crowned world champion. 'Michael! Michael! You have to go back a lap!' pleaded Wolff, to which Masi replied, 'Toto . . . Toto . . . this is a motor race.' It was an interesting choice of words given his previous discussion with Wheatley.

While Red Bull Racing were celebrating, Mercedes, with a barrister on hand, were already launching their appeal. Normally, team representatives such as the team manager, team principal or sporting director would attend any post-race investigation, but Mercedes had taken things up a notch with legal representation, seemingly anticipating controversy. There was a four-and-a-half-hour wait, dampening the mood considerably in the Red Bull racing camp, before the official result was announced: Verstappen was the champion, albeit still facing further legal challenge from Mercedes.

Looking back to that race now, Horner recalls the sterling work Pérez did to push Hamilton back into a battle with Verstappen, and lets slip that his world champion was driving with cramp! He says: 'I had spoken before the race of Checo [Pérez] strategically driving for a team in a way that Mark Webber didn't,' says Horner, with reference to how Webber did not help Vettel in the Brazilian GP of 2012, 'and he did it. I don't think any of us expected him to hold up Lewis in the way that he did, enabling Max to get on the back of his car, without which Mercedes would have had the chance to pit Hamilton for tyres [as Hamilton would have been so far ahead he would have had the time to do so and keep the lead] and it would have been a slam-dunk [win for Hamilton]. And then there was the Latifi shunt . . . I'd even said to Sky F1, "We're going to need something from the racing gods to turn this one around," and I didn't know I had a direct line! When Max went through, none of us expected it to happen. I don't think even Lewis expected it. Max told us afterwards he actually got cramp in his left leg and couldn't feel the brake pedal and was like, "I'm gonna send it anyway." And it took Lewis completely by surprise.'

When I ask if he had feared the title would be taken away given Mercedes' legal process, Horner replied: 'It was strange who they had in there for the hearing with the stewards. There's Adrian and myself with Jonathan, and on the other side you've got one of the top QCs in the country quoting legal terms. But they raised the protest, which they later chose not to pursue because the race director had done what he was entitled to do as the referee.'

Horner also recalls the party once the dust had settled in Abu Dhabi. 'We had a boat that had been hired for a bunch of sponsors and it was the first time the team could celebrate a win because of the Covid restrictions. I could see people in a hot tub. Max was stood in the middle of the party and couldn't even move his feet. A few days later, I got Covid. I was struck down with it and chucked into isolation for Christmas!'

Mercedes dropped their legal challenge a week after the end of the season. Verstappen was now, officially, the champion of the world.

CHAPTER 20

BACK-TO-BACK SUCCESS

– 2022 –

After the dramatic end to the previous season, the winter was a much-needed time for everyone associated with Red Bull Racing to reflect on their incredible achievement. The team had performed consistently, and both drivers had worked together to put an end to Mercedes' dominance. Masi's handling of the final race, however, was still lighting up news stories and TV debates across the world. His decision-making process was the subject of a lengthy FIA investigation. Those final few laps in Abu Dhabi had proved such a controversial end to the campaign that it had split fan bases across social media and called the sporting integrity of F1 into question.

There is a common belief that the FIA, who act as referees for the series, are the same as F1: they aren't. Put simply, Liberty Media have a licensing agreement with the FIA, who own the rights to F1. The FIA then act as the governing body for the series and are responsible for the safety and integrity of the championship. As a result of the Abu Dhabi fallout, there was intense scrutiny of

Masi, who had gone back to his native Australia in the middle of the furore and dodged media requests for interviews. The pressure was immense. Interestingly, I was in the same hotel bar as him the night before the race: he looked anxious, and I remember thinking at the time how I would not want to have the job of officiating the titanic battle between Verstappen and Hamilton. The speculation about whether Verstappen would be stripped of his title had ended with Mercedes' decision not to continue with their legal challenge. However, the controversial end to such a gripping season had undoubtedly tarnished the final result.

Horner was keen to move on and called for people to focus on the season, rather than the finale. 'Dietrich felt Max was very deserving. He was very proud of what he'd done and what the team had achieved. I think that it was such an epic year. It was probably the most competitive season in Formula One in the last 30 years, and great for Red Bull, for Max, for Honda, to come out on top,' he said in an article I published in the *Sun*. 'Yes, we got a little bit lucky with the safety car at the end of the race, but so much bad luck had gone against us throughout the season. These things, I've always said, tend to balance themselves out over the course of a season, and I think Max led more than 50 per cent of the laps in the year, more than every other driver combined. He had more pole positions, more race wins, and for me he was totally deserving.'

At the launch of the RB18, Horner revealed his concern that the intensity of the title fight in 2021 would result in his team being behind schedule for the start of the 2022 season. The parts' production line had been switched back to supporting the development of the RB17, as upgrades were hurried through to aid Verstappen in his fight for wins. It was a different scenario for a team such as Ferrari, who were not in the championship battle and could concentrate all their efforts on producing a strong car for the first race of the new season. 'We're aiming to build on what we achieved last year,' said Horner. At this point he was yet to see the car designs of his competition and how they had interpreted the new rules that had come in for 2022. He continued, 'The target is to retain the title and the big unknown is: have we missed something with the regulations and has another team stolen a march?'

Horner's concerns were compounded as the new season would see the sport usher in a sweeping set of new regulations. It was usual for the rulebook to be tweaked each year; however, this time there were major changes relating to key design aspects of the cars. The new rules – or, if we are being more precise, the new 'aerodynamic philosophy' – had been brought in with the aim of improving the spectacle of F1, by creating more chances for drivers to overtake. A conventional F1 car uses downforce created by air running over the bodywork that presses the car downwards and closer to the ground, enabling drivers to take the corners quicker. A by-product of the downforce is that the huge rear wings cause turbulence in the car's wake, which in turn makes it difficult for another driver to follow closely behind, as the dirty air causes the pursuing car to buffet about. I often think the best way to visualise this is to think of the blast of air behind a large aircraft when it takes off, or even the waves in the sea in the wake of a powerful vessel. The new philosophy from the 2022 season was to use the underside of the car to create the downforce which sucks the car to the ground. The air is then expelled upwards from the rear wing, forming a mushroom cloud above the car. Thanks to this new design, all the turbulent air is no longer put out behind the car and into the path of the car following behind. The theory behind the move was that the pursuing car would be able to follow much more closely and have more of an opportunity to overtake now the air was smoother.

The regulations had been worked on for a number of seasons but the implementation had been delayed due to the financial concerns and limitations caused by the Covid-19 pandemic. The smaller teams on the grid were concerned that the lack of racing and subsequent sponsorship could see them struggle to remain in operation, let alone develop new car parts. Now they were coming into force at a time when F1 was also introducing new rules on the teams' spending. The larger teams were spending in excess of $300 million per season, while those at the back would spend considerably less, creating an unfair advantage. A budget cap, or cost cap as it was also known, had been stipulated from the 2021 season onwards, and had been set at $140 million for 2022. Each component that was designed, manufactured and tested would come out of the spending pot, creating a difficult balancing act for the teams.

One welcome addition for Red Bull Racing in 2022 was the new lucrative title sponsorship with Oracle, which would see the American computer technology company add their name to the team. The additional funding would allow the team to continue to develop their factory, primarily the Red Bull Powertrains side of the business with support from Honda, as they looked to produce their own engines. The turbulent time with Renault engines and subsequent difficulty in finding a suitable replacement had had a lasting impact on the team. To prevent such a repeat, Red Bull Racing had invested heavily in building a facility on their campus in Milton Keynes to produce their own power units. It would mean the team could produce the chassis and power unit at the same location, allowing for swifter decision-making and a better synergy between the two components that make up an F1 car.

The new investment would also be spent on driver wages, one of the crucial aspects missing from the cost cap. Verstappen, of course, was already under contract but his maiden title had seen him rewarded with a bumper new payday and, more importantly for Red Bull Racing, a contract that would run until 2028, offering them continuity. The deal, with a reported wage of between £40 million and £50 million a year, was heralded by the media as the largest driver contract in the sport's history. The 24-year-old was quoted in the official press release to accompany the news on 2 March, saying: 'I really enjoy being part of the Oracle Red Bull Racing team, so choosing to stay to the 2028 season was an easy decision. I love this team and last year was simply incredible. Our goal since we came together in 2016 was to win the championship and we have done that, so now it's about keeping the number one on the car long-term.' In the same release, Horner said the new long-term deal showed the team's commitment to Verstappen as they entered the new season. 'To have Max signed with Oracle Red Bull Racing through to the end of 2028 is a real statement of intent,' he said. 'Our immediate focus is on retaining Max's world championship title, but this deal also shows he is a part of the team's long-term planning. With the Red Bull Powertrains division working towards the new engine regulations for 2026, we wanted to make sure we had the best driver on the grid secured for that car.'

Ahead of the season-opener in Bahrain, the FIA published the eagerly awaited findings of their investigation into Masi's handling of the Abu Dhabi Grand Prix. The FIA report focused on the handling of the final few laps of the race, citing how only five cars were able to unlap themselves under the safety car, and not all the unlapped cars as per the regulations, admitting there had been a mistake without mentioning any names. The report said: 'The process of identifying lapped cars has up until now been a manual one and human error led to the fact that not all cars were allowed to unlap themselves.' It stopped considerably short of providing any real details that weren't already known, but it did stipulate a change of leadership.

Masi lost his job as the F1 race director and was replaced by former DTM race director Niels Wittich and World Endurance Championship race director Eduardo Freitas, with the duo alternating between races. Nobody was surprised to see Masi removed from his role; the fallout from the 2021 Abu Dhabi Grand Prix had been so controversial that it would have been difficult for him to return to the position. However, it is worth noting that Masi was indeed exonerated from blame: 'The report finds that the race director was acting in good faith and to the best of his knowledge given the difficult circumstances, particularly acknowledging the significant time constraints for decisions to be made and the immense pressure being applied by the teams.' Later in the season, Freitas was also stood down and Wittich placed solely in charge, in a bid to ensure consistent decision-making, rather than factoring in two different opinions.

In the Bahrain Grand Prix itself, Horner's premonition that other teams would be quicker out of the blocks came true as Ferrari's

Charles Leclerc took pole position and converted it to victory, ahead of his teammate Carlos Sainz. Meanwhile, both Red Bull drivers were forced to retire. Verstappen and Pérez had been running in second and fourth place respectively until their cars developed a fuel pump issue, and they suffered a double retirement for the first time since the 2020 Austrian Grand Prix. 'It looked like there was no fuel coming to the engine and everything just turned off,' said Verstappen afterwards as his title defence got off to the worst possible start with no points.

A missile attack on a nearby fuel depot caused panic and subsequent safety fears at the following race in Saudi Arabia at the end of March. Plumes of black smoke could be seen in the distance from the track. Yemen's Houthi movement allegedly claimed responsibility for the attack, which happened during first practice. The F1 drivers held an emergency meeting with F1 chiefs and the organisers, who tried to reassure them they were safe from harm. The Grand Prix Drivers' Association, the body which represents the drivers, held a further meeting that ran long into the night as they weighed up whether they would race or not. Eventually, they agreed to go ahead, but it was a rare moment of solidarity between the drivers and sparked a wider debate about safety.

And the race itself? In qualifying, Pérez took pole position while Verstappen qualified in fourth behind both Ferraris, as the Italian team continued to look strong in the early stages of the season. But a late resurgence from Verstappen saw him overtake Leclerc for the victory, after the two traded first place on a number of occasions. Despite starting on pole, Pérez finished fourth behind both Ferraris.

Verstappen was then dealt another setback in the Australian Grand Prix when he was forced to retire again with a fuel problem, this time a leak. He had been running in second place behind Leclerc, who would win the race from pole position, while Pérez was second. Verstappen was pragmatic in his post-race media session, saying: 'We'll try to forget today. It doesn't look like there's a quick fix, so we need to work hard. I'll talk to the team when I'm back home.' Red Bull Racing responded by flying the broken engine to Japan where it would undergo a forensic examination by Honda to identify why it had failed.

Verstappen and Red Bull Racing's luck changed considerably over the next few races with wins for the Dutchman in Imola for the Emilia Romagna Grand Prix, the Miami Grand Prix and the Spanish Grand Prix, moving him into the lead in the drivers' championship ahead of Leclerc. This created an interesting dynamic, given Verstappen and Leclerc had raced each other since they were kids and there was a mutual respect between the two. Mercedes had come into the season with a car that was not competitive and they were plagued by poor performance – which was totally unexpected given how strongly they had finished the previous season – so it was shaping up to be a battle with Ferrari for wins.

Ahead of the race in Miami, Horner said: 'Last year there was a lot of needle, a lot going on off track as well as on track, whereas this year seems much more focused on what's going on on track. And I think the racing has been great between Charles and Max. The first four races have been epic. Inevitably it will boil over at some point as it gets more competitive and the stakes get higher in the second half of the year. But certainly what we've seen so far has been very respectful racing – hard racing but fair racing.'

In Monaco, it was Pérez who was victorious while Verstappen was third. The Mexican was rewarded with a new contract in the days following his win, which had moved him within 15 points of his teammate in the championship. Pérez was proving to be a solid foil for the Dutchman, outscoring his previous teammates – Sainz, Kvyat, Ricciardo, Gasly and Albon – and the media were homing in on whether he would be in a position to challenge Verstappen for the title. Horner was adamant that the two would not come to blows in the same way Webber and Vettel had done when they had fought for the same honour. 'You can see there's a great respect,' he said ahead of the Azerbaijan GP. 'There's a friendship between the two and they work very well together as a pairing. They work as a team. I think the dynamic in the team is as good as it has ever been.'

The question whether Pérez could be a contender was promptly answered by Verstappen, who won the next two races in Azerbaijan and Canada, the latter the scene of an extraordinary row between Wolff and Horner. There had been a rumour of a flare-up between the two but what was actually said only came to light after the Netflix series was released the following year, as the TV cameras had been given special access to the usually off-limits team principals' meeting. It was clear that Wolff was unhappy with Mercedes' problems and wanted the regulations changed to suit his team's difficulties with porpoising – that is, when a car bounces aggressively on its suspension as it races. This problem had been created by the new aerodynamic rules that had been brought in and it seems Mercedes had particularly struggled to adapt their car to prevent the issue. A change to the rules would not only benefit Wolff's team but would also negate Red Bull Racing's advantage, as their car was suffering far less than their rivals' when it came to porpoising. Horner reacted with a very matter-of-fact: 'If you've got a problem, change your fucking car!' It prompted an exasperated Wolff to declare that Pérez, too, had reported problems with his car, adding he had evidence 'printed out', with his open hand almost symbolising the piece of paper he was referencing. It was an amusing exchange between the two, and the other team bosses in the room chuckled in the background. As for the race in Montreal, the RB18 took its third pole of the season with Verstappen out-qualifying second-placed Alonso in a rain-hit session. In the race, Verstappen would take a win from Sainz while Pérez retired on the ninth lap with a gearbox problem.

The following month at Silverstone, Verstappen was leading the British Grand Prix until he struck a piece of debris on track and was forced to make a pit stop, which dropped him out of the lead. A later inspection revealed that the piece of carbon from another car had also damaged the underside of his car, causing it to lose downforce and impact his performance, so that he came home in seventh place, while Pérez was second. In Austria, Verstappen battled Leclerc for the win but had to settle for second, while Pérez retired. So far this season, then, it was fair to say the results were mostly in Verstappen's favour but things were not always going his way. But what happened at the next race in France signalled the start of a phenomenal run from Verstappen that would dictate the course of the championship.

Red Bull Racing's decision to use a low-downforce set-up, maximising top speed, allowed the Dutchman to head to a comfortable win. While there are rules pertaining to the overall car design, teams are able to operate within specific margins, which allows them to make changes to their cars to suit particular tracks. In this instance, Red Bull Racing opted for a smaller-than-usual rear wing that meant their car had less downforce and less drag, which equated to a higher top speed. Nearest challengers Ferrari had gone for the opposite option, a high-downforce car design that allowed them to take the corners faster – but the Red Bull Racing cars would power past them on the straights. That said, Leclerc had taken pole ahead of Verstappen and Pérez, but the race pace of the RB18 was vastly superior and the low-downforce option proved to be a smart tactical decision from Red Bull Racing. Verstappen was also aided by a crash for Leclerc on lap 17, bringing out the safety car. At the restart, he powered away from the rest of the field to take the chequered flag from Hamilton, who was ten seconds behind in second place while Pérez was fourth.

After another win in Hungary at the end of July, there was no doubt about the potent combination of Verstappen plus a Red Bull Racing F1 car, but few expected to see him win the Belgian GP in August. At this race, the team chose to add new unscheduled engine components to his car. The rationale for this was in part due to the failures Verstappen had experienced at the start of the season with those two retirements in Bahrain and Australia. Honda and Red Bull Powertrains had been working hard on refining and improving their designs to increase power and improve reliability. But taking a new power unit and gearbox in the Belgium GP meant that Verstappen accumulated hefty grid-penalty points – introduced as a way to reduce costs by forcing teams to make reliable parts that could be reused, rather than build new engines for each race. Once the penalties were tallied up, he would be starting the race in 14th place on the grid, despite qualifying on pole. Even though the new parts in his car would bring a performance gain, it would take a superhuman effort to pass all those cars.

He delivered it – moving up to eighth place on the opening lap alone. He passed Albon, then Ricciardo. Vettel was next, on the sixth lap. He overtook Alonso on lap seven. He took the outright lead on lap 18 when he passed Sainz, while Pérez also passed the Ferrari man to move into second place. Verstappen crossed the line in P1 nearly 18 seconds ahead of his teammate, giving Red Bull Racing the unlikeliest of one-two finishes. Verstappen then added wins in his home GP in Holland and in Monza to make it five consecutive victories on his way to glory.

Verstappen's title celebrations got off to a faltering start at the Japanese Grand Prix. The previous year he'd had to wait to discover if he would hold on to his title pending the Mercedes appeal. This time, there was uncertainty during a confusing exchange with TV interviewer and former racing driver Johnny Herbert. Verstappen was told he'd won the title by virtue of a five-second time penalty for Leclerc, which demoted the Ferrari man to third place. He asked: 'Are you sure?' – seemingly not trusting the news – before the FIA confirmed it some four minutes later. Looking somewhat awkward, Verstappen was perched on a flashy red throne, draped with fake sheepskin. It was a tacky moment to celebrate the achievement that had come as no surprise given his spectacular run of form. He'd won the Japanese GP by a whopping 27 seconds from Pérez in a race that had been time-limited to 28 laps due to a two-hour rain delay. It was a fitting performance with which to clinch the title with some four races to go.

'It's crazy, very mixed emotions,' he said in the post-race press conference. 'During the race, I had no clue what they were going to decide with the points. So, of course, the main target was to win the race. Once I crossed the line, I was like, "OK, that was an amazing race with good points again, but not world champion yet." Then I did my interview after and my mechanics started to cheer and I was like, "What's going on?" Then I realised Pérez was second instead of Charles – but still I didn't know if it was full points, half points or whatever. But then the FIA came to me and said I was the world champion.'

The confusion stemmed from a change to the rules regarding reduced points for races that do not go the full distance. Because the race was cut short in Suzuka, the assumption was that Verstappen would get 19 points for his win – not the full 25 – with Pérez getting 14 for second place and Leclerc 12. Article 6.5 says: 'If a race is suspended and cannot be resumed, points for each title will be awarded.' However, because the race did resume after the rain, the reduced-point rule did not apply and Verstappen was the champion. Horner admitted they were confused as Wheatley thumbed through the rulebook: 'We thought we would be one point short, so to win the title is beyond our wildest dreams. Max has been dominant from the first race of the season. The team also raised it to a new level.'

A week later, Red Bull Racing were brought crashing back down to earth with a telephone call confirming they had breached F1's budget cap. They protested their innocence, but the FIA found them guilty of overspending by £1.8 million, of which £1.4 million was due to an overpayment of tax, meaning the team had crept over the limit by just £432,652. Horner was understandably upset. The punishment was a £6 million fine and a 10 per cent reduction in aerodynamic research for the next 12 months, which would limit their development of the RB19. Horner took the news badly: 'We've been given a significant penalty, both financially and sportingly – £6 million is an enormous amount of money – and the draconian sporting penalty is a 10 per cent reduction in our ability to utilise our wind tunnel and aerodynamic tools. I've heard people say that is an insignificant amount, but it is an enormous amount. For some of them, it will never be enough, even if you burned down our wind tunnel!'

It was also worth noting the FIA's statement, which confirmed: 'There's no evidence Red Bull sought to act in bad faith, dishonestly or in a fraudulent manner, nor has it wilfully concealed any information.'

Horner added: 'We make no apology for the way we acted and take it on the chin. There are lessons to be learned and we accept some mistakes were made on our side. But there was no intent, nothing dishonest and certainly no cheating, which has been alleged in certain corners. We have taken a public pounding through accusations from other teams. Our drivers have been booed and it's time now to stop and move on.'

Further bad news followed when the team was plunged into mourning on the eve of the United States Grand Prix in Austin, with the devastating news that Mateschitz had died at the age of 78. There had been speculation about his health and then the news broke in the paddock on the Saturday. 'It's very, very sad; what a great man,' said Horner. 'What he achieved and what he has done, for so many people around the world in different sports, is second to none. So many of us have so much to be grateful to him for, the opportunities he provided and the vision that he had, the strength of character and never being afraid to chase your dreams. That's what he did here in Formula One, proving that you can make a difference.' Horner confirmed that Mateschitz had got to see Verstappen win his second world title two weeks earlier following his win in Japan. The team were incredibly sombre and wore jeans as a mark of respect to Mateschitz – he always dressed in jeans and was not one for suit trousers.

Ahead of the Abu Dhabi Grand Prix, which he would go on to win, I caught up with Verstappen to ask about his record-breaking season. He was in a bullish mood. He'd been blasted on social media and by some TV reporters, who had struggled to get over the controversial end to the 2021 season. It had clearly grated on him and he got it off his chest in an article we ran in the *Sun*:

'I feel like people seem to struggle with what I'm achieving. So last year, it was "rigged". It was "stolen". Well, if you look over the whole season, because it's not a one-race championship, I think I did pretty well. This year, [his critics say] it's all about the car. And then the budget-cap stories. It's not going to change my life but it's a shame because I'm here to race. I'm a real racer. I'm not here for the bullshit.

If I said, "I don't care if I'm liked or not," people would say, "What an arrogant prick." When I grew up, racing was not about being liked. It was about winning. That's all I honestly care about. Somehow, being honest and straightforward and saying what I think ends up with me being not liked. But I find it better being like that than to be two-faced, nice to the media or fans and then being different in the background. The Max you see here is the same as at home. When I go out with my friends and family and we go bowling, I don't like losing – I accept I am bad at it, but I am competitive.'

If there was anyone left in the paddock who hadn't got the memo about Verstappen's competitiveness by now, the next season was about to underline the message even further.

CHAPTER 21

TOTAL DOMINATION

– 2023 –

Despite having lived through and reported on every race, it is surprisingly difficult for me to put into words the magnitude of Red Bull Racing's success in the 2023 season. Verstappen won his third world championship at Qatar in the sprint race – F1 had rolled these sprint races out to six venues in 2023, with the top eight riders still earning extra points before the full Grand Prix the following day. In winning the title on the Saturday, Verstappen had done so some six races before the end of the season, while the team had already achieved their sixth constructors' title at the previous race in Japan.

Of course, there have been dominant spells in F1 before: McLaren in 1988, when they won 15 of the 16 races that season, and Mercedes in 2016, when they won 19 of the 21 races. However, what the RB19 achieved is something else altogether. As I write this final chapter, three days after returning from the season finale in Abu Dhabi, I find the statistics mind-boggling and I admit how frequently

I had overlooked them while managing the workload of covering the sport from week to week.

The RB19 scored a total of 860 points over the year, beating the previous record of 765 set by Mercedes in 2016. It scored 21 wins out of 22, plus won five out of six sprint races – the highest winning percentage in a season. Red Bull Racing also became the first team to win over 20 races in a season and set a new benchmark of achieving 15 consecutive wins – a run that stretched from Abu Dhabi 2022 to the 2023 Italian GP. Above all, this was a long 22-race season, not like in the 1980s or 1990s where there were only 16 rounds – it would have been 23 but for the late cancellation of the Emilia Romagna Grand Prix due to flooding in the area, despite the teams having already made the journey to Italy. Those 22 races saw a triple-header across two continents – three back-to-back races on consecutive weekends in Austin Texas, Mexico City and São Paulo in Brazil: an F1 first. Plus, after only a handful of days off after taking the long flight back home to Europe from São Paulo, the season finished with yet another two races back-to-back, meaning an 11-hour flight to Las Vegas followed immediately by the Abu Dhabi Grand Prix, which involved a 17-hour-plus journey and a 12-hour swing in time zones between the two destinations. Over the final five races, which only spanned six weeks, the total distance travelled was an incredible 33,500 miles. The 2023 season was a test of human endurance, the likes of which the sport had not seen before. It is only when you contemplate both the sustained success of the team, performing week after week at the highest level without mistakes, alongside the rigours of the schedule that you can really appreciate the achievement.

Over the winter, the team had confirmed a 'long-term strategic technical partnership' with Ford to work with Red Bull Powertrains. It was a landmark moment. The engine dilemma that had plagued the team since splitting with Renault was now finally resolved. The US car giant would work with the team in the run-up to the new engine rules that are set to be introduced in 2026. Both the Red Bull Racing cars and the AlphaTauri team, known as Visa Cash App RB or VCARB from 2024 onwards, would then be powered by Ford power units. In preparation, Ford's staff would work with Red Bull Racing to develop and produce the power units that would feature increased electrical power and 100 per cent sustainable fuel. It was obviously ironic that the chosen partner was Ford, the company Red Bull had purchased the team from in the first place in 2004. However, at the time, Red Bull had no choice but to find a new power unit supplier. Despite their success with Red Bull Racing, Honda had stood firm about their plans to move away from F1 as the sport did not fit in with their core objectives. However, midway through 2023, there was a final twist in the tale when the Japanese company performed a U-turn on their decision to leave F1 and announced they will now partner with Aston Martin from 2026.

The season kicked off in Bahrain and the paddock was unanimous about one thing: Red Bull Racing would win the team's championship and Verstappen would retain his drivers' title. Pre-season testing had gone well for the team and the Dutchman had become a formidable driver. It had also become apparent that Mercedes were not quick enough, so Aston Martin and Ferrari offered the only real threat. The media were running with the narrative that Red Bull were not only favourites, but also had the potential to win every single race.

Understandably, Horner dismissed claims that his team would run away with both titles again. 'We have 23 races and we have had one test,' said Horner ahead of the Bahrain Grand Prix curtain-raiser. 'We don't know what the other teams have been doing on engine modes or fuel loads. It is impossible to say. We can only focus on ourselves and we had a good pre-season test, completing our objectives. After a double championship last year, the motivation is sky high.'

Verstappen took pole and won in Bahrain with Pérez behind him in second. The Dutchman's win was comfortable; he crossed the line nearly 40 seconds ahead of Alonso, who was third. It was a crushing victory and one that set the tone for the rest of the campaign. George Russell, who was seventh in his Mercedes, was exasperated and in his post-race media session declared, 'Red Bull have got this championship sewn up. I don't think anyone will be fighting with them this year. They should win every single race. That is my bet.' It was remarkable hearing such a confident prediction after only one race of a long season. In the following race, Verstappen suffered a driveshaft problem meaning he qualified down in 15th place. He recovered to finish second behind Pérez, but it silenced talk that he would win the lot.

Verstappen did win in Australia before Pérez won again in Azerbaijan, sparking new speculation about a two-horse race for the drivers' championship. Could the Mexican mount a challenge for the title? Little did we know at the time, but the defeat for Verstappen in Baku proved to be a turning point in his season. Reflecting on this period after winning the title in Qatar some six months later, he revealed that he used the race in Azerbaijan as a mini test where he made changes to the car's performance by adjusting the settings from his cockpit, which he felt gave him a better understanding of how to get the best out of the car. He said, 'Of course, I didn't win that race in Baku but I tried out a lot of stuff and different tools in the car. That's why throughout the race I was a little bit inconsistent. But at one point, I got into a good rhythm with what I found, before I damaged my tyres a bit too much. But it was like, "OK, that's quite interesting for the next races," and it has helped me on every track since.'

Verstappen won again in Miami. And in Monaco, where he excelled in the wet. After the race in Monte Carlo, I asked Horner in the post-race debrief whether his team could remain undefeated for the season, another 16 races. 'You are trying to get me to do an Arsène Wenger here, aren't you?' he replied, with reference to the former Arsenal football manager who had guided his team through the 2003–4 Premier League season without a single defeat. He added: 'There is so much jeopardy – you saw it here with the weather. There are so many factors that can go wrong and the competition is so strong that anything can happen.' We did not know it at the time, but those victories in Miami and Monaco were just the start of a rather special winning run for Verstappen, during which he racked up ten straight wins in a row.

In the middle of this extraordinary run, following his success in Montreal where he won by 9.5 seconds over Alonso, I caught up with Horner at the team's Milton Keynes HQ. Verstappen's win had not only moved him 69 points clear of Pérez in the drivers' championship, he had also secured Red Bull Racing's 100th victory in Formula One. Horner was sitting in his office in his team's HQ and before we started our interview for my column in the *Sun*, his attention was caught by someone behind me. It turns out his accounting team were being scrutinised by the FIA and the inspection was taking place at this very moment. The previous year Red Bull Racing had been punished for exceeding the budget cap with a fine and reduction in wind-tunnel testing time, so it was imperative that the accounting all stacked up this year. When we started the interview, I brought him back to his remark that 100 wins is 'not bad for a subsidiary of a fizzy drinks company'. He responded: 'I still think we are seen as a newcomer because we have not got the same heritage as Ferrari and Mercedes and so on. We are just different. With the 100 victories and what we have achieved, people do see us differently now, but it probably still sits uncomfortably for some of those manufacturers. If you produce beautiful cars like Ferrari do, how does a fizzy drinks company, as we were once called, produce a better car? It is David versus Goliath. Don't ever tell us something can't be done because everything is possible.'

We discuss his presence at all the wins, having never missed a race, and he points out that I too had been there for most of them. 'I enjoy it just the same as I did from day one,' he said. 'The excitement of going racing, the passion and competitive spirit, is just the same. Reaching 100 wins is a landmark I could never have imagined when I first drove in here to the factory on that first day in January 2005.

'Formula One was always my goal and ambition and, having got there, I was determined to make a success of it. It was about sticking to the core principles that had served me well in Formula 3000. It was about picking the right people, having a belief and taking a risk but never losing sight of what the goal was. I liken it to [successful football manager] Sir Alex Ferguson at Manchester United. You cannot afford to stay stagnant for too long. You have to have continuity and progression. People's roles have all evolved, including mine, and if you stand still you are going backwards. We are in a halcyon moment for the team. We are a forward-facing organisation. We rarely look over our shoulder. We have to keep pushing. The one thing that is guaranteed in sport is that everything goes in cycles. We are in one at the moment, but we know it will come to an end at some point. The trick is to make that cycle as long as possible.'

Verstappen won in Austria, Silverstone, Hungary, Belgium, the Netherlands and then Italy to make it ten wins in a row, eclipsing Vettel's total by one. To put the achievement in perspective, Michael Schumacher's longest streak of victories was seven, while Hamilton has so far peaked at five. The success had seen Verstappen quickly fill the team's new trophy cabinet in their factory HQ. 'We ordered a new cabinet and we've already filled it. I'm superstitious. I don't like empty cabinets,' said Horner in Monza. 'We're making history and it's not often you get the chance to do that. We had seven tough years where we never lost focus of what our goal and objective was, so to get back into a situation where we're winning again, is very special for the whole team.'

Verstappen saw his winning run ended in Singapore by Sainz, after what proved to be a rogue bad weekend for the team. It was a race that would ultimately stop them from achieving a 100 per cent first-place record. The Singapore Grand Prix started badly, with both Verstappen and Pérez qualifying outside the top ten. It was the first time in five years that neither of the team's cars had made Q3 – the top-ten shootout for pole position. In the race itself, Verstappen finished fifth and Pérez in eighth, but perhaps what was even more unexpected than their defeat was the grace with which the team accepted it. 'Everything needs to be perfect to win every race in a season. I knew this day would come and it's absolutely fine,' said Verstappen afterwards. 'Everyone sees how dominant we can be and they don't realise how difficult it really is. We need to get a lot of things right.' Horner echoed Verstappen's comments, adding: 'We knew that the run would come to an end at some point and we reflect on the job well done by the team. Congratulations to Ferrari. Carlos drove a great race and managed to hold on for the win.'

In the following race in Japan, Verstappen's victory over Norris sealed the team's constructors' championship title, while he retained his own world crown in the Saturday sprint race in Qatar. He did not win the 30-minute race – he was second behind McLaren's Oscar Piastri – but the seven points were enough to see him crowned world champion for a third time, and with six races still to go. As he crossed the line he was congratulated by Horner: 'Max, you are a three-time world champion. That's unbelievable . . . Incredible year for you.' Verstappen replied: 'Yeah, unbelievable, guys. I don't know what to say. Thank you for providing me with such a car. It's been a lot of fun this year. To be able to achieve something like this, I can't thank you all enough. Besides all the performance-related stuff, it's just really enjoyable to work with you all. That's the most important thing in the end.'

His victory, which had long been on the cards following his impressive wins, had felt inevitable. Now it was confirmed, and he planned to celebrate with a few drinks. When quizzed about being a three-time world champion following his result in the sprint race, Verstappen said: '[It's] something of course I never really dreamt of, a very proud moment for myself, my family. To be able to experience all of this together with everyone in the team is amazing. This one [championship] is the best one. The first one was the most emotional one, as that's when your dreams are fulfilled in F1. This one has been my best year: consecutive wins and stuff; the car itself has probably been in the best shape. This one is probably the one I'm most proud of because of the consistency. I keep trying to improve and of course I don't necessarily think I've become a faster driver, but as you have more experience in the car, you grow as a driver and as a person in life. All these things help you a lot in dealing with every high-pressure situation throughout a weekend, or when something is thrown at you in difficult conditions.'

It was remarkable how relaxed Verstappen was about his achievement. He had just turned 26 and was now a three-time world champion: the same as F1 greats Ayrton Senna, Sir Jackie Stewart, Jack Brabham, Niki Lauda and Nelson Piquet, who is the father of Verstappen's long-term partner Kelly Piquet. He took it all in his stride with maturity. He also remained relentlessly focused and still planned on winning all the final six races. 'Of course I want to win as much as I can,' he said. 'I don't know how long this is going to last. I enjoy the moment. We'll see where we end up, but it's way more than I thought I could achieve so it's perfect.'

Verstappen's father Jos was clearly glowing with pride when he spoke to a few journalists in the paddock on the Saturday evening following his son's title success. He was asked whether a third world title made up for all the hard work when his son was a kid. 'Of course,' he said. 'That's something I have talked with him about a lot, but it's not only about winning a world championship. In the last years of go-karting he had something that I would say was special. You can still see it now, it's unbelievable. For me, he's the same Max as three or four years ago. The only difference is he has a fantastic car around him, he knows the people that he works with, and I think that makes it look easy, but you still have to be there every weekend. To win one world championship is something very special, but to win three in a row is even more special.'

Despite the jubilation for the reigning champion, it was not all rosy in the Red Bull camp. While Verstappen was hitting a rich vein of success, Pérez had struggled. Since his two wins early in the season, his form had tumbled. He had crashed out in Japan and Mexico and, while Verstappen won the last seven races, Pérez achieved just one podium – a third place in Las Vegas. After the race in Qatar, where he was a lowly tenth, Horner admitted the team 'really need to sit down with Checo because he's really not hitting that form at the moment'. Questions had been raised within the media about whether he would remain at the team. Marko, too, had been critical of his driver. 'We desperately need him to find his form to keep that second place in the championship,' Horner added. 'We all know what Checo's capable of and we want to support him to get back into a position where he was, finishing second place to Max.' The question would remain an open one as the season drew to a close.

The final race of the year in Abu Dhabi provided another moment to reflect on the team's achievements over the course of the season. Horner was asked by a journalist in a press conference ahead of the last race about whether Verstappen had found a new level of performance. He gave a telling response, saying: 'Max has just been incredible this year. I don't think any of us thought, after 2022, that we'd manage to better that. He has broken all records and I think as a driver, the way he's grown, he's just constantly evolving. His capacity within the car just gets greater and greater, to read a race, to be able to look after the tyres, to know when are the key moments, to absolutely deliver. And time and time again, he's done that.'

Horner also praised Verstappen's relentlessness. He could have taken his foot off the gas after securing the title in Qatar. The hard work had all been done and he was no longer required to operate at the highest level. However, he did not do that. He continued to press for the victories and achieve the fastest laps. During the Abu Dhabi Grand Prix there was a moment where in frustration he squeezed past Hamilton and Russell in the pit lane. He was not doing it to show off or be controversial, he was simply desperate to get out on track and have more time refining and honing his car's performance. It was the mark of a dedicated world champion.

'The way he works with the team, and you can see that since winning the championship back in Qatar, he's not lifted off [the gas] at all,' said Horner as he continued to praise his driver. 'He's absolutely pushing all the way to this chequered flag in Abu Dhabi. With the records he's now achieved – becoming the third most-winning driver in Formula One, a three-time world champion, with the statistic of most wins in a season, and everything that he's done – you have to start to talk about him among the greatest names in the sport. He's earned his position there. And what's phenomenal is that he's done it at 26 years of age. He's got a lot of racing still ahead of him.'

Verstappen completed the phenomenal season with another victory in Abu Dhabi. It was his 19th of the season. He had become the first driver in F1 history to lead over 1,000 laps. He'd scored a total of 575 points – a total of 92.7 per cent of the points available to him over the course of the 22 races. He had won over 86 per cent of the races. He achieved the most consecutive victories in F1 (10), took the most podiums in a season (21), achieved the most wins from pole position in a season (12) and completed the most hat tricks – achieving pole position, win and setting the fastest lap (6). He was also the only driver to finish every race in the 2023 season.

In the final press session, Horner lamented missing the win in Singapore that had prevented a clean sweep of victories: 'This car is going to go down in the history books as a very, very special car,' Horner said of the RB19. 'To have won 21 races out of the 22, just missing out on Singapore, it leaves room for improvement,' he said wryly. 'We know our opponents; this will have motivated them more than ever to come back at us hard and nothing stands still in this sport. Everything moves so quickly. You could see, as we weren't developing, the opposition coming closer and closer. We're going to hopefully take all of these lessons out of this car and apply it into our 20th car, RB20, next year and try to defend these two titles: the drivers' and the constructors' championships.'

With that in mind, perhaps it is fitting to end with a rare quote from Mateschitz as Red Bull Racing move into their 20th year. It featured in an article published in German publication *Stern* in 2004, sent to me by one of Mateschitz's close friends, Stefan Aufschnaiter, who says it was the first interview the Red Bull magnate had done. In the article, it explains how Mateschitz denied ever saying he wanted his drink to become as big as Coca-Cola. He was not interested in what had gone on before, but what was on the road ahead. 'Coca-Cola has a 100-year history behind it,' he's quoted as saying. 'We have a 100-year future in front of us.'

AFTERWORD
– March 2024 –

And that is where this book was due to end – a triumphant conclusion to 2023 and a segue into a celebration of their 20th anniversary. Only, this is Formula One. And if there is one thing the last 13 years of working in this sport have taught me, it is to always expect the unexpected.

On 5 February 2024, news broke that Christian Horner was the subject of an internal investigation initiated by Red Bull's HQ in Austria following a complaint of inappropriate behaviour. The details were very thin but, needless to say, the implications were enormous.

Over the next few weeks, unfounded speculation lit up the internet and news channels, as the lack of information had created a vacuum. I received messages on my phone from various TV and radio stations seeking my availability to come on and speak about the subject. However, I decided to decline all of them. Anything that I knew as fact would be used in my writing and I would not be contributing to the rumour mill.

One of the most memorable days was 15 February and the launch of Red Bull Racing's new car, the challenger for the 2024 season. It was held in Milton Keynes at the team's factory and, unlike Mercedes and Ferrari, who had both opted for an online-only launch, Red Bull Racing threw open the doors to their HQ.

Despite what was going on behind the scenes, Horner was centre stage and was joined by Verstappen and Pérez as they launched the car. In the media round table, Horner was quizzed about the investigation. He made it clear that he denied all of the accusations and that he would be in Bahrain the following week for pre-season testing. I noticed, as mentioned in my article for the *Sun*, that he looked – and understandably so – very tired.

He was indeed on the pit wall during testing. In the build-up to the season-opening race, also in Bahrain, the big question, however, remained the prospective outcome of the internal investigation. It had been widely reported that there would be some news ahead of the race.

On 28 February, at around 6.25pm local time, the private jet taking Horner to Bahrain landed and, around five minutes later, there was a short 89-word statement from Red Bull GmbH in Austria saying that the grievance from the claimant had been dismissed. After weeks of media second guessing, it looked like the matter had been drawn to a close. However, what happened 24 hours later, almost to the minute, proved that would not be the case.

I was sitting in the Red Bull Racing hospitality unit having a conversation about the previous few weeks and the impact, if any, it had upon those working inside the team. I had expected the mood to be that of relief now the internal investigation had been completed, with the grievance dismissed and the statements released. However, that was not the case. There was a nervousness, a strange uneasiness and a sense that something was about to happen. Quite what was unknown.

Then I retreated to the press room to find it buzzing with excitement. There really is no place better to work than a press room when a story is breaking. Sitting in my inbox was an email sent from an address that merely gave the day's date. The subject heading was 'Christian Horner investigation evidence' and attached was a link to a Google Drive. I've sat through countless training modules at work telling me not to open suspicious attachments, yet not everyone else in the press room was so hesitant. The content of the drive – as has since been widely reported – was a series of WhatsApp exchanges, none of which, as I write this, are known to be genuine. A statement from Horner said: 'I won't comment on anonymous speculation. But to reiterate I have always denied the allegations.' He also reiterated that he had complied with the internal process and was 'fully focused on the start of the season'.

The buzz created by the email was soon replaced with a feeling that I can only describe as sadness. Sad because the content of the initial grievance had now been lost and become part of what appeared to be an orchestrated smear campaign designed to have maximum impact on an individual's very existence. It had gone beyond Horner's role as team boss of Red Bull Racing and now seemed to be a deliberate attempt to completely destroy him.

Internally, the cracks that had started to form were blown wide open following the race, which incidentally was won by Verstappen with Pérez in second place. The on-track success was forgotten in the wake of some remarks made by Verstappen's father, who had effectively called for Horner to be replaced. The widely reported quote was: 'There is tension here while he remains in position. The team is in danger of being torn apart. It can't go on the way it is. It will explode.' As a result, Max Verstappen has unfortunately been pulled into the argument.

It has since been labelled a civil war, be it Horner versus Verstappen Snr and Helmut Marko, or indeed whether it stretches into the upper echelons of Red Bull. Right now, as this book goes to print, there are still so many unknowns: will Horner stay on? What about Verstappen? What happens next to this all-conquering team?

All of which is a fitting end to a story of the unpredictability of Formula One and one of its most successful teams, which started with such little. However, there is one thing that is for sure, the last few months have simply been another element to Red Bull Racing's incredible story.

ACKNOWLEDGEMENTS

My thanks to the following:

To my wife Hayley, thank you for your love and support – you have constantly been a beacon of positivity throughout my career.

To my children, Teddy and Rose. Travelling the world to cover F1 is an incredible experience but also requires some sacrifices in the form of missing family events, special moments and birthdays, yet you have never once complained when I've been away.

To Lorna Russell, my excellent editor, who made the process so enjoyable from start to finish.

And to Melanie Michael-Greer, my agent, for listening to all my ideas in the first place and for keeping things on track.

I'd also like to thank all those who have contributed to this book, with a special thanks to Paul Smith at Red Bull Racing for supporting this project.

And to Christian Horner for all your time. It was a privilege writing about the team's incredible rise and success. I am sure there is even more to come . . .

IMAGE CREDITS

All images are the copyright of Mark Thompson/Staff or the following rightsholders at Getty Images:

Clive Rose/Staff (Image 3), Bryn Lennon/Staff (Image 4), Peter Parks/Staff (Image 10), Paul Gilham/Staff (Image 11), Fred Dufour/Staff (Image 15), Manan Vatsyayana/Stringer (Image 16), Philippe Lopez/Staff (Image 17), Darren Heath Photographer/Contributor (Image 20), Peter J Fox/Contributor (Images 22, 24), Getty Images/Stringer (Image 27), Dan Istitene - Formula 1/Contributor (Image 30), NurPhoto/Contributor (Image 32)

INDEX

24 Hours of Le Mans race 9, 65

A1-Ring 167
Abiteboul, Cyril 169, 185, 228, 233
Abu Dhabi 3, 98, 113, 126–7, 157,
    174, 175, 180, 183, 188, 203,
    240–1, 250, 265–71, 272–3,
    288–9, 297–9
Abu Dhabi Grand Prix 140–2, 235,
    254–7, 277, 286, 289, 298
Agathangelou, Ben 36
Albert Park, Melbourne 32, 40–1,
    243, 245, 247
Albon, Alexander 239–40, 245, 249,
    250–3, 283
Alfa Romeo 252
Alguersuari, Jaime 122, 162
Alonso, Fernando 43, 55–7, 66, 73,
    82, 104–5, 113–14, 122, 125–6,
    134, 136, 139–40, 143, 149,
    150, 171, 173, 219, 229–30, 281,
    283, 291–2
AlphaTauri team 250–2, 290
AM-RB 001 (Aston Martin
    Valkyrie) 191
APA 31
Arab Spring 119
Arden 25, 26–7, 179
Armstrong, Lance 17

Arrivabene, Maurizio 192
Arrows 10, 53, 65
Aston Martin 191, 214, 217, 252, 290
Aufschnaiter, Stefan 299
Austin, Texas 142, 157, 160, 187–8,
    209, 228, 262–3, 285, 289
Australia 105, 121, 163, 166, 175,
    243, 243–8, 282, 291
Australian Formula Ford
    Championship 63
Australian Grand Prix 66, 79, 89,
    146, 164, 191, 212, 235–6, 243,
    245, 247–8, 279
Australian Grand Prix Corporation
    (AGPC) 248
Austria 8, 29, 213, 237, 241, 249–50,
    281, 294
Austrian Grand Prix 5–6, 166–7,
    211, 224–7, 240, 259, 278
Autosport 17, 18, 81, 113, 120
Azerbaijan 209, 236, 291–2
Azerbaijan Grand Prix 213, 220–1,
    226, 258, 280

Bahar, Dany 14–15, 22
Bahrain 52–3, 55, 80, 94, 103–5,
    119–20, 132–5, 154, 165–6,
    191–2, 212, 217, 252, 255,
    282, 290

Bahrain Grand Prix 133, 218, 250–1, 277–8, 291

Bahrain International Circuit 255

Baku City Circuit 220–1, 223, 226, 291

Balding, Clare 65

Baldwin, Alan 28, 75

BAR F1 26

BAR Honda 46, 93

Barcelona 39, 79, 94, 106, 109, 162, 178, 200, 217, 236, 258

Barretto, Lawrence 73

Barrichello, Rubens 43, 58, 89, 92, 95–9, 235

Baumschlager, Raimund 29

BBC 12, 13, 138, 142

BBC Formula One coverage 81

BBC News 12, 36–8

BBC Sport 57

Beavis, Glenn 225

Belgian Grand Prix 45, 211, 228, 240, 260–1, 282–3

Belgium 126, 156, 170, 294

Bell, Townsend 26

Benetton 33–4, 65–6, 68

Benetton, Luciano 66

Berger, Gerhard 8, 9, 53–4, 83

Bernoldi, Enrique 10

Bianchi, Jules 217

BMW 67, 72, 73, 74–5, 83, 113

Bottas, Valtteri 194, 205, 213, 225, 236, 238, 241, 260

Brabham, Jack 296

Brabham F1 207

Brawn, Ross 89, 182, 205, 246, 247, 262

Brawn GP F1 team 88–9, 94, 98, 101, 102, 182

Brazil 85, 98, 112–13, 127, 143, 148–50, 155, 157, 202–3, 211–12, 240–1, 289

Brazilian Grand Prix 85–6, 180, 263, 270

Briatore, Flavio 21, 34, 65–6, 68, 109, 222

British Formula Ford 30, 63

British Grand Prix 17, 80–2, 95, 98, 111–12, 124, 135, 154–5, 184, 235, 238, 250, 259, 281

Brixworth Mercedes factory 160

Brown, Oliver 150–1

Brown, Zak 228

Brundle, Martin 55–6, 59, 107

BT Sports 65

Budapest 240

Buddh International Circuit 156

'Budgie Nine' 202

Button, Jenson 57, 66, 79, 89–90, 92, 95, 99, 104, 111, 122, 126–7, 132, 137, 182, 198–9, 229

Caesars Palace Grand Prix 96

Campaign Asia-Pacific (magazine) 209–10

Campese, David 64

Canada 108, 134, 166, 170, 212–13, 280

Canadian Grand Prix 49, 72, 80–1, 110, 123–4, 138, 154, 223–4

Carey, Chase 205, 206, 210–11, 243

Carlin 162

Champ Car series 12–13

Chiesa, Dino 178–9

China 106, 121, 132, 150–1, 153–4, 165, 166, 174–5, 183, 194, 212, 219, 236

Chinese Grand Prix 71, 76, 91–4, 192–3, 240, 244

Circuit of the Americas 142

Circuit de Catalunya 39

Circuito de Jerez 38–9

Coca-Cola 18, 300

Concorde Agreements 55, 207, 208–9

constructors' championship 112–14, 122, 126, 152, 156, 175, 188, 203, 288

Cooper, Adam 17

Cosworth 12, 13, 36

Coulthard, David 30–1, 107
  2005 season 32, 37–44, 46
  2006 season 48–9, 55–6, 58–9
  2007 season 60–1, 68, 69–71
  2008 season 79–83, 85–6, 155
  F1 retirement 80–3, 85–6, 155

Covid-19 pandemic 243–9, 255, 271, 275

Credit Suisse 10

CVC Capital Partners 209

Daily Express (newspaper) 104

Daily Telegraph (newspaper) 150

Davidson, Anthony 17, 79

Delta Topco 205

Dennis, Ron 16, 21, 45, 49, 188, 221–2

'Dieselgate' scandal 186–7

Docking, Alan 63

Domenicali, Stefano 172, 205

Donohue, Geoff 87

Doornbos, Robert 41, 59

Drive to Survive (Netflix show) 23, 161, 232–4, 280

Dutch Grand Prix 211

Ecclestone, Bernie 12, 27, 187, 188, 190, 201, 205–11

Ecclestone, Fabiana 201, 210

Ecclestone, Slavica 208

Eintracht Frankfurt 131

Emilia Romagna Grand Prix 279, 289

Energy Station, Monaco 45, 48, 56, 59

Enge, Tomáš 26

ESPN 226–7

European Grand Prix 38, 45–6, 69–70, 72, 98, 110

Evening Standard (newspaper) 120

F1.com 7, 73

F1's 70th Anniversary Grand Prix 250

Fangio, Juan Manuel 157

Fédération Internationale de l'Automobile (FIA) 42, 55, 79–80, 89, 134, 136–8, 142, 147, 163–4, 169, 181, 184, 187, 198, 208, 234–5, 237, 244–9, 256, 258, 264–5, 272, 277, 283–5, 293

fitness tests 72

GT Championship 1998 64

Ferguson, Sir Alex 294

Ferrari 8, 10, 21, 42, 43, 78, 82, 89, 101, 113, 118, 122, 125, 146, 156, 215, 231, 274, 293

2006 season 55, 56–7

2012 season 134–6, 138–9, 143

2014 season 162, 171–3

2015 season 180, 184

2016 season 192–3, 200

2018 season 217, 219–20, 226–7

2020 season 242, 243

2022 season 277–8, 282, 283

2023 season 290, 295

engines 54, 85, 180, 183, 185–7, 190, 252

and Verstappen 198

Fisichella, Giancarlo 58, 66

Forbes magazine 17–18

Force India 192

Ford Motor Company 4, 10–16, 17, 28, 33, 88–9, 94, 290

Formula 3000 (now Formula Two) 9, 17, 21, 22, 24, 25, 26, 30, 31, 37, 38, 65–6, 68, 293

Formula BMW 162

Formula One Commission 211

Formula One Constructors Association (FOCA) 207

Formula One Group 205–6

Formula One Management (FOM) 207–8

Formula One Promotions and Administration (FOPA) 207–8

Formula One World Drivers' Championship 9

Formula Renault 74, 162–3

Formula Three (F3) 23, 24, 31, 63–4, 74, 158, 162, 174, 198, 235

Formula Three Euro Series 74

Formula Two 9, 207, 235

see also Formula 3000

Forsythe, Gerald 12–13

Fortec 24

France 258, 258–9, 281

Freitas, Eduardo 277

French Grand Prix 9, 66, 237

Fuller, Simon 123

Gasly, Pierre 194, 228–9, 235–6, 239–40, 250

German Grand Prix 34, 82, 95–7, 98, 136, 239

German Touring Car series 81

Germany 156, 237, 240, 241

Ghosn, Carlos 144, 165–6
Glock, Timo 72–3
GP3 179–80, 194
Grand Prix 9, 12, 43–4, 69, 72, 82,
    83, 90, 104, 113, 117, 119, 140,
    168, 181, 196, 207–8
    see also specific Grands Prix
Grand Prix Drivers' Association 278
Greenwell, Joe 11
Grosjean, Romain 217, 251
Guardian (newspaper) 103

Haas F1 team 28, 45, 233, 251, 252
halo cockpit canopy 216–17,
    251, 262
Hamilton, Lewis 75, 147, 150, 157,
    161, 165, 194, 204, 236,
    294, 298
    2010 season 104–5, 111–12
    2011 season 121–4, 126
    2012 season 131–2
    2015 season 178–81
    2016 season 198, 199, 202, 203
    2017 season 211–12, 215
    2018 season 219, 225, 234
    2019 season 231, 236, 237,
        238–41
    2020 season 242–3, 245, 249, 255
    2021 season 254–70, 273
Handkammer, Kenny 33–5, 68–9,
    106
Harlow, Winnie 223–4
Hartley, Brendon 162

Hartstein, Gary 117
Haug, Norbert 64
Heidfeld, Nick 17, 74, 89
Herbert, Johnny 283
High Performance Podcast 27–8
Hispania Racing F1 Team 163
Hockenheim 34, 65, 70, 82, 83,
    136, 137, 237
Holland Grand Prix 283
'Holzhaus' 5
Honda 57–8, 89, 178, 183, 188, 218,
    224, 227, 229–30, 235, 242,
    251–2, 258–9, 273, 275, 279,
    282, 290
    see also BAR Honda
Hong Kong 244–5
Horner, Christian 5, 21, 22–8,
    29–31, 47–50, 63–4, 196
    2005 season 32–4, 36–41, 44, 46,
        47–8
    2006 season 52–6, 58–9, 61, 68
    2007 season 71, 75–6
    2008 season 77, 80, 81, 82
    2009 season 88, 93, 97
    2010 season 106, 108, 110,
        112–13, 116–17
    2011 season 118, 119, 123, 125,
        127–8
    2012 season 130, 131–8, 142, 157
    2013 season 145–6, 148–9, 150,
        153, 154–5, 157–8
    2014 season 165, 166, 169, 171,
        173–4, 176–7

Horner, Christian – *cont.*
  2015 season 177, 180–8
  2016 season 190–1, 193, 200–1, 203
  2017 season 213, 214
  2018 season 218, 219, 221–4, 226, 227–8, 233
  2019 season 234, 237–40
  2020 season 243, 246–7, 249–50, 252–3
  2021 season 254–6, 259–60, 263–4, 267–8, 270–1, 273–4
  2022 season 276, 277–81, 284–6
  2023 season 291, 292–5, 297–9
  and the death of Mateschitz 285–6
  and Ecclestone 210–11
  and Verstappen 198, 199, 200–1
  and Vettel 74–5, 76, 82–4, 171, 173–4, 193
  and Webber's departure 154–5
Horner, Garry 25
Houthi movement 278
HRT 132, 163
Hülkenberg, Nico 192
Hungarian Grand Prix 98, 137, 213–14, 239
Hungaroring 184
Hungary 136–7, 156, 170, 184, 239, 250, 260, 282, 294

Ilmor 185
Imola 257, 279
Independent (newspaper) 93–4

India 127, 138, 140, 156–7
Indian Grand Prix 139, 160
Indycar series 216, 217
Infiniti 144, 170, 183, 184
Istanbul Park 122
Italian Grand Prix 9, 85, 156, 261, 289
Italy 12, 98, 126, 162, 228, 289, 294
ITV 59

Jaguar 10–13, 15, 17, 20, 27–8, 175
Jaguar Racing 2, 6, 12–13, 15–16, 19, 28–9, 32–3, 46, 53–5, 61–2, 66–8, 78, 236
Japan 85, 98, 108, 116–17, 126, 138, 156, 173, 214, 288, 295, 297
Japanese Grand Prix 75, 103, 169–70, 174, 196, 198, 217, 230, 261, 283–4, 286
Jerez, Spain 36, 38–9, 67, 77, 101, 102, 130, 177–8
Jones, Alan 96
Jordan 12, 15, 27, 33, 41, 53, 73
Jordan, Eddie 27, 222

Kalkhoven, Kevin 12–13
Karthikeyan, Narain 132, 163
karting 63, 158, 162, 178–9, 196–7
Klien, Christian 16, 37–9, 41–3, 46, 55, 59, 61, 163
Knutson, Dan 70
Korea 116, 126, 138, 156
Kovalainen, Heikki 89–90, 110

Krating Daeng ('Red Bull') (drink) 7–8
Kristensen, Tom 25
Kubica, Robert 72, 73–4, 90
Kumpen, Sophie 196–7
Kvyat, Daniil 170, 174, 178, 220, 240, 280
    2015 season 178–9, 183–4, 188
    2016 season 191–6, 198–9, 218
    2019 season 238
    2020 season 251
    background 178–9
    joins Red Bull Racing 179–80
    nicknamed 'the Torpedo' 192
    relegation in favour of Verstappen 194–6, 198–9

Las Vegas 289, 297
Latifi, Nicholas 254, 266, 267, 270
Lauda, Niki 13, 28–9, 181, 185, 190, 207, 220, 236, 252, 296
Lawson, Liam 194
Le Mans 9, 25, 65, 154, 162
Leclerc, Charles 5–6, 237, 243, 278–9, 281–2, 284
Lewis-Evans, Stuart 206
Liberty Media 205, 209–11, 231–2, 243, 272
Liuzzi, Tonio 37–9, 41–2, 44, 46, 163
Liuzzi, Vitantonio 17, 26
Lotus 156, 198, 207
Lowndes, Craig 25

Lucas, George 44–5
Lucid Motors 33
Lüthi, Joachim 207

Magnussen, Kevin 229
Malaysia 79–80, 121, 132, 149, 157, 164, 165, 214
Malaysian Grand Prix 90–1, 105–6, 146–9, 151, 202, 225
Malone, John 205
Manchester United 294
Mansell, Nigel 49
March 9
Marchionne, Sergio 185–6
Marko, Helmut 9–10, 15, 19–21, 24–6, 28–9, 73–4, 80, 82–3, 108, 116, 145, 166, 180, 193–4, 197–8, 225–6, 260, 297
Marshall, Rob 33
Martini Porsche 9
Masi, Michael 235, 246, 256, 261, 265, 267–9, 272–3, 277
Massa, Felipe 42, 79, 104, 135
Mateschitz, Dietrich 1, 2–4, 6–10, 14–18, 21, 28–9, 30–1, 35–7, 299–300
    2005 season 37, 40, 44, 45, 46, 48
    2006 season 53–4
    2008 season 79
    2009 season 94, 97
    2010 season 113–14, 116
    2011 season 118
    2013 season 148, 150

Mateschitz, Dietrich – *cont.*
  2017 season 214
  2018 season 226–7
  2021 season 273
  background 7
  and Coulthard 82
  death 6, 285–6
  and Horner 146
  launches Red Bull 8
  looks to develop Red Bull engine
    division 185
  net worth 18
  and Newey 49, 50–1
  purchases Jaguar Racing 6
  questions Red Bull's F1
    involvement 177
  and the Red Bull Ring 167–8
  and Toro Rosso 66
  and Vettel 83–4
  and Webber 61–2, 67, 116, 154–6
McKenzie, Bob 104
McLaren 16, 17, 21, 30, 31, 67, 68,
    77, 101, 113, 118, 150, 181, 188,
    189, 198, 215, 226, 228
  1988 season 288
  1998 season 1
  2005 season 41–2, 44–6
  2006 season 47–8, 50–1, 58
  2008 season 78
  2010 season 104, 105, 109
  2011 season 121–4, 126
  2012 season 132
  2013 season 145

  2015 season 178, 229–30
  2020 season 245–6, 248
  2023 season 295
  and Honda 218, 224, 229–30, 251
McRae, Donald 103
Medland, Chris 232–3
Melbourne 32, 39–41, 43, 66, 69,
    121, 123, 131, 148, 163, 165,
    180–3, 191, 218, 231, 234–6,
    243–6
Mercedes 64–5, 102, 104, 113, 145,
    160–1, 165–6, 169, 172, 190,
    217–20, 227, 231–2, 252, 293
  2012 season 254
  2015 season 178, 180–8
  2016 season 190, 198–200, 288–9
  2017 season 204–5, 212, 215
  2018 season 225
  2019 season 234, 236, 237–9, 241
  2020 season 242, 247, 249,
    250, 255
  2021 season 257, 259–60, 263,
    265–73, 283
  2022 season 279–81
  2023 season 290, 291
Mercedes-Benz 64, 185
Mercedes-Benz Grosser Preis von
    Deutschland 237–8
Merwe, Alan van der 251
Mexican Grand Prix 160
Mexico 214, 228, 297
Mexico City 262–3, 289
Miami 292

Miami Grand Prix 279

Milton Keynes 2, 28–30, 34, 43, 54, 59–62, 68, 94–5, 101, 148, 161, 176–7, 193, 221, 230, 276, 292–3, 294

Minardi 16, 46, 53, 54, 66

Mirror (newspaper) 57

Mol, Olav 200

Monaco 12, 80, 94, 106, 122, 134–5, 137, 166, 183–4, 202–3, 228, 236, 280, 292

Monaco Grand Prix 44, 48, 55–9, 67, 81, 122–3, 133, 136, 206, 222–3, 225, 257

Monaghan, Paul 33

Monte Carlo 80, 94–5, 133, 292

Montezemolo, Luca di 139

Montoya, Juan Pablo 17, 25, 30, 42–3, 63, 68

Montreal 110, 154, 224, 292

Monza 85, 109, 173, 180, 207, 250, 261, 283, 294

Morsicani, Angelo 179

Morsicani Racing 179

Mosley, Max 21, 207

Motorsport (magazine) 23, 24

Mugello, Tuscany 250

Murray, Gordon 207

Nakajima, Kazuki 86

NASCAR series 52

National Speed Sport News (magazine and website) 70

Neal, Ann 63, 64, 65–6, 111

Netflix 23, 161, 232–4, 254, 280

Netherlands, The 294
    see also Holland Grand Prix

Newey, Adrian 33, 46, 47–53, 67, 138, 166, 270
    2009 season 89, 93, 94–5, 101
    2010 season 100–1, 108
    2011 season 119
    2012 season 133, 137, 142, 143, 149
    2013 season 157
    2014 season 169
    2015 season 177, 187
    2016 season 190–1
    and Aston Martin 191
    and RB3 69
    and RB4 77, 78
    and RB5 94–5, 101
    and RB6 101
    and RB8 145
    and RB9 145

Newey, Marigold 49

Nissan 144, 183

Norris 295

Nürburgring 46, 70

Observer (newspaper) 9

Opel 28

Oracle 275, 276

Österreichring (A1-Ring) 167

P1 Engineering 23

parc fermé rules 263

Parry-Jones, Richard 12, 13
Pepsi 18
Pérez, Sergio 'Checo' 1, 132, 145
   2021 season 255, 257, 260, 266, 270
   2022 season 278–84
   2023 season 291, 292, 294–5, 297
   signed to Red Bull 252
Peterson, Ronnie 9
Petrov, Vitaly 122
Piastri, Oscar 67, 295
Pink 40–1
Piquet, Kelly 296
Piquet, Nelson 207, 296
Pirelli 258
Pitchforth, Dave 19, 20, 22, 28, 36
Porsche 9, 154–6, 189
Portugal 257
Portugal Grand Prix 1995 30
Prodrive 26
'Project Pit Lane' 248
Prost, Alain 1, 156, 208, 261
Purnell, Tony 13–15, 17, 19–22, 28,
   36, 45, 48, 51–2, 94
Putin, Vladimir 210

Qatar 265, 288, 291, 295, 297, 298
Qatar Grand Prix 194, 263–4, 288
Queens Park Rangers (QPR) 68

Racing Point 252
Rahal, Bobby 13
Räikkönen, Kimi 10, 42, 58, 96, 98,
   141, 156, 171, 192, 200–1

Red Bull Advanced Technologies 191
Red Bull Applied Technologies 54
Red Bull drinks company 13–15,
   18, 19–21, 23, 27, 37, 123, 126,
   299–300
   HQ, Fuschl am See 15
Red Bull GMbH Formula One
   team 9
Red Bull Junior Team 9, 10, 16, 18,
   53, 74, 83, 84, 170, 179, 184
Red Bull Powertrains 4, 275, 276,
   282, 290
Red Bull Racing 1–3, 5–6, 17, 22–3,
   29–31, 34–6
   2005 season 32–3, 36–46, 48, 54
   2006 season 52–9, 61–2, 68–9
   2007 season 60, 69–72, 75–6, 77
   2008 season 77–86
   2009 season 2, 69, 87–99, 174–5
   2010 season 2, 100–14, 115–16,
     175, 199
   2011 season 117–28, 129
   2012 season 129–43, 149–50,
     157, 270
   2013 season 144–58, 175
   2014 season 160–1, 163–6,
     168–75, 176–7, 204
   2015 season 177–8, 180–8
   2016 season 188, 189–92,
     199–203, 218
   2017 season 211–15
   2018 season 216–28, 232–3
   2019 season 229–32, 234–41

2020 season 242–3, 245–53

2021 season 254–71, 272–3, 275, 283

2022 season 273–87

2023 season 1, 288–99

and Adrian Newey 47–53, 67

driver development programme 9

first podium finish 55–6, 58–9

and Ford 4, 290

Honda engines 224, 229–30, 242, 251–2, 258–9, 275, 282

looks to develop own engine division 185

as media target 35–6

rise of 2

sister team *see* Toro Rosso

spirit behind 6

sponsors 8, 9, 144, 189, 275

Red Bull Racing cars 19

DM01/DM02 3

R5 20

RB1 19, 36, 39, 54

RB2 52

RB3 52, 69, 77, 78

RB4 77–80, 85–6

RB5 92, 94–5, 101

RB6 101, 110

RB7 117

RB8 132–7, 142, 143, 145

RB9 145, 157

RB10 170

RB11 177–8, 217

RB12 (Red Bull Racing-Tag Heuer) 189

RB14 217, 222

RB15 234

RB17 273–4

RB18 273–4, 281–2

RB19 285, 288–9, 299

RB20 299

Red Bull Ring 83, 167–8, 237, 248–9

Red Bulletin (lifestyle magazine) 64

Reitzle, Wolfgang 13

Renault 21, 23, 33–4, 43, 54–5, 58, 68, 77, 117, 122, 128, 150, 160, 164–6, 168–9, 171–2, 179–80, 182–5, 188–9, 195–6, 212, 214, 217–18, 224, 227–8, 233, 248, 252, 275, 290

Renault Nissan Alliance 144

Renault team 227–8

Ressler, Neil 13

Reuters 28, 75

Ricciardo, Daniel 132, 280, 283

2014 season 163–6, 168, 170, 173

2015 season 178, 184, 188

2016 season 191–3, 200–3

2017 season 211–15

2018 season 216, 217–21, 223–4, 225–8, 233

background 161–3

hired by Red Bull to replace Webber 156, 161, 163

quits Red Bull Racing 225–8

Ricciardo, Giuseppe (Joe) 161, 162
Ricciardo, Grace 161–2
Richards, Dave 25–6
Rindt, Jochen 9, 206–7
Roberts, Ian 251
Rocquelin, Guillaume ('Rocky') 33
Roeske, Britta 130
Rosberg, Keke 57
Rosberg, Nico 61, 86, 104–5, 116,
    163, 165–6, 178–80, 198–9,
    203–5, 211, 257
RSM Marko 9
Russell, George 255, 261, 291,
    298
Russia 178, 199, 209, 212, 262
Russian Grand Prix 192, 218

Sainte-Dévote 95
Sainz, Carlos, Jr 178–9, 191, 278,
    280–1, 283, 294–5
Sakhir Grand Prix 252
Salmela, Pyry 194–6
São Paulo 113, 127, 143, 240,
    265, 289
Sauber 10, 14, 42, 58, 72, 74, 132,
    180, 218
Sauber, Peter 72
Saudi Arabia 265, 278
Saudi Arabian Grand Prix 264
Saunders, Graham 22
Saunders, Nate 226–7
Schack, Ole 22, 92
Schneider, Bernd 64

Schumacher, Michael 30, 42–3,
    55–7, 73, 102–4, 127, 150, 157,
    172–3, 222, 294
Schwarzenegger, Arnold 180–1
Senna, Ayrton 1, 8, 30, 150, 203,
    208, 212, 261, 296
Senna, Bruno 143, 148, 149
Sepang 121
Shanghai 71, 91, 94, 121, 132, 152
Silver Arrow 255
Silverstone 39, 65, 80–1, 95–6, 98,
    111, 135–6, 191, 234, 250, 259,
    260–1, 281, 294
Singapore 85, 98, 126, 138, 156,
    184, 299
Singapore Grand Prix 116, 173,
    294–5
Sky F1 264, 270
SLEC Holdings 208, 209
Smith, Mark 33, 34, 36
Sochi, Russia 160
Spa 162, 180, 201, 240
Spain 80, 94, 106, 122, 165, 166,
    202, 236
Spanish Grand Prix 38, 39,
    198–201, 212, 222, 257, 279
Speed, Scott 72, 73
Speedweek (news site) 187
Spielberg 167–8
sprint races 288, 289
Steiner, Guenther 28–33, 39, 44–5,
    52, 233
Stern (magazine) 299–300

Stewart, Sir Jackie 11, 29, 296
Stoddart, Paul 53
Strang, Simon 81
Styrian Grand Prix 249–50
Subaru 26
Sun (newspaper) 130, 267, 273, 286–7, 293
Super Nova Racing 65–6
Suzuka 126, 171, 174, 284

TAG Heuer 189, 190, 200, 212
Tasmania 87, 117
Taylor, Rob 36
T.C. Pharmaceutical 7
Tesla 33
Theissen, Mario 72, 73
Times, The (newspaper) 120
Todt, Jean 21, 57, 187, 235, 247
Toleman team 66
Toro Rosso 53–5, 59–60, 66, 72–4, 162–3
  2007 season 103
  2008 season 79–80, 82–5, 173, 174
  2009 season 94, 179
  2011 season 122
  2013 season 156, 161, 180
  2014 season 161, 170, 180
  2015 season 184, 198, 230
  2016 season 190, 191, 194
  2018 season 218, 228
  2019 season 228, 238, 239–40
  and Honda 224

renamed AlphaTauri 250
and Verstappen 173–4, 178, 196, 198
Tost, Franz 72, 83
Toyota 41, 43, 58, 89
Tremayne, David 7, 93–4
Trulli, Jarno 58
Turkey 80, 99, 146–7, 199
Turkish Grand Prix 95, 107–8, 109, 111, 122, 148
Tyrell 53

United States 160
United States Grand Prix 72, 142, 180, 187–8, 194, 209, 234, 285

V8 Supercars series 235
Valencia 110, 115–16
Van Diemen 63
Vergne, Jean-Éric 132
Vermeulen, Raymond 197, 242
Verstappen, Jos 33–4, 196–7, 296–7
Verstappen, Max 33–4, 156, 158, 168, 173–4
  2015 season 178, 184, 186, 198
  2016 season 189, 191–2, 194–6, 198–203
  2017 season 211–15
  2018 season 216, 218–26, 228, 234
  2019 season 229, 231, 234, 235–41
  2020 season 242–3, 245, 249–53

Verstappen, Max – *cont.*
  2021 season 254–71, 273–4, 283
  2022 season 276, 278–84, 286–7
  2023 season 1, 5–6, 288, 290–2, 294–9
  approaches Red Bull for sponsorship 197–8
  background 195–8
  and *Drive to Survive* 234
  and Ferrari 186
  joins Red Bull Racing programme 198
  Red Bull Racing debut 189, 194–6, 199–201
  world champion 271, 276, 284, 286, 288, 295–7, 298
Vettel, Sebastian 72–5, 184, 215, 221, 252, 280, 294
  2007 season 103–4
  2008 season 78–80, 82–5
  2009 season 87, 88, 89–99, 174
  2010 season 100, 102, 103–14, 116, 174, 175, 199
  2011 season 118–24, 126–8, 129
  2012 season 130–3, 135–43, 149–50, 270
  2013 season 144–9, 150–8, 175
  2014 season 164–6, 168–74, 204
  2016 season 192–4, 200, 218
  2018 season 219, 220
  2019 season 234, 238, 241
  2021 season 257
  2022 season 283

advertising work 130–1
and Ferrari 180
highlights 174–5
leaves Red Bull Racing 169–75, 176, 178, 204, 213
natural leader 194
youngest ever F1 world champion 114
Vierula, Antti 194
Villeneuve, Jacques 57–8, 264–5
Vincini, Roly 23
Visa Cash App RB (VCARB) 290
Volkswagen Audi 186–7

Webber, Alan 62–3
Webber, Mark 16–17, 43, 58, 60–71, 75–6, 85, 162, 178, 280
  2007 season 103–4
  2008 season 79, 80, 83, 85
  2009 season 87, 89–99
  2010 season 100–1, 103–14, 115–17, 199
  2011 season 119–28
  2012 season 130, 132, 134–6, 142, 143, 149–50, 270
  2013 season 144–9, 150–6
  cycling injuries 87–9, 96–7, 116–17
  and Ferrari 138
  quits Red Bull Racing 154–6, 170, 225, 226
Wheatley, Jonathan 33, 267–70, 284
Whiting, Charlie 70, 234–5

Whitmarsh, Martin 150
Williams 16–17, 30–1, 43, 58, 60–1,
    66–8, 74, 77, 89, 93, 113, 142–3,
    180–1, 184, 205, 254–5, 266
Williams, Sir Frank 17, 207
Williams, Richard 9
Willis, Geoff 93–4
Wilson, Justin 217
wind tunnels 51–2
Wings for Life charity 86
Wirdheim, Björn 26
Wittich, Niels 277

Wolff, Toto 181–2, 185, 187–8,
    205, 232, 236, 249, 252,
    256–60, 262–3, 268–9,
    280–1
Wurz, Alex 61, 69

Yas Marina Circuit 254
Yoovidhya, Chaleo 7
Young, Byron 57

Zanardi 178–9
Zehnder, Beat 73

ABOUT THE AUTHOR

BEN HUNT has been a journalist for twenty years and has covered motorsport for more than a decade. He is now chief motorsport writer at *Autosport* and cohosts the F1 podcast *Inside the Piranha Club*. He lives in England.